The Datafied Society

The Datafied Society

Studying Culture through Data

Edited by
Mirko Tobias Schäfer & Karin van Es

Amsterdam University Press

The publication of this book is made possible by a grant from Utrecht Data School and Open Access Fund at Utrecht University.

Cover design: Template Visual Design Studio with a photo by Pat Pilon
Lay-out: Crius Group, Hulshout

Amsterdam University Press English-language titles are distributed in the US and Canada by the University of Chicago Press.

ISBN	978 94 6298 717 3 (Paperback)
ISBN	978 94 6298 136 2 (Hard cover)
e-ISBN	978 90 4853 101 1
DOI	10.5117/9789462981362
NUR	670

Table of Contents

Acknowledgements   9

Foreword   11

Introduction   13
New Brave World
Karin van Es & Mirko Tobias Schäfer

Section 1   Studying Culture through Data

1. Humanistic Data Research   25
An Encounter between Epistemic Traditions
Eef Masson

2. Towards a 'Humanistic Cinemetrics'?   39
Christian Gosvig Olesen

3. Cultural Analytics, Social Computing and Digital Humanities   55
Lev Manovich

4. Case Study   69
On Broadway
*Daniel Goddemeyer, Moritz Stefaner, Dominikus Baur &
Lev Manovich*

5. Foundations of Digital Methods   75
Query Design
Richard Rogers

6. Case Study   95
Webs and Streams – Mapping Issue Networks Using Hyperlinks,
Hashtags and (Potentially) Embedded Content
Natalia Sánchez-Querubín

Section 2 Data Practices in Digital Data Analysis

7. Digital Methods   109
    From Challenges to *Bildung*
    Bernhard Rieder & Theo Röhle

8. Data, Culture and the Ambivalence of Algorithms   125
    William Uricchio

9. Unknowing Algorithms   139
    On Transparency of Unopenable Black Boxes
    Johannes Paßmann & Asher Boersma

10. Social Data APIs   147
    Origin, Types, Issues
    Cornelius Puschmann & Julian Ausserhofer

11. How to Tell Stories with Networks   155
    Exploring the Narrative Affordances of Graphs with the *Iliad*
    Tommaso Venturini, Liliana Bounegru, Mathieu Jacomy &
    Jonathan Gray

12. Towards a Reflexive Digital Data Analysis   171
    Karin van Es, Nicolás López Coombs & Thomas Boeschoten

Section 3 Research Ethics

13. Get Your Hands Dirty   183
    Emerging Data Practices as Challenge for Research Integrity
    Gerwin van Schie, Irene Westra & Mirko Tobias Schäfer

14. Research Ethics in Context   201
    Decision-Making in Digital Research
    Annette Markham & Elizabeth Buchanan

15. Datafication & Discrimination   211
    Koen Leurs & Tamara Shepherd

Section 4 Key Ideas in Big Data Research

16. The Myth of Big Data   235
    Nick Couldry

17. Data Point Critique   241
    Carolin Gerlitz

18. Opposing the Exceptionalism of the Algorithm   245
    Evgeny Morozov

19. The Need for a Dialogue with Technology   249
    Mercedes Bunz

Tools   255

Notes on Contributors   257

Index   265

Acknowledgements

A few years back we embarked on an expedition into the rapidly transforming landscape of data research, the narratives of big data and the
practices emerging with novel data resources, tools and new directions of
social and cultural inquiry. This book represents our own experiences and
impressions of this journey. We were out there on unfamiliar and at times
even uncharted territory. Often we depended on the help of more learned
colleagues who generously shared their knowledge, gave us directions or
helped with problems. Many of them became authors for this book and we
would like to thank them for trusting us with collecting their contributions
and presenting them in a joint volume.

The editors wish to thank the Utrecht Data School staff Thomas Boeschoten, Irene Westra, Iris Muis, Daniela van Geenen and Gerwin van
Schie for their input and for providing an intellectually stimulating work
environment. With the Utrecht Data School we have created a place where
ambitious and enthusiastic students can meet to join us in this exploration.
We are grateful for having the rare opportunity of conducting research
together with students from whom we can learn so much and whose
insatiable curiosity is an inspiration as well as a constant reminder of why
we became teachers in the first place. Our gratitude extends also to the
Institute of Cultural Inquiry and the open access fund at Utrecht University
for enabling us to make this book open access.

A special thanks to William Uricchio, Fernando van der Vlist and Eef
Masson for their helpful comments and advice at various stages of the editing process. Finally, we are particularly grateful to Nicolás López Coombs
for helping us with the editing and the formatting of the book, but most
importantly for keeping an eye on our timeline.

Mirko Tobias Schäfer & Karin van Es
Anywhere but in their office, 2016

Foreword

Over the past few years, many books have heralded a 'data revolution' that will change the way we live, work, think and make money (Kitchin 2014; Mayer-Schönberger & Cukier 2013). Datafication – transforming all things under the sun into a data format and thus quantifying them – is at the heart of the networked world. Data are also at the centre of our media practices: data feed the many applications we use on a variety of platforms, they flow from users and devices to services and platforms, making connections and scaling audiences at an unprecedented rate. Networked connectivity runs on data – the new oil of the information economy. Just as electricity changed industrial processes and domestic practices in the nineteenth century, a data-driven paradigm will constitute the core of twenty-first-century processes and practices.

It is therefore no surprise that data have moved to the centre of media research and have become protagonists in media narratives. Some scholars have heralded Big Data as the engine of unprecedented technological and social progress; for others, this framing marks yet another myth in the history of media technologies. In a society where many aspects of language, discourse and culture have been datafied, it is imperative to scrutinize the conditions and contexts from which they emanate. Researchers from the humanities and social sciences increasingly realize they have to valorise data originating from Web platforms, devices and repositories as significant cultural research objects. Data have become ontological and epistemological objects of research – manifestations of social interaction and cultural production. *The Datafied Society: Studying Culture through Data* approaches datafication as a process of mediatisation, and provides a theoretical and methodological toolkit for those wanting to study culture through data.

In developing new research skills, academics not only expand their own corpora of research objects; they also significantly change – and boost – their own role in society. As data are increasingly considered to be at the heart of the knowledge economies, data-savvy scholars from the humanities and arts (often in collaboration with information and computer scientists) have ignited critical public debates. Their perspectives on data science are important in that they bring the question of responsibility to the fore. Questions of responsible data production and use, but also questions of meaning attribution, ethics, privacy, data power and transparency of data handling now constitute the core of this new paradigm. As much as scholars need to tackle the challenges for research ethics standards when working with big data, they also need to critically revisit their own position as experts who can influence public debates, policymaking and commercial activities.

For humanities scholars and students, the transformation towards a datafied society means they have to be able to deploy new research skills and methods that come along with this paradigm shift. Significantly, students need to be educated to become critical data practitioners who are both capable of working with data and of critically questioning the big myths that frame the datafied society. It also means they have to leave the academic ivory tower and enter the new world of 'data practices' to witness how they transform institutions, shape business models, and lead to new forms of governance or civic participation.

The Datafied Society: Studying Culture through Data provides students from the humanities in general (and media studies in particular) with a comprehensive overview of data practices relevant to media researchers. The book contains a broad overview of methods available, most prominently so-called Cultural Analytics and digital methods. A number of well-respected contributors show how specific social interactions and cultural practices in a data-fuelled society can be thoroughly studied and analysed, not only by exploring new analytical tools but also by critically assessing the various approaches, encouraging readers to develop a balanced understanding of how the datafied society works and how it can be looked upon from different angles. Several engaging case studies show the rich potential of what the analysis of data practices has to offer to media studies scholars. In the best tradition of this young field, critical reflection goes hand in hand with exploring new theoretical venues.

As our world gets increasingly connected and mediatised, input and expertise from the humanities and social sciences becomes essential to understanding the dynamics, ethics and pragmatics of a datafied society. This book is an important contribution towards meeting the challenges of the platform-driven, data-fuelled world in which we have all come to live.

José van Dijck
Professor of Comparative Media Studies, University of Amsterdam
11 April 2016

Introduction

New Brave World

Karin van Es & Mirko Tobias Schäfer

Optimistic reporting about 'big data' has made it easy to forget that data-driven practices have been part of the emerging information society since the nineteenth century (Beniger 1989; Porter 1996; Campbell-Kelly 2003). In lieu of an illustrative metaphor, the label 'big data' is used to describe a set of practices involving the collection, processing and analysis of large data sets. The term enables members of the general public to engage in debates, albeit often uninformed, on the ongoing transformation of our knowledge economy, but it disguises more than it reveals. Nevertheless, despite its vagueness, the term captures something of significance about contemporary Western societies, where economic value is generated through the processing of information and the monetization of knowledge. To develop a critical understanding of this current situation and its societal consequences, it is important to debunk the exceptionalism inherent in the 'big data' paradigm. For starters, we must stop feeding the hype about it and lay out what we know: the phenomenon we are dealing with is not 'big data', but 'the computational turn' (Berry 2012; Braidotti 2013). This turn began in the 1950s with the introduction of electronic computers and continues unabated today. It concerns the datafication of everything: all aspects of life are now transformed into quantifiable data (Mayer-Schönberger & Cukier 2013). As the social is extensively mined, its data are used to predict human behaviour and automate decision-making processes. As José van Dijck claims, 'datafication as a legitimate means to *access, understand* and *monitor* people's behaviour is becoming a leading principle, not just amongst techno-adepts, but also amongst scholars who see datafication as a revolutionary research opportunity to investigate human conduct' (2014: 198). Data analysis promises an 'objective' way to grasp the complex and dynamic reality we live in. Visualized via colourful dashboards, info-graphics and charts, it puts forth, persuasively and seductively, a seemingly accurate and unbiased assessment of reality. However, the translation of the social into data involves a process of abstraction that compels certain compromises to be made as the data are generated, collected, selected and analysed (Langlois et al. 2015).

The New Empirical

Because datafication is taking place at the core of our culture and social organization, it is crucial that humanities scholars tackle questions about how this process affects our understanding and documentation of history, forms of social interaction and organization, political developments, and our understanding of democracy. That datafication is a phenomenon that urgently demands investigation was acknowledged in sociology more than a decade ago, but this recognition did not necessarily lead to the adoption of novel data practices or the reassessment of existing research agendas. In a programmatic article, Andrew Abbott (2000) pointed out the challenges for researchers when confronted with new data resources available on an unprecedented scale:

> There is little question that a gradual revolution in the nature of knowledge is taking place: a slow eclipsing of print by visual representation, a move toward knowledge that is more experimental and even aleatory, an extensive commodification of important parts of previously esoteric knowledge. (298)

This forecast has been borne out by the developments of the past decade and a half, and these processes of change have indeed intensified. The Google search engine and commercial social media platforms such as Facebook, Twitter, YouTube and Instagram continually generate data from the interactions of millions of users. Access to data/tools is sold to marketeers and is employed to target, predict and manage these platforms' users. So-called application programming interfaces (APIs) make parts of vast databases accessible to third parties, including researchers. Concurrently, an industry has emerged whose companies collect, sell, combine and analyse data sets for all kinds of purposes, ranging from targeted advertising and market research to credit ratings, risk assessments and mass surveillance. The collection of data from massive data sets also yields a glimpse of a future when certain sorts of businesses will thrive on the exploitation of vast amounts of stored information.

The large corpus of empirical data and available tools for data collection and analysis is changing the ways knowledge is produced (Weinberger 2013; Meyer & Schroeder 2015). For the humanities, this transformation requires not only that we critically inquire into how technology affects our understanding of knowledge and how it alters our epistemic processes, but that we also employ the new data resources and technologies in new ways of scholarly investigation. Although data sets can provide new insights that offer opportunities for fine-grained detail previously not available, their possibilities are frequently overestimated (e.g. Anderson 2008; Schmidt &

Cohen 2014). Within academia, the blind trust in models, methods and data has been consistently criticized; recent big data enthusiasm has motivated a cohort of critical scholars to raise the alarm yet again (e.g. Couldry 2014; Gitelman 2013; boyd & Crawford 2011; Pasquale 2015). In this light, Rob Kitchin in *The Data Revolution: Big Data, Open Data, Data Infrastructures and Their Consequences* (2014) identifies four fallacies sustaining big data empiricism:

1. Big Data can capture the whole of a domain and provide full resolution;
2. there is no need for a priori theory, models or hypotheses;
3. data can speak for themselves free of human bias or framing;
4. meaning transcends context or domain-specific knowledge. (133-137)

The unquestionable allure of new forms of empiricism makes it important for us to continue to acknowledge that humanities scholars' epistemological assumptions are different from those of their counterparts in the hard sciences. The purpose of humanities data research is not empirical validation and hypothesis testing, but the development of questions and the discovery of insights (Ramsay 2003: 173). Rather than import questions and methods from the hard sciences, we must develop our own approaches and sensitivities in working with data that will reflect the humanities' traditions.

The Humanities Scholar Revisited

There has been a tendency in academia to classify the emerging research practices of the digital humanities as a new specialism, a new field that can be neatly contained, whether within a department, an academic minor or research group. This position is troubling: computer-aided methods and data practices are not some new object like films or games once were. 'Digital humanities' is merely the *nom de guerre* of the computational turn in the humanities. Datafication and computerization will come to affect all research agendas and inform the skill sets of students and scholars alike. We predict that the term 'digital humanities' will sound increasingly pleonastic and will eventually disappear – it will lead not to the replacement of established methods in the humanities, but rather to an expansion in the curricula we study and the methods we use.

Widely associated with computational methods, the digital humanities have been criticized from within the humanities as a whole. In "The Dark Side of the Digital Humanities" (2014), Richard Grusin discusses the tensions between scholars of the traditional humanities and those engaged in digital humanities, which have been based on the idea that the latter 'make things'. In this assertion he sees a devaluation of critique (or other modes of humanistic inquiry). The current focus on the digital humanities' ability to 'build' or to 'make' things rather than to critically comment on issues is misleading (not least because critique takes many forms, including making, building and application). At the core of this debate – though often it is not made explicit – is the question of how to approach the object of research. It has frequently been claimed that studying culture through data would necessitate thorough training in programming so as to allow researchers the wherewithal to 'look' into the 'black box' of the technology they are using, but such an emphasis misses the mark. Since the emerging algorithmic culture is characterized by the translation of rules and procedures into software, we need to develop an understanding of the mathematical concepts and models driving these programmes not in order to fully master them but rather to understand them sufficiently enough to approach new research objects from a critical perspective. We endorse Nick Montfort's understanding of programming as a means to develop intellectual capabilities that help us grasp how procedures of everyday life are translated into machine-readable language (Montfort 2016).

With regard to Grusin's call for humanities scholars to engage in critical inquiry, we are aware of the pressures brought on by academia's relentless corporatization and the overall neoliberal trend in society. Fields in the humanities are increasingly confronted with the demand that they justify their research activities. In such a climate it is tempting to employ computer-aided methods and quantitative analysis to feign a more 'scientific' appearance. Employing popular but meaningless terms such as 'big data' is symptomatic in this regard. However, the computational turn offers the humanities an incredibly important opportunity to study the contemporary transformation of society. We believe that access to large-scale empirical evidence and to analytic tools enables humanities scholars not only to describe this transformation empirically, but also to develop conceptual frameworks for understanding its impact. Understanding the 'digital humanities' as something instrumental, merely covering ways of doing research instead of conceiving of it as a more encompassing scholarly reaction to an increasingly datafied society, would simply mean following the folly of policymakers who believe that technological advancement will solve social problems.

As humanities scholars, we engage with 'the situated, partial, and constitutive character of knowledge production' (Drucker 2011: n.p.). The increasing translation of aspects of everyday life into machine-readable information can be seen as yet another process of mediatisation that media scholars in particular are well suited to scrutinize. This does not mean that they can sit back and rely on their distinct methods and skills. On the contrary: the data revolution (Kitchin 2014) raises issues concerning research questions, methods and ethics. It calls for new literacies and the development of codes of conduct that make transparent the role of computational methods, that tackle ethical issues in data collection and sharing, and that address the role of humanities scholars in public debate and interdisciplinary cooperation.

To become 'experts' in data practices and simultaneously investigate how datafication affects institutions in our society, we need to work directly in the very fields where transformation through these practices manifests itself; whether as embedded researchers, activists or active participants applying scholarly expertise in the diverse contexts afforded by various social institutions. Here application and making are not only critical practices but also constitute learning acts. In response to the new demands of our times, we founded the Utrecht Data School at Utrecht University in the Netherlands. This research and education platform allows us to conduct data research with our students in areas that are rapidly changing through the advancing information processing technologies commissioned by companies, governments and non-profit organizations. But we are not a mere service provider: by initiating debates among stakeholders and policymakers, we can inform opinion-making processes and express critique as much in the application of data practices as in public debate. Unlike preaching from the pulpit of the academic lecture hall, our engagement in the field is risky. Nevertheless, we are convinced that the humanities have much to offer in societal debates about data through their profound understanding of cultural complexity and their critical inquiry into knowledge technologies.

Investigating the Datafied Society

This book is a collection of scholarly investigations into computer-aided methods and practices. While several contributors offer essays representing their skills, methods and exemplary research projects, others reflect on the sensibilities and competencies that scholars need to develop in order to study contemporary culture through data. This includes an expert understanding of the specific role of data analysis tools and data visualization in the process of knowledge production. In academic research, but also in many sectors of business and other areas of society at large, data analysis unfolds via computer interfaces that display results that users often mistakenly regard as objective assessments. Such environments need knowledge workers who can grasp the processes of knowledge generation, from data collection through the various stages of analysis to visualization. These experts should be positioned to question the data sets as well as the mathematical models which determine the analysis.

In their historical investigation, Lorraine Daston and Peter Galison (2007) show that objectivity emerges as a symptom of epistemological fear: 'fear that the world is too labyrinthine to be threaded by reason; fear that the senses are too feeble and the intellect too frail; fear that memory fades, even between adjacent steps of a mathematical demonstration; fear that authority and convention is blind [...] Objectivity fears subjectivity, the core self' (373-74). The emergence of objectivity in scientific discourse also shaped a distinct self-understanding of the scientist. Delegating image creation to machines, the twentieth-century scientist became the expert reader of images whose 'trained judgement' afforded an accurate analysis and an alteration of the image for the depiction of patterns, the categorization of families of objects and so forth.[1] Daston and Galison note that contemporary scientific images are changing, both in quality and functionality. 'The image-as-tool seems to enter the scene inseparably from the creation of a new kind of scientific self – a hybrid figure, who very often works toward scientific goals, but with an attitude to the work that borrows a great deal from engineering, industrial application, and even artistic-aesthetic ambition' (2007: 413). One might add that over the past two decades of internet culture, open-source software development and online collaboration have also affected academic inquiry, which unfolds at the crossroads of universities and maker labs, hackathons or start-ups. Our current enthusiasm for computer-aided methods and data parallels the technology-induced crisis in representation and objectivity analysed by Daston and Galison. Their concerns must be taken into account in order to critically reflect upon the purported objectivity of computer-calculated results and visualizations.

The persuasive power of such claims to objectivity works on all levels of management and policymaking and requires that the scientific self be an eager advocate for critical inquiry into the working mechanisms of computer-aided and data-driven analysis. The media philosopher Vilém Flusser warned of the inscribed promise of scientific accuracy and objectivity in 'techno-images' (1997). The unbalanced enthusiasm for

---

1   See, for example, Daston and Galison (2007: 371).

data practices as processes for the development of accurate and 'neutral' (hence objective) results might prove just as problematic. As has been eloquently pointed out by David Gelernter, in discussing the uncritical reading of a map of potential ash distribution following the eruption of the Icelandic volcano Eyjafjallajökull in 2010, uncritical acceptance of computer-calculated results might have dangerous consequences: 'Firstly we'll be covered in an ash cloud of anti-knowledge and secondly a moral and intellectual passivity will emerge that won't doubt or argue against the images' (Gelernter 2010). This does not mean that we should reject those practices, but rather that we should employ them while being informed about their limitations, questioning their social impact and grasping their role in the epistemic process. The task ahead is to inform users, policymakers and the general public about the many factors that make up a data set, shape analysis and generate visualizations – and the many ways to read these digital analytics.

Although primarily directed at upper graduate students and researchers in the media studies, *The Datafied Society* is a useful collection of essays for anyone interested in studying culture during the era of the computational turn. The edited volume has been structured into four parts: (1) Studying Culture through Data; (2) Practices; (3) Concerns; and (4) Key Ideas in Big Data Research.

Part 1, 'Studying Culture through Data', covers different research methods. In her contribution, Eef Masson explores how two sets of epistemic traditions that used to be relevant to more or less distinct groups of scholars – hermeneutic and empirical – encounter each other in humanistic data research. She discusses how recent literature that reflects on the current state of the digital humanities tends to focus either on returning to the core, interpretative tasks of humanists or on bridging the two epistemic traditions. The tension between these traditions is also addressed in the contribution by Christian Gosvig Olesen, who argues that Cinemetrics, Cultural Analytics and ACTION, which quantify and visualize stylistic patterns in films and other cultural products, promote an inductive, exploratory form of analysis, and thus challenge the perception that cinemetric methodology is primarily a scientistic mode. These tools possess the potential to make cinemetrics more compelling to film scholars, who have been sceptical of its approach due to its association with a positivist epistemology.

The focus then shifts to Cultural Analytics, with Lev Manovich's proposed alternative to the distinct traditions carved out by Social Computing and Digital Humanities. Manovich successfully avoids taking sides between the goals and methods of the humanities and of the sciences and instead explores how to toggle between the two disciplinary paradigms in order to pursue opportunities missed by both. He discusses the project he heads up, *On Broadway*, as an exemplary use of Cultural Analytics. The project uses data and images from various sources such as Twitter and Instagram posts, New York City taxi trips and data of economic indicators to create a novel view of city life.

The next two contributions focus on digital methods. First, Richard Rogers investigates the role of query design in digital methods, discussing how digital methods repurpose mediums and outputs for social (and medium) research. He explores how Google can be employed as an epistemological machine in research and discusses query design as a distinct analytical approach. Then, Natalia Sánchez-Querubín examines issue networks as part of the digital methods initiative to 'follow the medium'. She explores how streams of hashtags rather than hyperlinks can provide a way for redoing issue network analysis for social media.

Part 2 is dedicated to data practices in digital data analysis. It considers how researchers can engage with the datafied society. In his contribution, William Uricchio explores how algorithms paired with big data redefine long-held subject-object relations, raising important epistemological questions. He makes suggestions as to how the humanities agenda can be revised so that the new order's implications can be properly understood. In the following chapter, Bernhard Rieder and Theo Röhle discuss what they regard as the five main challenges of digital methods and explore the concept of the 'digital Bildung' (Berry 2011) as a means of facing these challenges. Taking up three examples, they demonstrate that the tools we have come to use mobilize a wide array of knowledge. The singular focus on code as a form of knowledge that is required when working with data distracts from considering what is actually coded. The 'content' of software is not code per se but rather a procedure *expressed* in code; and knowledge about these procedures is what needs to be developed.

The next contribution zooms in on the tools used in digital data analysis, as Johannes Paßmann and Asher Boersma consider an approach to algorithmic black boxes. They develop a concept of transparency that outlines the skills necessary for researchers to deal with the parts of the box that remain 'black' or opaque. Next, Cornelius Puschmann and Julian Ausserhofer show us different aspects of APIs from the perspective of social scientists using them for data collection. They describe the origin of APIs in software development, conduct a survey of popular Web APIs by type, and discuss issues with regard to the reliability, validity and representativeness of data retrieved from APIs before offering speculation about future developments in this area. Tommaso Venturini et al. then reflect on a particular way of analysing data through the visualization of networks. They illustrate the narrative and storytelling potential of networks by examining the *Iliad's* network of characters, thus moving away from a discussion of the mathematical properties of networks to a reflection on how networks mediate and structure the phenomena they represent. Lastly, Karin van Es, Nicolás López Coombs and Thomas Boeschoten advocate for reflexive data analysis. They provide a series of questions about the various stages involved in doing digital data research that underscores how data and data visualizations are constructed by researchers and the tools they use.

Part 3 is dedicated to ethics, encompassing concerns ranging from moral issues that need to be tackled when embarking on research to reflections on how big data discriminates. Gerwin van Schie, Irene Westra and Mirko Tobias Schäfer discuss research ethics in light of their own experience in scraping patient data from an online platform. They reflect on the strained relationship between existing ethical guidelines and big data research, particularly in relation to the idea of informed consent. They propose a research structure that allows big data research to be conducted in an ethical manner. Taking a broader view, Annette Markham and Elizabeth Buchanan consider their previous work to provide a cohesive framework for assisting internet researchers, review boards, students and ethicists in ethically navigating the murky waters of internet research. Concluding this section, Koen Leurs and Tamara Shepherd explore the social biases of data sets and discuss the extent to which inequality, racism and prejudice are reflected in data sets.

Part 4, 'Key Ideas in Big Data Research', comprises a series of four short interviews exploring two topics; first, with Nick Couldry and Carolin Gerlitz on the challenges in researching the datafied society. Couldry specifically tackles the 'myth of big data' and Gerlitz the problems of making data points countable and comparable. With Evgeny Morozov and Mercedes Bunz, we then consider how algorithms affect everyday life. Morozov opposes the exceptionalism of algorithms; Bunz stresses the need to engage in dialogue with technology and to learn how to understand 'algorithmic thought'.

The chapters in this book can be read separately, but, taken together, they make a contribution that will stimulate and engage humanities scholars via their perspectives on debates and reflections on the theory and practices of digital data research. In addition to enhancing understanding of the field itself, they provide some hands-on guidelines to help direct research in an ethical and transparent manner, promoting awareness of how researchers and their tools affect knowledge production.

References

Abbott, Andrew. 2000. "Reflections on the Future of Sociology." *Contemporary Sociology – Journal of Reviews*. 29 (2) (March): 296-300.

Berry, David M. 2012. "Introduction: Understanding the Digital Humanities." In *Understanding Digital Humanities*, ed. David M. Berry, 1-20. New York: Palgrave Macmillan.

boyd, danah, & Crawford, Kate. 2012. "Critical Questions for Big Data: Provocations for a Cultural, Technological, And Scholarly Phenomenon." *Information, Communication & Society* 15 (5): 662-679.

Braidotti, Rosi. 2013. *The Posthuman*. Cambridge: John Wiley & Sons.

Couldry, Nick. 2014. "Inaugural: A necessary disenchantment: myth, agency and injustice in a digital world." http://onlinelibrary.wiley.com/doi/10.1111/1467-954X.12158/abstract.

Daston, Lorraine & Peter Galison. 2007. *Objectivity*. Cambridge, MA: The MIT Press.

Dijck, José van. 2014. "Datafication, dataism and dataveillance: Big Data between scientific paradigm and ideology." *Surveillance & Society* 12 (2): 197-208.

Drucker, Johanna. "Humanities Approaches to Graphical Display." *Digital Humanities Quarterly* 5 (1).

Flusser, Vilém. 1997. *Medienkultur*. Frankfurt a.M.: Fischer.

Gelernter, David. 2010. "Gefahren der Softwaregläubigkeit: Die Aschewolke aus Antiwissen." *Frankfurter Allgemeine Zeitung*, April 26. www.faz.net/aktuell/feuilleton/debatten/digitales-denken/gefahren-der- softwareglaeubigkeit-die-aschewolke-aus-antiwissen-1606375.html.

Gitelman, Lisa & Virginia Jackson. 2013. "Introduction." In *"Raw Data" Is an Oxymoron* ed. Lisa Gitelman, 1-14. Cambridge, MA: The MIT Press.

Grusin, Richard. "The Dark Side of Digital Humanities: Dispatches from Two Recent MLA Conventions." *Differences: A Journal of Feminist Cultural Studies* 25 (1): 79-92.

Kitchin, Rob. 2014. *The Data Revolution: Big Data, Open Data, Infrastructures and Their Conse-quences*. London: SAGE.

Mayer-Schönberger, Viktor & Kenneth Cukier. 2013. *Big Data: A Revolution that Will Transform How We Live, Work, and Think*. London: John Murray Publishers.

Meyer, Eric T. & Ralph Schroeder. 2015. *Knowledge Machines: Digital Transformations of the Science and Humanities*. Cambridge, MA: The MIT Press.

Montfort, Nick. 2016. *Exploratory Programming for the Arts and Humanities*. Cambridge, MA: The MIT Press.

Pasquale, Frank. 2015. *The Black Box Society*. Cambridge, MA: Harvard University Press.

Ramsay, Stephen. 2003. "Toward an Algorithmic Criticism." *Literary and Linguistic Computing* 18 (2): 167-174.

Weinberger, David. 2014. *Too big to know: Rethinking knowledge now that the facts aren't the facts, experts are everywhere, and the smartest person in the room is the room*. Basic Books.

Section 1
Studying Culture through Data

1.   Humanistic Data Research

An Encounter between Epistemic Traditions

Eef Masson

> *The majority of information graphics [...] are shaped by the disciplines*
> *from which they have sprung: statistics, empirical sciences, and*
> *business. Can these languages serve humanistic fields where*
> *interpretation, ambiguity, inference, and qualitative judgment take*
> *priority over quantitative statements and presentations of 'facts'?*
> – Johanna Drucker[1]

Introduction

Humanities scholars, in many cases, do not seek to establish unassailable, objective truths. Unlike their colleagues in the natural sciences, historians, literary scholars or media scholars often do not proceed by measuring or testing observable phenomena in order to conclusively demonstrate tendencies or relations between them (although there are certainly some who do).[2] Instead, they approach their objects of study from interpretive and critical perspectives, acting in the assumption that in doing so they necessarily also preconstitute them. However, with the introduction of digital research tools, and tools for data research specifically, humanistic scholarship seems to get increasingly indebted to positivist traditions. For one, this is because those tools, more often than not, are borrowed from disciplines centred on the analysis of empirical, usually quantitative data. Inevitably, then, they incorporate the epistemic traditions they derive from.[3] Another reason

---

1   Drucker 2014: 6-7.

2   For evidence of the latter, see for instance Bod 2013, which traces empirical tendencies in humanities scholarship from Antiquity to the present. Bod argues that there is an 'apparently unbroken strand in the humanities that can be identified as *the quest for patterns in humanistic material on the basis of methodical principles*' (7) – a strand which, in his view, contemporary philosophy of the humanities tends to ignore (7, 10). Arguably, this pattern-seeking tendency is more central to some disciplines (for instance, linguistics) than to others (e.g. literary studies).

3   Knorr Cetina provides an in-depth analysis of the operation of what she terms epistemic 'cultures' (1999). I prefer to use another noun here, because I consider much more basic conceptions as to how knowledge is or can be produced. (Knorr Cetina, indeed, is interested in the minute ontological and methodological differences between, very specifically, the natural

is that data research in the humanities is necessarily interdisciplinary: it involves collaborations between scholars with backgrounds in different fields – and therefore, different views on how knowledge takes shape.

Over the past decades, this encounter between scholarly traditions has led to a number of frictions. While some humanists have adopted digital tools in the hopes of making their results more verifiable, others have questioned the underlying assumptions, arguing that they threaten to undermine the very project of the humanities. By succumbing to the lure of scientism, those commentators fear, humanists run the risk of forgetting what they excel at – critical interpretation – and by the same token, of impoverishing their practice. At the same time, debates emerging from the encounter between research traditions have also engendered a series of profound developments in terms of how data research is performed.

In the past 20 years, the use of digital tools in humanities projects has become increasingly widespread.[4] In the early years, those tools were seen as mere aids: technical devices that could support the actual scholarly work, as performed by human researchers (Berry 2012: 3). At the time, the practice was most often referred to as 'humanities computing'. In the late 1990s, the denominator 'digital humanities' became more common. According to N. Katherine Hayles, this change in name 'was meant to signal that the field had emerged from the low-prestige status of a support device into a genuinely intellectual endeavour with its own professional practices, rigorous standards, and exciting theoretical explorations' (2012: 43).[5]

Although generalizations on the topic are contested, many agree that this shift in function was accompanied by a series of transformations in the nature and focus of the scholarship conducted. Early adopters, in many cases, were interested in the computer's capabilities for encoding, searching and retrieving large amounts of text, and for automating their analysis. Their research was focused predominantly on the detection of patterns and structures in an abundance of empirical data and geared towards

sciences; see pp. 3-4 of her introduction.) By using the term 'traditions' I seek to highlight the relation between attitudes towards data research, and assumptions and practices that long predate the use of computers in humanities scholarship.

4   The 'origins' of this practice are often traced to the 1940s, but the use of digital tools has grown more popular with the introduction of the World Wide Web (in the early 1990s). See for instance Hayles 2012: 42.

5   For a more profound analysis of the (then-recent) lexical shift from 'humanities computing' to 'digital humanities', see Svensson 2009. The author here examines 'how [the field's] naming is related to shifts in institutional, disciplinary, and social organization' (n.p.). Matthew Kirschenbaum for his part has highlighted on several occasions the tactical impulse behind this change in name (e.g. Kirschenbaum 2012).

generating quantitative results (Evans & Rees 2012: 23; Hayles 2012: 43).[6] Towards the end of the last decade, projects with a qualitative slant also became more common, and practitioners increasingly sought to answer interpretive questions. In the 2009 version of their 'Digital Humanities Manifesto', Jeffrey Schnapp, Todd Presner and Peter Lunenfeld observe that digital humanists, at the time, not only began to tackle a broader range of research objects than previously – advancing from digitized printed text to media forms and practices in the widest sense, including born-digital ones – but harnessed 'digital toolkits in the service of the Humanities' core [...] strengths: attention to complexity, medium specificity, historical context, analytical depth, critique and interpretation' (2). Inevitably, this entailed an interest also in matters of methodology: practitioners increasingly engaged in reflection on the underpinnings of computational approaches, both technical and epistemological.

As these trends continue, the role of information technologies for humanities research is being thoroughly reimagined. Computers, software and data are increasingly seen as generative: they are taken to afford new forms of scholarship, centring on questions that so far have lain outside the scope of academic endeavours. By the same token, humanities research and digital methods or tools are more often thought of as inextricably intertwined. Leighton Evans and Sian Rees, in their contribution to the introductory volume *Understanding Digital Humanities* (2012), claim that we are currently beginning to see the emergence of a 'field influenced by computation as *a way of* accessing, interpreting, and reporting the world' (29; emphasis added). For David M. Berry, editor of the volume, 'computational technology has become the very condition of possibility required in order to think about many of the questions raised in the humanities today' (3). These days, the most ambitious of digital humanities practitioners see computation as an opportunity to profoundly transform cultural criticism, and humanities research more broadly.

---

6   Such research, of course, is still being conducted today. The following URLs provide access to some examples of recent projects in quantitative data research, in the fields of history, literary studies, and linguistics respectively: http://www.herts.ac.uk/digital-history/cliodynamics-lab (the webpage of the Cliodynamics Lab at the Digital History Research Centre of the University of Hertfortshire, UK; cliodynamics uses mathematical modeling techniques to study historical dynamics in the social, cultural, and/or economic domain); http://novel-tm.ca/ (the website of NovelTM, a North-American inter-university initiative devoted to mining patterns in novels); http://research.dbvis.de/text/research-areas/digital-humanities/linguistic/ (the webpage for the Linguistic Data Analysis research area of the Data Analysis and Visualization Group at the University of Konstanz, Germany).

In this chapter I discuss in an exploratory manner how, over the course of the past two decades, humanistic data research has served as the backdrop to an encounter between two sets of epistemic traditions – hermeneutic and empirical – that had previously wielded their influence in more or less distinct areas of academic practice.[7] First, I identify some of the sites for this encounter, touching successively upon the tools scholars work with, the methodological underpinnings for those tools, and practices of cross-disciplinary collaboration. Next, I consider the frictions this encounter entailed, zooming in on some major points of critique directed at practitioners (most of them, indeed, concerning the status of interpretation in data research). Finally, I briefly contemplate how this criticism eventually helped shape developments in the digital humanities at large (as briefly outlined above).[8] As I shall argue, efforts to set new agendas for digital research are motivated in part by a wish to reclaim some of the core tasks of humanists – tasks often seen as interpretive in nature – but also, in some cases, to bridge the gap between disparate epistemic traditions.[9] While this chapter considers the humanities more broadly, I take my examples primarily, though not exclusively, from the study of media, and in particular film (historical), research.

7   I should stress, here, that 'areas of practice' does not mean 'disciplines'. Both traditions, indeed, co-exist within the same academic departments – although in those cases, they are often relevant to different groups of practitioners. Compare also Bod 2013: 351.

8   It might be useful to explicate here that the denominator 'digital humanities' is commonly used to refer to a broader category of practices than the 'humanistic data research' mentioned in my chapter title. For instance, the term is often also used by those involved in the creation or curation of online collections, or to refer to alternative (i.e. non-print) forms of knowledge production and dissemination. I shall use the terms alternately, depending on which category my claims are more relevant to.

The website of the Alliance of Digital Humanities Organizations (ADHO, an umbrella organisation for national and international associations of digital humanists) gives a useful overview of information on and resources for digital humanities research; see especially the sections 'publications' (http://adho.org/publications) and 'resources' (http://adho.org/resources, which lists key conferences and platforms, such as blogs). The City University of New York's Digital Humanities Resource Guide (http://commons.gc.cuny.edu/wiki/index.php/The_CUNY_Digital_Humanities_Resource_Guide) also references publications, events and tools, and provides links to leading centres for digital humanities research. The website of centerNet, a network of digital humanities centres, provides a more inclusive listing of research initiatives worldwide (http://dhcenternet.org/centers).

9   Christian Gosvig Olesen's chapter in this volume, which can be read as a companion piece to this text, demonstrates that in spite of such attempts, projects in humanistic data research still vary greatly in terms of how they deal with the empiricist underpinnings of the tools they work with.

Tools, Methods, Cooperations

In the epigraph to this chapter, Johanna Drucker points out that tools for
information visualization are inevitably indebted to the disciplines from
which they derive. The same, one might add, applies to tools for data scraping, and for the cleaning, sorting or otherwise processing of collected data.
For digital humanists, this is particularly relevant, as the tools they use are
rarely purpose-produced (or if they are, then they tend to refashion tools
that were designed to serve the needs of other disciplines). For example, the
Cultural Analytics toolkit developed by Lev Manovich's Software Studies
Initiative, featured in this book, includes among others the application
ImagePlot. This tool is an extension of the open-source image-analysis
program ImageJ (previously known as 'NIH Image') that was originally
developed for use in medical research (among others for the viewing of
tomography scans and X-rays, but later also in biological microscopy; see
Schneider, Rasband & Eliceiri 2012). Other examples are software initially
designed for use in the geosciences (mapping tools for instance), to perform
statistical operations in the study of economics, or even, to serve as aids in
the business and management sectors.

At the most basic level, the indebtedness Drucker speaks of can be understood as a set of built-in presuppositions about how knowledge is obtained.
In this context, it is important to consider not only the assumptions of the
practitioners for whom the tools were designed (in the above examples:
health or geoscientists, or economists) but also those of the software engineers who conceived them. In their contribution to *Understanding Digital
Humanities*, summarized in their chapter for this book, Bernhard Rieder
and Theo Röhle point out that the 'digital helpers' humanists use 'rely on
sets of assumptions, models, and strategies' that determine how 'units of
analysis, algorithms, and visualisation procedures' are defined (2012: 70).
These models and strategies derive in turn from such fields as statistics,
information or computer science, or mathematics: disciplines that even the
most experienced digital humanists can be only minimally familiar with. In
the tools themselves, moreover, they necessarily take on a technical form,
which means that they are not easily 'readable', *even* for experts (75-76).
In spite of this, the conceptual underpinnings of one's methods and tools
profoundly affect the results of the data processing done, and how these
should be interpreted (see also Drucker 2012).

In the absence of readily legible clues as to their epistemic foundations,
computational research tools are often assigned such values as reliability
and transparency (Kitchin 2014: 130). As Rieder and Röhle observe, the

automated processing of empirical data that they enable seems to suggest a neutral perspective on reality, unaffected by human subjectivity (2012: 72). Drucker, a specialist in the history of graphics, makes a similar point, focusing more closely on practices of data visualization. She argues that the tools used for this purpose are often treated as if the representations they render provide direct access to 'what is'. This way, the distinction between scientific observation ('the act of creating a statistical, empirical, or subjective account or image') and the phenomena observed is being collapsed (Drucker 2014: 125; see also Drucker 2012: 86).

Considering the association of digital methods and tools with such profoundly positivist ideals, it is hardly surprising that initially, it was primarily humanists already inclined towards empirical work who elected to use them. Computational methods were attractive to them because these promised more reliable, accurate or 'scientific' answers to their research questions than they had previously been able to obtain. In his contribution to a volume on computation in literary studies, Stephen Ramsay detects such motivations in projects since the 1980s, and even earlier (2008). Recent examples from media studies that seem similarly inspired are film historian Yuri Tsivian's efforts to automate quantitative approaches to the analysis of silent film style (dealt with at some length in Christian Gosvig Olesen's chapter in this volume) or the work of such practitioners of New Cinema History as John Sedgwick, who attempts to measure the historical popular-ity of films (2009; 2011).[10] However, as the use of digital methods gets more pervasive, the promise of mechanically obtained objectivity and transpar-ency seems to entice even those humanists who traditionally premised their scholarship on constructivist, rather than positivist, principles. As I discuss further on, this has provoked a good deal of criticism.[11]

Aside from the chosen methods and tools, cooperation is also an important factor in the encounter between epistemic traditions in humanistic data research. As many authors have argued, collaboration in digital projects between scholars in different fields is the rule rather than the exception (e.g. Hayles 2012: 51). One reason for this is that using digital tools, and in some cases also their development or fine-tuning, requires different sets of skills than most humanities researchers have. In addition, digital projects tend to be increasingly large-scale and take ever more complex forms; as such, they require a broad range of specialist (disciplinary) expertise. As Schnapp, Presner and Lunenfeld point out, such projects are about the building of

10   For an introduction to the concerns of New Cinema History, see Maltby 2011.
11   For a critique of the statistical analysis of film (style) specifically, see Gunning 2014.

'bigger pictures' (2009: 4) and therefore require combinations of perspectives, some of those not even humanistic at all. Regardless of the participants' motivation to succeed, this inevitably means that they have to negotiate the terms of their cooperation and, in particular, find ways to reconcile their disparate epistemic positions. Experience shows that even explicating those positions and communicating about them to others – whether these 'others' are software developers and computer scientists, or colleagues in other academic fields, in or outside the humanities – is not self-evident (e.g. Heftberger 2012: n.p.; Sculley & Pasanek 2008: 409-410; Van Zundert et al. 2012).

Resistance and Critique

As they engage in data research, humanists not only have to explain their ways to collaborators with different scholarly backgrounds. Over the years, they have had to justify themselves also to colleagues in their own specialist fields. For as long as humanities scholars have made use of digital tools, they have met with critique from fellow practitioners. At its most fundamental, this critique stems from the perception that the projects conducted do not do justice to the critical-interpretive legacy of much humanities research.[12] Roughly speaking, critics here divide into two groups. On the one hand, there are the sceptics, who are convinced that there is nothing to gain from the use of digital tools in the disciplines they engage in. Usually, these commentators have not tried their hands at digital research themselves, but voice their apprehension in reaction to work done by peers.[13] On the other, there are those scholars who, although recognizing the potential of computational approaches for addressing humanities concerns, make a case for a more critical engagement with the tools, methods, questions and results that are used or obtained, and especially their positivist underpinnings. Some of them even argue for a radically different approach to data research: one that could ultimately meet the hermeneutic standards of much 'traditional' humanities work.

   At least two sets of arguments, used by members of both groups, are relevant here. First, there is a concern that much data research practice today

12   There are also other points of critique, which do not follow as directly from the friction between epistemic traditions discussed above. For example, some have argued that the proliferation of digital projects leads to an 'instrumentalization' of humanities (teaching and) research (e.g. Grusin 2014).

13   A piece that exemplifies this position is literary critic and *New Republic* editor Adam Kirsch's contribution on the 'false promise' of the digital humanities (2014), which attests to a rather profound awareness of current debates on the topic.

does not involve the kind of interpretive intervention that the humanities are known for. Evans and Rees for instance wonder whether some practitioners might be getting caught in a logic of 'abstracted empiricism' (a term they borrow from sociologist Charles Wright Mills) 'which focuses so minutely on macro data that it fails to refine meaning' (2012: 29). The reasoning here is that researchers are so in awe of their data and visualizations that they 'forget' to also attribute meaning. Other critics react instead to the claim that digital scholars do not actually *need* to do this: that it is enough that they discover patterns (Hayles 2012: 51; Kitchin 2014: 131) as these already 'show us what we would never have been aware of' without our digital tools (Currie in Evans & Rees 2012: 21). For many, this assumption undermines the fundamental humanistic premise that knowledge gets produced in an encounter between a subject and his or her sources or data. To them, a kind of 'post-human' scholarship 'in which human interpretation takes a back seat to algorithmic processes' (Hayles 2012: 48) seems highly undesirable.

A second set of arguments in contrast relate to the observation that the results of data research are always, necessarily, a product of interpretation. The critique here centres on practitioners' inability or unwillingness to recognize this, or to consider it in their process. As Hayles points out, interpretation inevitably comes into play – whether it is humans or machines who do the 'reading' of data. The reason is that it is the former who create programmes, use them, and in doing so, make sense of the results (Hayles 2012: 47). Drucker, speaking more specifically of information visualizations, takes this a step further, arguing that the very data we use are already infused with interpretation. Rendering information in graphical form, she claims, 'gives it a simplicity and legibility that hides every aspect of the original interpretative framework on which the [...] data were constructed' (2014: 128). Drucker's point here is that data are always preconstituted, shaped by the parameters for their selection. Others have stressed that these parameters are never neutral, but construct the world as profoundly ideological (e.g. Posner 2015).[14] Therefore, we are well-advised to think of them not as *data* (given) but rather as *capta* (taken), 'constructed as an interpretation of the phenomenal world' rather than inherent to it (Drucker 2014: 128).[15]

14   Tara McPherson extends this argument to the computational systems – the technologies and their functionalities – that digital humanists work with (2012). See also McPherson in Jenkins 2015: n.p.

15   The term *capta*, as used in this way, is preferred also by Rob Kitchin (2014: 2), who in turn attributes it to one H.E. Jensen, writing in 1950. Alexander Galloway makes an argument similar to Drucker's, however without using the term (2011: 87-88).

New Agendas

Over time, such criticism has profoundly affected how data researchers have viewed their practices and responsibilities, and even more crucially, how they have approached their research. These days, more and more digital humanists find it mandatory to consider methodological and epistemic issues *as part of* the studies they conduct. Doing digital research, these scholars are convinced, requires explicit reflection on the status of one's data (how are they shaped by parameters for selection and how does this affect what one can learn from them?), one's methods and tools (which overt and covert assumptions about the world and how we know it do they incorporate, and how does this shape one's results?), and the interpretations one makes (how do they relate to calculation and representation; how do they tie in with the here and now; are alternative interpretations possible as well?). D. Sculley and Bradley Pasanek, in a piece on data mining and machine learning in the humanities, argue that these methods force us to 'trade in a close reading of the original text [a common pursuit in the traditional humanities] for something that looks like a close reading of experimental results' (2008: 417).[16] This requires in turn that we navigate the ambiguities and contradictions our softwares produce (*ibid.*).

Some authors however find such measures insufficient. Among others, they suggest that even those who stress the limitations of their methods or tools often concede in the process to what is ultimately a positivist ideal of establishing facts, even if they conceive of it as an unattainable one (e.g. Ramsay 2008). Instead, these commentators plead for a better integration of computational methods with the core activities of humanities research, so as to ultimately redeem its characteristic strengths. One way of doing this is to use the computer's calculation and visualization powers not to test preconceived hypotheses, but to probe data in an exploratory manner. Scholars in various fields have argued that one of the great merits of digital tools is their capacity for *ostranenie*: for 'making strange', or defamiliarizing us from, our objects of study – and by the same token, for calling into question our most profound assumptions about them (e.g. Ramsay 2008: n.p.; Schnapp, Presner & Lunenfeld 2009: 10; Manovich 2012: 276).[17] Embracing

16 'Machine learning', in this sentence, refers to the use of computational methods for making predictions on the basis of data.

17 *Ostranenie* is a concept theorized among others by the Russian Formalist Victor Shklovsky. He used it to refer to the techniques writers deploy in transforming everyday into poetic language, in order to induce a heightened state of perception in their readers.

this potential requires that one uses one's tools not to solve existing scholarly problems, but to raise new questions, trigger new ideas, or as a prompt to try out alternative perspectives on the same objects (not necessarily with the help of digital tools).[18]

Another way of reconciling humanistic interests with the possibilities of computation is to exploit, as Daniel Chávez Heras puts it, software's affinity with 'notions of infinity, contingency or paradox' (2012: 10). The author draws inspiration here from Drucker's proposal for a 'speculative computing' (Drucker & Nowviskie 2004). Much digital humanities work today, Drucker argues, is premised on automation: the mechanistic application of set procedures, according to an unchanging logic. The problem with such procedures is that they inevitably restrict the user's interpretive options. In her view, humanists should invest instead in tools that enable 'augmentation' (a term by Douglas Engelbart): the extension of their intellectual and imaginative capabilities. The objective here is to bring forward in the research sequence acts of – active, openly performed – interpretative intervention. Rather than making do with tools that limit interpretation to a 'reading' of that which has already been sorted and measured (according to a set of often hidden parameters), humanities researchers should work towards a kind that could, for instance, integrate their own engagements with data into the calculations and representations performed or generated by computers. Of course, such an approach not only reclaims some of the characteristic strengths of humanities scholarship (at least, as perceived by the above-mentioned critics) and puts them centre stage, it also forces far-reaching transformations in terms of how this research is performed (in Drucker's case, for example, a shift from a text-based to a fundamentally visual *modus operandi*).[19]

---

18   Note however that this approach has also been criticized, most famously by the literary theorist Stanley Fish, in a blog post for the *New York Times* (2012) which he wrote partly in reaction to Stephen Ramsay's *Reading Machines* (2011). In this piece Fish attests to his preference for the sort of deductive approach – one that involves reasoning on the basis of a hypothesis – that Kitchin calls 'hegemonic within modern science' (132). The above pleas, in contrast, open the way for a more inductive approach, where the use of algorithms serves an exploratory purpose. For more on this topic, see also Scheinfeldt 2012 (which sees room in digital humanities research for both principles and procedures).

19   David J. Bodenhamer, in an article on the use of GIS technologies for historical research, imagines a similarly flexible kind of representation (multilayered and structurally open) but specifically for geospatial information. In his piece, he adds to Chávez Heras' and Drucker's arguments that it would also help (re)position scholarship, and the spatial humanities in particular, as a conversation or negotiation between (many) experts or contributors (2013: 10-12).

Demands for a more profoundly humanistic digital practice are countered by parties who see computational methods rather as an opportunity for a more comprehensive integration of the humanities and the sciences – and in some cases, even the arts and technology. Further integration is necessary, they argue, because it can help safeguard the humanities' central role in our contemporary society (e.g. Schnapp, Presner & Lunenfeld 2009: 11) or even ensure the continuity of scholarly practice as such (Lin 2012: 296). Although formulations vary, the observation is often made in this context that cooperation in digital projects should evolve from its current inter-disciplinarity to a more profound 'transdisciplinarity', which 'radicalises existing disciplinary norms and practices and allows researchers to go beyond their parent disciplines, using a shared conceptual framework that draws together concepts, theories, and approaches from various disciplines into something new that transcends them all' (*ibid.*: 298).

Inevitably, pleas such as these suggest that the situations their authors envision have not quite materialized in practice. Today still, the participants of projects in humanities data research relate in very different ways to the research traditions they encounter, either through their various collabora-tions or in the tools they use. (And, as Olesen's piece in this volume suggests, dissent on how data research should be conducted also occurs between scholars working in the same specialist fields.) Moreover, they attest to the fact that it is a lot easier to formulate requirements for a truly humanistic data research than to devise the methods and tools that meet them.

References

Berry, David M. 2012. "Introduction: Understanding the Digital Humanities." In *Understanding Digital Humanities*, ed. David M. Berry, 1-20. New York: Palgrave Macmillan.

Bodenhamer, David J. 2013. "Beyond GIS: Geospatial Technologies and the Future of History." In *History and GIS: Epistemologies, Considerations and Reflections*, ed. Alexander von Lünen & Charles Travis, 1-13. Dordrecht: Springer.

Bod, Rens. 2013. *A New History of the Humanities: The Search for Principles and Patterns from Antiquity to the Present.* Oxford: Oxford University Press.

Chávez Heras, Daniel. 2012. "The Malleable Computer: Software and the Study of the Moving Image." *Frames Cinema Journal* (1). Accessed 8 October 2015. http://framescinemajournal. com/article/the-malleable-computer/.

Drucker, Johanna. 2012. "Humanistic Theory and Digital Scholarship." In *Debates in the Digital Humanities*, ed. Matthew K. Gold, 85-95. Minneapolis: University of Minnesota Press.

—. 2014. *Graphesis: Visual Forms of Knowledge Production.* Cambridge, MA: Harvard University Press.

Drucker, Johanna & Bethany Nowviskie. 2004. "Speculative Computing: Aesthetic Provocations in Humanities Computing." In *A Companion to Digital Humanities*, ed. Susan Schreibman, Ray

Siemens & John Unsworth, Chapter 29. Oxford: Blackwell. Accessed 4 December 2016. www.digitalhumanities.org/companion/view?docId=blackwell/9781405103213/9781405103213.xml&chunk.id=ss1-4-10&toc.depth=1&toc.id=ss1-4-10&brand=default.

Evans, Leighton & Sian Rees. 2012. "An Interpretation of Digital Humanities." In *Understanding Digital Humanities*, ed. David M. Berry, 21-41. New York: Palgrave Macmillan.

Fish, Stanley. 2012. "Mind Your P's and B's: The Digital Humanities and Interpretation." *Opinionator* (*New York Times* blog), 23 January. Accessed 8 January 2016. http://opinionator.blogs.nytimes.com/2012/01/23/mind-your-ps-and-bs-the-digital-humanities-and-interpretation/?_r=0.

Galloway, Alexander. 2011. "Are Some Things Unrepresentable?" *Theory, Culture & Society* 28 (7-8): 85-102.

Grusin, Richard. 2014. "The Dark Side of Digital Humanities: Dispatches from Two Recent MLA Conventions." *differences* 25 (1): 79-92.

Gunning, Tom. 2014. "Your Number Is Up! Questioning Numbers in Film History (or Can Numbers Provide Answers?)." Lecture, conference "A Numerate Film History? Cinemetrics Looks at Griffith, Sennett and Chaplin (1909-1917)", University of Chicago, 1 March. www.youtube.com/watch?v=VvwC_3FyRAo.

Hayles, N. Katherine. 2012. "How We Think: Transforming Power and Digital Technologies." In *Understanding Digital Humanities*, ed. David M. Berry, 42-66. New York: Palgrave Macmillan.

Heftberger, Adelheid. 2012. "Ask Not What Your Web Can Do For You – Ask What You Can Do For Your Web! Some Speculations about Film Studies in the Age of the Digital Humanities." *Frames Cinema Journal* (1). Accessed 30 September 2015. http://framescinemajournal.com/article/ask-not-what-your-web-can-do-for-you/.

Jenkins, Henry. 2015. "Bringing Critical Perspectives to the Digital Humanities: An Interview with Tara McPherson (Part Three)." *Confessions of an Aca-fan: The Official Weblog of Henry Jenkins*, 20 March. Accessed 4 December 2016. http://henryjenkins.org/2015/03/bringing-critical-perspectives-to-the-digital-humanities-an-interview-with-tara-mcpherson-part-three.html#sthash.n5oN3MRV.dpuf.

Kirsch, Adam. 2014. "Technology is Taking Over English Departments: The False Promise of the Digital Humanities." *New Republic*, 2 May. Accessed 8 January 2016. https://newrepublic.com/article/117428/limits-digital-humanities-adam-kirsch.

Kirschenbaum, Matthew. 2012. "Digital Humanities As/Is a Tactical Term." In *Debates in the Digital Humanities*, ed. Matthew K. Gold, 415-428. Minneapolis: University of Minnesota Press.

Kitchin, Rob. 2014. *The Data Revolution: Big Data, Open Data, Data Infrastructures and Their Consequences*. London: Sage.

Knorr Cetina, Karin. 1999. *Epistemic Cultures: How the Sciences Make Knowledge*. Cambridge, MA: Harvard University Press.

Lin, Yu-Wei. 2012. "Transdisciplinarity and Digital Humanities: Lessons Learned from Developing Text-Mining Tools for Textual Analysis." In *Understanding Digital Humanities*, ed. David M. Berry, 21-41. New York: Palgrave Macmillan.

Maltby, Richard. 2011. "New Cinema Histories." In *Explorations in New Cinema History: Approaches and Case Studies*, ed. Richard Maltby, Daniel Biltereyst & Philippe Meers, 3-39. Chichester: Wiley-Blackwell.

Manovich, Lev. 2012. "How to Compare One Million Images?" In *Understanding Digital Humanities*, ed. David M. Berry, 295-314. New York: Palgrave Macmillan.

McPherson, Tara. 2012. "Why Are the Digital Humanities So White? Or Thinking the Histories of Race and Computation." In *Debates in the Digital Humanities*, ed. Matthew K. Gold, 139-160. Minneapolis: University of Minnesota Press.

Posner, Miriam. 2015. "What's Next: The Radical, Unrealized Potential of Digital Humanities." Keynote lecture, Keystone Digital Humanities Conference, University of Pennsylvania, 22 July. http://miriamposner.com/blog/whats-next-the-radical-unrealized-potential-of-digital-humanities/.

Ramsay, Stephen. 2008. "Algorithmic Criticism." In *A Companion to Digital Literary Studies*, ed. Susan Schreibman & Ray Siemens, Chapter 26. Oxford: Blackwell. Accessed 22 September 2015. www.digitalhumanities.org/companionDLS/.

—. 2011. *Reading Machines: Toward an Algorithmic Criticism*. Urbana-Champaign: University of Illinois Press.

Rieder, Bernhard & Theo Röhle. 2012. "Digital Methods: Five Challenges." In *Understanding Digital Humanities*, ed. David M. Berry, 67-84. New York: Palgrave Macmillan.

Scheinfeldt, Tom. 2012. "Where's the Beef? Does Digital Humanities have to Answer Questions?" In *Debates in the Digital Humanities*, ed. Matthew K. Gold, 56-58. Minneapolis: University of Minnesota Press.

Schnapp, Jeffrey, Todd Presner & Peter Lunenfeld. 2009. "The Digital Humanities Manifesto 2.0." Accessed 22 September 2015. www.humanitiesblast.com/manifesto/Manifesto_V2.pdf.

Schneider, Caroline A., Wayne S. Rasband & Kevin W. Eliceiri. 2012. "NIH Image to ImageJ: 25 Years of Image Analysis." *Nature Methods* 9 (7): 671-675.

Sculley, D. & Bradley M. Pasanek. 2008. "Meaning and Mining: The Impact of Implicit Assumptions in Data Mining for the Humanities." *Literary and Linguistic Computing* 23 (4): 409-424.

Sedgwick, John. 2009. "Measuring Film Popularity: Principles and Applications." In *Digital Tools in Media Studies: Analysis and Research; An Overview*, ed. Michael Ross, Manfred Grauer & Bernd Freisleben, 43-54. Bielefeld: transcript.

—. 2011. "Patterns in First-Run and Suburban Filmgoing in Sydney in the mid-1930s." In *Explorations in New Cinema History: Approaches and Case Studies*, ed. Richard Maltby, Daniel Biltereyst & Philippe Meers, 140-158. Chichester: Wiley-Blackwell.

Svensson, Patrik. 2009. "Humanities Computing as Digital Humanities." *Digital Humanities Quarterly* 3 (3). Accessed 8 January 2016. http://digitalhumanities.org/dhq/vol/3/3/000065/000065.html.

Zundert, Joris van, Smiljana Antonijevic, Anne Beaulieu, Karina van Dalen-Oskam, Douwe Zeldenrust & Tara L. Andrews. 2012. "Cultures of Formalisation: Towards an Encounter between Humanities and Computing." In *Understanding Digital Humanities*, ed. David M. Berry, 279-294. New York: Palgrave Macmillan.

Acknowledgments

Many thanks to Christian Gosvig Olesen, Karin van Es, Mirko Tobias Schäfer and Markus Stauff for their comments on an earlier version of this article, and to Christian for his useful reading tips.

2. Towards a 'Humanistic Cinemetrics'?

Christian Gosvig Olesen

In recent years, film scholars have increasingly developed quantitative methodologies to produce data visualizations for a historical analysis of film style. Through methods of Cultural Analytics, Cinemetrics (2005) and ACTION (2014), which can be described as cinemetric or stylometric, scholars measure, quantify and visualize stylistic patterns in, for instance, editing, light or sound. These are used to investigate historical developments in film aesthetics and narration and to produce statistical profiles of films, directors or national cinemas.

Characterized by scientific rigour, deduction and hypothesis-testing, Cinemetrics' quantitative framework has been perceived as introducing a new empiricism or positivism in film historical research (Christie 2008). A significant reason for this is that the tool resuscitates a scientific paradigm of historical style analysis initiated in the 1970s to produce evidence for research on film editing and shot types (*ibid.*). The recent quantitative, statistical approaches of Cultural Analytics and ACTION, which build on this paradigm as a conceptual departure point, have equally been associated with a positivist epistemology (Manovich 2012a; Casey & Williams 2014). Yet, as I will argue in this article, their emergence is engendering an inductive, exploratory form of Cinemetrics which necessitates a change in the perception of cinemetric methodology as being primarily scientist. As I shall discuss further on, their practices, in the words of Eef Masson, suggest 'prob[ing] data in an exploratory manner' and highlight how data visualization defamiliarizes our objects of study by foregrounding their constructed nature (see the chapter by Mason in this publication, p. 33). In these aspects it seems they qualify as humanistic data research but that they still need to be fully recognized and distinguished as such. By attending to the development and deployments of Cultural Analytics and ACTION in comparison to Cinemetrics, my article takes further steps in this direction.[1] This, I argue, may open a critical path for contemporary, statistical style analysis and contribute to increased methodological pluralism in data-driven film historical research.

---

1   The developers of Cultural Analytics and ACTION, respectively, have emphasized their practices as more exploratory than Cinemetrics through blog posts and conference papers. It is these steps that I wish to acknowledge and theorize further by situating them within the discussion of scientism vs. hermeneutics in the present volume.

To introduce such a distinction is important because film studies, unlike history, sociology or literary studies, have tended to develop digital tools at a slow pace, arguably because digitized films for many years remained too data-heavy objects for automated analysis.[2] Consequently, data-driven research on film is characterized by less methodological pluralism than other disciplines and in particular lacks critical, quantitative methodologies. It seems however, that there is a desire for the latter among film historians. As Yuri Tsivian, co-founder of Cinemetrics, has observed regarding the tool's potential users, '[...] not every student of film history is ready or eager to masquerade as a scientist' (2008: 765). Furthermore, as discussed by Masson in Chapter 1 in this publication, many humanities scholars broadly speaking tend to wish to reflect their critical legacy and interpretative frameworks in their conceptualization of digital tools. In this regard, distinguishing and theorizing Cultural Analytics and ACTION as 'humanistic cinemetrics' based on what I see as their exploratory, critical *modus operandi* may provide a fruitful departure in this direction and make them more widely compelling to film scholars.

To present this argument, I draw on the theory of history of Michel de Certeau. De Certeau, responding to enthusiastic claims that had surrounded quantitative, computational history throughout the 1970s, reminded his colleagues that these methods remain technically and socially biased towards the specific traditions and institutions they emanate from (1986). When historians adopt the computer's scientific procedures, he argued, they essentially express and respond to their contemporary concerns and historical fictions, producing a 'science fiction' which combines scientific and poetic gestures of interpretation (*ibid.*: 215). Therefore he argued that historians should challenge the 'neutral' aura of computational history by remaining acutely aware of its institutional processes of knowledge production and limitations, and seek to reflect the latter in their methods (*ibid.*). Through this theoretical lens I analyse how the underlying social and technical processes of Cinemetrics, Cultural Analytics and ACTION attribute meanings to data visualizations as epistemic images in order to elicit the tools' differences.

My article is divided into three parts. First, I provide a historical discussion of statistical style analysis' epistemology by tracing cinemetric practices back to its foundational ideas in film studies in the 1970s. Second, I focus

---

2   However, it should be noted that film scholars have engaged extensively with and adopted digital methods of text editions deriving from literary studies to develop scholarly DVD presentations of films and with GIS technologies from socio-economic history to study film distribution, exhibition and reception. Yet only little work has been done which intervenes analytically in digitized archival films to detect formal patterns.

on the software Cinemetrics as an emblematic development of computer-based style analysis which introduces scientific, visual analytics to produce evidence for stylistic history. Finally, I discuss how cinemetric theory and techniques have developed beyond this approach in Cultural Analytics and ACTION to highlight the poetic aspects of data visualization. In this section I argue that they gesture towards a humanistic data analysis which may open a critical, methodological avenue for film scholars.

Statistical Style Analysis and Representation of Filmic Structure

To understand where cinemetric tools come from it is necessary to go back to the 1970s. In this period, film historians began developing systematic, quantitative methods to study film style, as film studies was institutionalizing as an academic discipline (Bordwell 1997). As Harvard professor of film studies at the time Vlada Petric contended, the film histories used in academic curricula had described especially film editing and style's developments haphazardly without a firm, empirical basis (1975).[3] According to Petric, to reliably account for film editing's 'historical evolution', film historians should scrutinize archival films as 'primary documents' to produce extensive and precise analytical documentation of editing patterns from canonical films, genres and periods and disseminate them in 'visual/analytical' representations (*ibid.*: 23-24).

Concurrently, film scholar Barry Salt questioned contemporary style analysis which he perceived as relying too much on hermeneutics rather than systematized, scientific procedures (1974).[4] Salt instead envisioned a film history which would achieve a more objective, scientific foundation by embracing statistical methods and the natural sciences' attitude (1983). He suggested a form of Scientific Realism, which would observe and measure stylistic features such as cutting rates, camera movements and shot scales as real phenomena, to verify or disprove hypotheses about film editing's historical development.[5] In doing so, Salt aspired to discover if aesthetic or

---

3   Petric in particular addressed the film histories written by Georges Sadoul, Rachael Low, Lewis Jacobs and Lotte Eisner.

4   Specifically, Salt addressed Andrew Sarris's classic work *The American Cinema: Directors and Directions 1929-1968* (New York: E.P. Dutton, 1968). In his key work *Film Style & Technology. History & Analysis* (Starword, 1983) which also explains his method in greater depth than his 1970s articles, Salt developed this approach with attention to classic mainstream cinema.

5   Salt mentioned that he found inspiration for his Scientific Realism in the work of philosophers of science such as Karl Popper, Thomas Kuhn and Imre Lakatos, without however providing a detailed discussion of how exactly they informed his work.

narrative qualities followed recurrent or exceptional patterns (for example, slow versus fast editing) and to facilitate a comparative, historical analysis following uniform, scientific principles (*ibid.*).

Attending primarily to films' cutting rates, what Salt dubbed Average Shot Lengths (ASL), he developed statistical, reduced forms of representation to express his results. In doing so, he aspired to yield more objective insights into film editing's evolution and norms, to facilitate the comparative analysis of films (*ibid.*). For this, Salt relied in particular on the widely used method of lognormal distribution to create histograms of ASLs which visualized patterns in film directors' *oeuvres* or norms in films from specific periods (Salt 2006a).[6] Using lognormal distribution for film style analysis implies that shots are grouped into class intervals or bins out of their sequential order to establish normal distributions of shot lengths. This creates a histogram displaying the film structure as a curve with a simple shape which, according to Salt, is ideal for visualizing and comparing film structure and discerning patterns, or for instance identifying outliers – meaning shots of potential analytical interest.[7]

While widely known by now and influential in film studies, the rigour of Salt's method was hotly debated in the 1970s and 1980s. Film scholars like Kristin Thompson and David Bordwell pointed to several inconsistencies, such as the circumstance that Salt initially calculated ASLs using 30-minute samples, which he regarded as representative, and not entire films (Bordwell & Thompson 1985). This, they argued, led Salt to provide inaccurate data himself.[8] Furthermore, they felt Salt's approach exaggerated the general applicability of quantitative approaches and was essentially positivist, in spite of presenting itself as a softer, scientific method.[9]

6   Lognormal distribution analysis emerged in the late nineteenth century developed by British scientist Francis Galton as a response to contemporary probability statistics and has since been refined into several variants. A somewhat simplified explanation of its scope is that it calculates the probability of a phenomenon's occurrence from a given data set with the aim of predicting its future development. It is widely used for instance to predict price developments, the occurrence of illnesses or for weather forecasts. See: Theodore M. Porter, *The Rise of Statistical Thinking, 1820-1900* (Princeton: Princeton University Press, 1986), 139 and J. Aitchinson and J.A.C. Brown's classic *The Lognormal Distribution, with Special Reference to its Uses in Economics* (Cambridge University Press, 1957), the latter of which guided Salt in the conception of his method.

7   The terms 'bin' and 'interval' can be used interchangeably and in statistical style analysis refer to the different categories of shot lengths. Illustrative examples of Salt's histogram visualizations can be seen in his article 'The Metrics in Cinemetrics' which is accessible online. See: www.cinemetrics.lv/metrics_in_cinemetrics.php, last accessed 6 April 2016.

8   Bordwell calculated the ASLs of several entire films to compare them to Salt's results based on 30-minute samples, to support this criticism.

9   As they remarked, Salt seemed to suggest 'that science's strongest certainties are those which can be reduced to numbers' (*ibid.*: 225).

Nonetheless, Bordwell and Thompson endorsed Salt's method more broadly in light of how stylistic history had hitherto been produced. As they wrote:

> His demand for precision of description, including statistical representation, comes as a welcome alternative to the practices of a generation of historians who relied upon memory, reviews, and gossip for their evidence. (*ibid.*: 234)

This remark may be taken as a concise characteristic of the direction in which film historical research was pushed by Petric and Salt in the 1970s. Responding to a scholarly need to develop scientific approaches for film style's history, they developed statistical methods which have increasingly appealed to film historians drawn to empirical research in the following decades (Buckland 2008).

Having sketched the emergence of statistical style analysis in the 1970s, I shall now turn to a discussion of Cinemetrics, which develops Salt's concept of ASL into a more fully fledged scientific method.

Style Analysis as Scientific Data Research: Cinemetrics

Conceived by University of Chicago professor Yuri Tsivian together with computer scientist Gunars Cijvans, Cinemetrics was launched in 2005 as 'an open-access interactive website to collect, store and process digital data related to film editing' (Tsivian 2008: 766). It shares statistical style analysis' assumption that film editing is a key distinguishing feature of film art and places it within an even broader theoretical reference frame to underline how scholars, also long before the 1970s, studied film editing quantitatively.[10] Highlighting how great directors throughout film history have measured segments at the editing table to achieve the pinnacle of

10   See 'Cinemetrics Predecessors': www.cinemetrics.lv/topic.php?topic_ID=38. Last accessed 28 July 2015. Tsivian has recurrently pointed to early film theorist Hugo Münsterberg's measurements of cutting rates in the mid-1910s for studies of spectatorship and psychology. Kristin Thompson finds inspiration in German film critic Georg Otto Stindt's article 'Bildschnitt' (1926) which compared shot lengths in US and German fiction films. And film historian Frank Kessler highlights German film historian Herbert Birett's foundational work on film statistics initiated in the 1960s. For a representative example of Herbert Birett's statistical style analysis see: Herbert Birett, 'Alte Filme: Filmalter und Filmstil', *Diskurs Film. Münchner Beiträge zur Filmphilologie* 2 (1988): 69-87.

their art through variations in shot length, the website's presentation calls for a metric, computational approach to film style (Tsivian 2008).[11] Currently, Cinemetrics' database counts approximately 15,000 titles uploaded by more than a thousand users.[12] These uploads do not follow a unifying selection criterion nor apply standard details on provenance and technical specificities. They constitute a heterogeneous data mass which facilitates comparison between primarily limited corpora with uniform, technical standards rather than providing evidence for a universal, evolutionary film history as in the 1970s (*ibid.*).[13] Popular among scholars propagating statistical style analysis in the 1970s and 80s such as Salt, Thompson and Bordwell, as well as newcomers, Cinemetrics users seek to refine style analysis into a more scientifically sound theoretical approach based on computer-generated data visualizations. In the following, I shall attend to key aspects of this development through a discussion of the underlying processes of its data visualization, the Cinemetrics graph.

Though not the only visualization format used by cinemetricians, the Cinemetrics graph is the primary 'inscription device' and evidentiary image used for summarizing and distributing editing data among the site's community (Latour 1987: 68).[14] As a standard representation, it consists of a custom-made red graph plotted onto a grid of horizontal lines, using

11   In particular, Tsivian highlights the formally dense works of the avant-garde directors Abel Gance, Dziga Vertov and, perhaps most emblematically, Peter Kubelka's 'metric' cinema.

12   See: www.cinemetrics.lv/database.php, last accessed 11 June 2014. However, it should be noted that this number includes a fair amount of television programmes, music videos and film excerpts as well. This aspect has however prompted discussions among academic Cinemetrics users about the data's reliability and the possibility of introducing rankings of user data to ensure cleaner data. See discussion thread 'Data Ranking and Verification': www.cinemetrics. lv/topic.php?topic_ID=355, last accessed 30 July 2015.

13   In this aspect, Cinemetrics nurtures a piecemeal approach. In general, Cinemetrics is critical of the teleological, universalizing accounts which 1970s style analysis supported. Tsivian argues at length how the earlier teleological film histories' account of cinema becoming an accomplished art form only in the late silent era, obfuscates an understanding of early cinema's distinct modes of expression.

14   Some users, such as Mike Baxter and Nick Redfern, explore alternative visualization formats, using the open-source software *R*. British scholar Nick Redfern for instance finds order structure matrices to structure the data in such a way that it allows for easier identification of clusterings of shots in sequences within films and shifts between segments. See Mike Baxter, *Notes on Cinemetric Data Analysis* (Nottingham, self-published, 2014), 46. See: www. cinemetrics.lv/dev/Cinemetrics_Book_Baxter.pdf, and Nick Redfern, 'An introduction to using graphical displays for analysing the editing of motion pictures', p. 22, 24, www.cinemetrics. lv/dev/redfern_q2_opt.pdf, last accessed 11 December 2015. For background information on *R* see: http://cran.r-project.org/.

a classic statistical format as has existed for centuries (Drucker 2014).[15] Numbered shots appear as white bars from above in sequential order. The x- and y-axes represent the variables of time code and shot duration, respectively, and users can annotate and comment on each shot/bar.[16] While the principle of showing a film's shot lengths as bars, combined through a curve resembles in fundamental aspects Salt's idea to use a histogram for comparative analysis, there remain significant differences.

First of all, the Cinemetrics graph reflects adversary, scholarly positions on the key parameter ASL. Tsivian considers Salt's ASL problematic because it only offers a single datum per film as a basis for comparison (Tsivian 2013). A single datum does not convey how cutting rates shift in relation to depicted events or motifs giving little insight into internal film dynamics. Therefore, Cinemetrics represents shots sequentially and is also designed to reflect a wider array of parameters such as *cutting swing*, which measures how the cutting rate shifts throughout a film's segments and diverges from its overall ASL. It also shows a film's *cutting range*, which is the difference between its shortest and longest shots (*ibid.*). In this regard, Cinemetrics offers a way for scholars to identify and link editing statistics on specific shots to film narration in greater detail.

In addition to Tsivian, British media scholar Nick Redfern has challenged the ASL concept by suggesting Median Shot Length (MSL) as an alternative (2011). ASL represents a mean value and is calculated by dividing a film's duration with its number of shots to find its average. MSL, on the other hand, locates the middle value of the cutting range to define it as a film's norm. In practice, this means that MSL performs outlier correction of the film's longest and shortest shots, producing different values.[17] Redfern has argued that MSL gives a more accurate impression of the typical shot length one may expect to see in a film because it is less sensitive to extreme outliers. Opposing MSL, Salt contends that MSL alters the data to an undesirable degree in cases where outliers may be relevant,

---

15   As Drucker points out, 'before the seventeenth century, the number of statistical graphs – that is, visual expressions of variables charted against each other as abstract quantities – was extremely small', but flourished in the following centuries with René Descartes' work in analytical geometry.

16   For a representative example of the Cinemetrics graph made by Yuri Tsivian, see for instance his visualization of Alfred Hitchcock's Rear Window (US, 1954), added to the database 23 May 2009: http://cinemetrics.lv/movie.php?movie_ID=3166, last accessed 6 April 2016.

17   Redfern gives examples of two Josef von Sternberg films, *The Lights of New York* (USA, 1928) and *Scarlet Empress* (1934). For the former the ASL is 9.9 seconds and MSL 5.1 seconds. For the latter the ASL is 9.9 and MSL 6.5.

stressing that ASL is also more widely accepted among cinemetricians (Salt 2013).[18] This discussion is reflected in the graph where MSL is included as an alternative to the ASL to enable comparison in each visualization. In this way, the graph accommodates internal adversary propositions on the function and value of the visual evidence's graphical properties (Amann & Knorr-Cetina 1990).

In different ways, these discussions of ASL negotiate the relation between data, representation and analytical purpose to determine an ideal 'analysability' of Cinemetrics' scientific image (Amann & Knorr-Cetina 1990: 107). This process can be seen as reminiscent of the way scientists debate how to fix their evidence in a representational form according to a shared set of assumptions and best practices. In this respect, Cinemetrics leans towards a scientist form of data research, following the natural sciences' attitudes to data visualization in the lineage of Salt's approach.

A second aspect of Cinemetrics that instantiates a scientist position is its emphasis on producing accurate data by eliminating potential inaccuracies caused by human reaction time. The tool's first 'classic' version launched in 2005 is semi-automatic and requires full user participation throughout a film's playback. During playback the user runs Cinemetrics in a separate window, clicking a 'Shot Change' button for every new shot to calculate the ASL and generate a graph. With Cinemetrics second version, Frame Accurate Cinemetrics Tool (FACT), which has currently only been released in a beta-version under testing, shot boundary detection has become more fine-grained and accurate by allowing users to pause and rewind so as to perform the shot segmentation with greater exactitude. Furthermore, while this is not integrated into FACT, users have expressed the overall ambition and projected as a future development – as also stated by Yuri Tsivian already in 2006 – to automate shot boundary detection in Cinemetrics in order to eliminate potential human inaccuracies, or to simply make the process of data collection quicker. However, there are different stances towards automatisation among cinemetricians and on whether human or computational annotation is most accurate or desirable. For instance, inspired by the key parameters of Cinemetrics' underlying theory, and to complement Tsivian's initiative, the related software Shot Logger – created by media scholar Jeremy Butler – goes a step further by offering automatic shot boundary detection developed in the PHP scripting language. However,

18   As Salt dryly remarks, 'Such an idea seems reminiscent of the Catholic church continuing its ban on the discussion of the idea of the earth going round the sun, even after the concept was in wide use'.

while FACT still only exists in a beta version which does not offer automatic shot boundary detection, it projects a new relation between the scholar and the viewing equipment previously used by creating a closer approximation of filmic structure through visual analytics of cutting rates in digital source material.

To conclude, Cinemetrics recasts statistical style analysis' methodology as articulated in the mid-1970s in central aspects. Salt's ASL analysis initially favoured comparison between films, representing each by a single datum. Cinemetrics, on the other hand, privileges a microscopic perspective on films, displaying text-internal, hitherto imperceptible dynamics as, in Tsivian's words, 'hard facts', from a wider range of perspectives, such as the MSL (Tsivian 2013). Cinemetrics enables scholars to closely study text-internal, micro-perspectives of single films and to switch to a macro-perspective to raise questions on film editing's historical development by comparing groups of films. One of Cinemetrics' great affordances is especially its micro-perspective, which was less prominent, if not absent, in 1970s sample-based style analysis, because it allows for a fine-grained analysis of the dynamic relationship between shot lengths and depicted events.

The display of internal dynamics and the FACT acronym's bold proposition that its procedures yield more accurate empirical data arguably advance style analysis' realism by assuming a closer approximation between film editing as a real-life phenomenon and its description (Salt 2006b). While Cinemetrics has its clear advantages for the study of film style based on editing data, it can however also be said to embody a scientist conception of data research, which humanities scholars more broadly would feel uncomfortable engaging with. In particular, the observer-independence which Cinemetrics' graph seems to imply and champion contradicts many humanities scholars' consideration of visual evidence as inherently ambiguous and contingent. Therefore, as I argued in my introduction, it is crucial to develop more critical, cinemetric approaches for film historians who do not regard scientific images as observer-independent and wish to reflect the ambiguity of their research methods in their results.

Cultural Analytics and ACTION – Gesturing Towards Humanistic Cinemetrics?

Cinemetric analysis has developed beyond Tsivian's initiative, in a variety of conceptually related, quantitative software applications. Some of these, Shot-Logger and Edit2000 for instance, as Cinemetrics, analyse ASL but produce differently styled graphs.[19] Others, such as Cultural Analytics or ACTION, draw on cinemetric theory to focus on different moving image features such as light, sound or colour. While sharing Cinemetrics' conceptual departure point in statistical style analysis their attitude towards data visualization differs fundamentally. They proceed inductively, without a preconceived theoretical framework and are less bound to tradition and established methodological operations. In this last section I would like to attend to these applications as practices that can be recognized as a form of 'Humanistic Cinemetrics' in their deployment of scientific data visualizations for style analysis.

Cultural Analytics is a research program which develops toolkits for visual analytics of cultural patterns in large image sets created within media theorist Lev Manovich's Software Studies Initiative (Yamaoka, Manovich, Douglass & Kuester 2011). Suggesting a middle way between scientist and hermeneutic approaches to visual analytics, it departs from the question, 'What will happen when humanists start using interactive visualizations as a standard tool in their work, the way many scientists already do?'[20] Its core application is ImagePlot, an extension of the open-source scientific visualization software ImageJ, first known as NIH Image, developed by the US National Institute of Mental Health.[21] Conceived by programmer Wayne S. Rasband in 1987 it advanced the combination of modern computation techniques with microscopy and gained widespread success in the natural sciences, because of its later translation into Java-programming (Schneider, Rasband & Eliceiri 2012).[22]

The software has always been open source, enabling users to tweak it and resulting in around 500 plug-ins by May 2012 (Schneider, Rasband & Eliceiri 2012). ImagePlot added four of these.[23] Manovich has developed ImagePlot's visual analytics approach within the 'Cultural Analytics' research program and initially conceived it for analysing the digital age's big data image sets, especially of amateur image sites such as Flickr and Instagram. In this regard, Manovich considered ImageJ capable of providing adequate 'super-visualization technologies' to match these sets' scale and discover patterns in them.[24]

19   See www.data2000.no/EDIT2000/ and www.shotlogger.org/, last accessed 10 April 2015.
20   See the project introduction 'Cultural Analytics': http://lab.softwarestudies.com/p/cultural-analytics.html, last accessed 27 September 2015.
21   'About NIH Image', see: http://rsb.info.nih.gov/nih-image/about.html, last accessed 22 April 2015. ImageJ followed the NIH Image software on the basis of which it was created.
22   According to Schneider, Rasband and Eliceiri, in the late 1990s Java programming became considered an 'operating system-agnostic' language, compatible between Macintosh and PC. The 'J' in ImageJ stands for Java. (pp. 671-672).
23   See: http://lab.softwarestudies.com/p/imageplot.html#features1, last accessed 11 May 2015.
24   'Cultural Analytics', op. cit.

Cultural Analytics' scope quickly expanded to digitized heritage collections, art history and moving images.[25] Regarding the latter, Cultural Analytics thinks along the lines of Cinemetrics by evoking how formally dense and complex film works necessitate statistical approaches for analysing filmic structures (Manovich 2013).[26] However, its distinguishing feature as a method is that it processes entire films as image sets instead of extracting metadata to produce reduced, statistical representations. It breaks down video files into sequences of separate images and seriates or layers them according to various image features in different visualization types. The ImageJ Montage visualization, for example, orders frames onto a grid according to their sequential order, from left to right, enabling a quick, comprehensive overview of movements between shots (*ibid.*).[27] Figurative in comparison to Cinemetrics' graph, it seems close to early scientific cinematography, such as Etienne-Jules Marey's and Eadweard Muybridge's sequential photography, in particular the latter's famous *The Horse in Motion* (1878) (Tosi 2005). It has been applied to films by Soviet avant-garde director Dziga Vertov to grasp his film's complex structures and for understanding his reuse of footage within different films. With another ImageJ visualization type, the Summary image, one can layer image sequences to visualize median values of colours in films.[28] Subsequently, with ImagePlot one may plot these visualizations or entire image sets on a y- and x-axis with different values.

Closer to Cinemetrics' reduced visual analytics, the recent project Audio-Visual Cinematic Toolkit for Interaction, Organization and Navigation

25 For examples of the wider array of visualization formats, see: http://lab.softwarestudies. com/p/research_14.html, last accessed 11 May 2015.

26 As in Cinemetrics Dziga Vertov's documentary theory is used to conceptualize the potential of digital tools, aligning their analytical potential with Vertov's conception of cinema as a machinic vision which unveils hidden structures of life to the human eye. Yet in contrast to Cinemetrics, Manovich has also prominently invoked Vertov's documentary theory to regard new media as dynamic and as privileging multiple viewpoints rather than positivism, by analogy to Vertov's staging of editing. See: Lev Manovich, *The Language of New Media* (Cambridge, MA: The MIT Press, 2001), 199.

27 See: http://lab.softwarestudies.com/2013/01/visualizing-vertov-new-article-by-lev.html, last accessed 6 April 2015. The visualization of Vertov's *The Eleventh Year* can be seen via the following link: www.flickr.com/photos/culturevis/3988919869/in/album-72157632441192048/, last accessed 6 April 2016.

28 For reasons of space I do not include a discussion of the Summary visualization here. For examples and an interesting recent application, I refer to film scholar Kevin L. Ferguson's use of Summary for studying the Western. See: Kevin L. Ferguson, 'What Does the Western Really Look Like?', https://medium.com/the-outtake/what-does-the-western-look-like-545981d93ae8, last accessed 27 September 2015.

(ACTION) developed by Michael Casey, Mark Williams and Tom Stoll at Dartmouth College also analyses patterns in film style. Using the open-source software Matplotlib and Python to visualize 'latent stylistic patterns' of colour, sound and movement it creates auteur and film profiles from a sample of 120 films.[29] Though not focused on film editing, it extends cine-metric theory to comprise other stylistic features and develops it by putting greater emphasis on machine learning processes in the hope of producing more precise, clean data (Casey & Williams 2014).[30] Using algorithms to extract for instance mean values of colour and sound, it charts the results onto order structure matrices or tabular diagrams where single data of mean values represent *auteur* profiles to enable comparison, much in the vein of Salt's original approach. In the latter format, directors are represented by their initials, AH for Alfred Hitchcock and JLG for Jean-Luc Godard for instance, and are classified according to their mean values of colour.

While conceptually related to Cinemetrics, these uses of visual analytics can be said to take different measures to distance themselves from its scient-ism. Manovich evokes statistician John Tukey's tradition of Exploratory Data Analysis (EDA) as an inductive approach, to underline that ImagePlot does not depart from a clearly defined hypothesis but uses visualizations for ex-ploratory purposes as a stepping stone to new research questions (Manovich 2012a).[31] According to Manovich, this produces open answers rather than finite, hard scientific explanations and encourages multiple interpreta-tions. Furthermore, Cultural Analytics also nods to literary scholar Franco Moretti's quantitative, historical approach as middle way between scientist methodological rigour and hermeneutics' 'free play' of subjectivity (Manovich & Douglass 2009; Moretti 2008). Arguably, this 'free play' manifests itself in an attitude towards data visualizations which does not regard them as hard evidence but equally contemplates their graphic features to highlight their abstract and constructed nature. Manovich, for example, underscores the limits of ImagePlot visualizations when he associates its graphic properties with the characteristic compositions of Soviet photographer Alexander Rod-chenko's avant-garde photography (Manovich 2012b). In doing so, he stresses how ImagePlot's visualizations may also be taken to render reality more unfamiliar to us rather than serving solely a revelatory, scientific function.

29   See https://sites.dartmouth.edu/mediaecology/content-partners/campus-partners/action/, last accessed 10 November 2015.

30   The project's white paper is available online and contains the list of the 120 films analysed within the project as well as the visualizations which I refer to here. See: https://securegrants. neh.gov/PublicQuery/main.aspx?f=1&gn=HD-51394-11, last accessed 6 April 2016.

31   See also Bernhard Rieder's and Theo Röhle's discussion of Tukey in this anthology.

Through a similar attitude, ACTION also seems to locate itself midway between the scientific and aesthetic contemplation of data visualizations to emphasize its contingencies (Casey 2014). This can be seen in the appropriation work *One Million Seconds* (US, 2014) which Casey produced using sound classifications of film samples analysed within ACTION.[32] Where Manovich associatively muses on ImagePlot's visualization in relation to Rodchenko, Casey uses Glenn Gould's famous recording of Bach's *Goldberg Variations* (1981) as a template from which film excerpts are retrieved based on their audio similarities with Gould's recording. Thus, Casey creates a frenetic video piece where glimpses of barely recognizable film excerpts replace each other in rapid succession based on their audio similarity to Gould's *Goldberg Variations*, in which both the films' and Gould's recording are audible.

While tentative, experimental gestures, both Manovich's and Casey's appropriations can be said to point to the uncertainty in their analytic and representational practices, inviting us to think critically about the meanings we assign to data visualizations. In this regard ImagePlot and ACTION differ from Cinemetrics because they do not strive towards best practices following positivist aspirations nor idealize data visualization for stylistic analysis. Whereas Cinemetrics' graph is perceived as a strong evidentiary image among its practitioners, ACTION and ImagePlot embrace the analytical potential of computational stylometry while stressing how data visualizations can also be perceived as abstract and, as discussed by Masson, defamiliarize our objects of study (Masson in this volume). In doing so, they arguably appreciate scientific, graphical expressions within a historically long-standing intersection of science and art to open for less formalized exploratory methodologies.[33] Consequently, Cultural Analytics and ACTION come across as more self-reflexive towards data's visual shapes and may be seen as congruent with a humanistic approach which, as Johanna Drucker defines it, 'calls to attention its madeness – and by extension, the constructedness of knowledge, its interpretative dimensions' (2014: 178).

Bearing in mind this observation, I would conclude by suggesting that Cultural Analytics and ACTION can also productively be considered

---

32 Michael Casey's video appropriation and description of the work can be accessed via the following link: https://vimeo.com/105909439, last accessed 14 May 2015.

33 On this subject see Caroline A. Jones and Peter Galison, 'Introduction' in Caroline A. Jones & Peter Galison (eds.), *Picturing Science, Producing Art* (Abingdon, New York: Routledge, 1998) and Monique Sicard, *La fabrique du regard. Images de science et appareils de vision* (*Xve-XXe siècle*) (Paris: Editions Odile Jacob, 1998).

consistent with de Certeau's notion of computational history as a 'science fiction' referred to in my introduction, by foregrounding both the scientific and poetic dimensions of its making (de Certeau 1986). Concretely, I take them to suggest, lending a characterization of de Certeau's historiography from Jeremy Ahearne, 'a method [which] is alternately scientific and anti-scientific. It oscillates between interpretation and something like anti-interpretation' (Ahaerne 1995: 35). Thinking along these lines when visualizing data, I believe, may especially enable film historians with reservations about style analysis' scientific realism to move in a new, critical direction which restores one of the fundamental tasks of the historian on their terms, namely to emphasize the ambiguity of the relationship between past and present and its construction (de Certeau 1986). In doing so, we may to a greater degree underline the enigmatic enterprise of (film) history making, while embracing computational methods in fruitful new ways to study filmic structures and directorial styles and review the way we understand the inner workings of films new and old.

References

Ahaerne, Jeremy. 1995. *Michel de Certeau. Interpretation and its Other.* Cambridge: Polity Press.

Amann, K. & K. Knorr Cetina. 1990. "The fixation of (visual) evidence." In *Representation in Scientific Practice,* ed. Michael Lynch & Steve Woolgar. Cambridge, MA: The MIT Press.

Baxter, Mike. 2014. *Notes on Cinemetric Data Analysis.* Nottingham, self-published. Available online: www.cinemetrics.lv/dev/Cinemetrics_Book_Baxter.pdf.

Birett, Herbert. 1988. "Alte Filme: Filmalter und Filmstil." *Diskurs Film. Münchner Beiträge zur Filmphilologie* 2.

Bordwell, David & Kristin Thompson. 1985. "Towards a Scientific Film History?" *Quarterly Review of Film Studies* 10 (3): 224-237.

Bordwell, David. 1997. *On the History of Film Style.* Cambridge, MA, and London, England: Harvard University Press.

Buckland, Warren. 2008. "What Does the Statistical Style Analysis of Film Involve? A Review of Moving into Pictures. More on Film History, Style, and Analysis." *Literary and Linguistic Computing* 23 (2): 219-230.

Casey, Michael & Mark Williams. 2014. *White Paper. ACTION: Audio-visual Cinematics Toolbox for Interaction, Organization, and Navigation of Film.* Hanover: Dartmouth College.

Casey, Michael. 2014. "Investigating Film Authorship with the ACTION Toolbox." Conference paper given at the 55 Annual conference of the Society for Cinema and Media Studies, 22 March.

Christie, Ian. 2006. "'Just the Facts, Ma'am?' A Short History of Ambivalence towards Empiricism in Cinema Studies." *Tijdschrift voor Mediageschiedenis* 9 (2): 65-73.

Daston, Lorraine & Peter Galison. 1992. "The Image of Objectivity." In *Representations,* 40.

De Certeau, Michel. 1986. "History: Science and Fiction." In Michel de Certeau, transl. Brian Massumi, *Heterologies. Discourse on the Other.* Minneapolis: Minnesota University Press. 217-218.

Drucker, Johanna. 2014. *Graphesis. Visual Forms of Knowledge Production*. Cambridge, MA, and London, England: Harvard University Press.

Chávez Heras, Daniel. 2012. "The Malleable Computer: Software and the Study of the Moving Image." *Frames Cinema Journal* 1 (1). n.p.

Jones, Caroline A. & Peter Galison. 1998. "Introduction." In *Picturing Science, Producing Art*, ed. Caroline A. Jones & Peter Galison. Abingdon, New York: Routledge.

Ladurie, Emmanuel Le Roy. 1979 [1973]. *The Territory of the Historian*, transl. Ben and Siân Reynolds. Sussex: The Harvester Press.

Latour, Bruno. 1988. *Science in Action. How to Follow Scientists and Engineers Through Society*. Cambridge, MA: Harvard University Press.

Manovich, Lev. 2001. *The Language of New Media*. Cambridge, MA: The MIT Press.

—. 2012a. "The Meaning of Statistics and Digital Humanities." *Software Studies* blog entry 27 November: http://lab.softwarestudies.com/2012/11/the-meaning-of-statistics-and-digital.html.

—. 2012b. "How to Compare One Million Images?" In *Understanding Digital Humanities*, ed. David M. Berry. New York: Palgrave Macmillan. 249-278.

—. 2013. "Visualizing Vertov." Available online: http://softwarestudies.com/cultural_analytics/Manovich.Visualizing_Vertov.2013.pdf.

Manovich, Lev and Jeremy Douglass. 2009. "Visualizing Temporal Patterns in Visual Media." Available online: http://softwarestudies.com/cultural_analytics/visualizing_temporal_patterns.pdf.

Moretti, Franco. 2008. *Graphs, Maps, Trees. Abstract Models for Literary History*. London: Verso.

Petric, Vladimir. 1974. "A Visual/Analytic History of the Silent Cinema (1895-1930)." Paper presented to the 30th Congress of the International Federation of Film Archives, May 25-27. Available online at: http://files.eric.ed.gov/fulltext/ED098639.pdf.

—. 1975. "From a Written Film History to a Visual Film History." *Cinema Journal* 14 (2), 20-24.

Porter, Theodore. 1986. *The Rise of Statistical Thinking, 1820-1900*. Princeton: Princeton University Press.

Redfern, Nick. "An introduction to using graphical displays for analysing the editing of motion pictures." Available online: www.cinemetrics.lv/dev/redfern_q2_opt.pdf.

—. "Films and Statistics – Give and Take. The average shot length as a statistic of film style". Available online: http://cinemetrics.lv/dev/fsgt_q1b.php.

Salt, Barry. 1974. "Statistical Style Analysis of Motion Pictures." *Film Quarterly* 28 (1).

—. 1983. *Film Style and Technology: History and Analysis*. London: Starword.

—. 2006a. *Moving into Pictures. More on Film History, Style, and Analysis*. London: Starword.

—. "Statistical Film Analysis (Basic Concepts and Practical Details)." Available online: www.cinemetrics.lv/articles.php.

—. 2006b. "The Metrics in Cinemetrics." Available online: www.cinemetrics.lv/metrics_in_cinemetrics.php.

—. "Films and Statistics – Give and Take. Graphs and Numbers." Available online: http://cinemetrics.lv/dev/fsgt_q1d.php.

Schneider, Caroline A., Wayne S. Rasband & Kevin W. Eliceiri. 2012. "NIH Image to ImageJ: 25 Years of Image Analysis." *Nature Methods* 9 (7): 671-675.

Sicard, Monique. 1998. *La fabrique du regard. Images de science et appareils de vision (XVe-XXe siècle)*. Paris: Editions Odile Jacob.

Tosi, Virgilio. 2005. *Cinema Before Cinema. The Origins of Scientific Cinematography*. London: British Universities Film & Video Council.

Tsivian, Yuri. 2008. "What Is Cinema? An Agnostic Answer." *Critical Inquiry* 34 (4), 754-776.

—. "Films and Statistics – Give and Take. Question 1: Median or Mean." Available online: http://
www.cinemetrics.lv/dev/fsgt_q1a.php.

—. "Taking Cinemetrics into the Digital Age (2005-now)." Available online: www.cinemetrics.
lv/dev/tsivian_2.php.

Yamaoka, So, Lev Manovich, Jeremy Douglass & Falko Kuester. 2011. "Cultural Analytics in
Large-Scale Visualization Environments." *Computer* 44 (12), 39-48.

3. Cultural Analytics, Social Computing and Digital Humanities

Lev Manovich

Social Computing vs. Digital Humanities

I define Cultural Analytics as the analysis of massive cultural data sets and flows using computational and visualization techniques. I developed this concept in 2005, and in 2007, the Software Studies Initiative[1] research lab was established to start working on Cultural Analytics projects.

Our work is driven by a number of theoretical and practical questions: What does it mean to represent 'culture' by 'data'? What are the unique possibilities offered by the computational analysis of large cultural data in contrast to qualitative methods used in humanities and social sciences? How can quantitative techniques be used to study the key cultural form of our era – interactive media? How can we combine computational analysis and visualization of large cultural data with qualitative methods like 'close reading'? Put another way, how can we combine the analysis of larger patterns with the analysis of individual artefacts and their details? How can computational analysis do justice to variability and diversity of cultural artefacts and processes, rather than focusing on the 'typical' and 'most popular'?

Eight years later, the work of our lab has become a tiny portion of a very large body of research. Thousands of researchers have published tens of thousands of papers analysing patterns in massive cultural data sets. This is data describing activity on most popular social networks (Flickr, Instagram, YouTube, Twitter, etc.), user-created content shared on these networks (tweets, images, video, etc.), and users' interactions with this content (likes, favourites, reshares, comments). Researchers have also started to analyse particular professional cultural areas and historical periods, such as website design, fashion photography, 20th-century popular music, and 19th-century literature. This work is being carried out in two newly developed fields: Social Computing and Digital Humanities.

Given the scale of that research, I am not interested in proposing Cultural Analytics as some alternative 'third way'. However, I think that the ideas this

---

1   Software Studies Initiative: www.softwarestudies.com.

term stands for remain relevant. As we will see, Digital Humanities and Social Computing have carved out their own domains in relation to the types of data they study, while 'Cultural Analytics' continues to be free of such limitations. It also attempts not to take sides vis-à-vis humanities vs. scientific goals and methods. In this article I don't take sides vis-à-vis humanities vs. scientific goals and methods. In this chapter I reflect on both paradigms, pointing out opportunities and ideas that have not yet been explored.

Digital Humanities scholars use computers to analyse mostly historical artefacts created by professionals, such as writers, artists and musicians. To take an example, one area of study could be novels written by professional writers in the 19th and 20th century. Yet for reasons of access, they stop at the historical boundaries defined by copyright laws in their countries. According to the United States copyright law, for example,[2] the works published in the last 95 years are automatically copyrighted. (So, for example, as of 2015, everything created after 1920 is copyrighted, unless it is recent digital content that uses Creative Commons licenses.) I have no qualms about respecting copyright laws, but in this case that means that digital humanists are shut out from studying the present.

The field of Social Computing is thousands of times larger. Here, researchers with advanced degrees in computer science study online user-created content and user interactions with this content. Note that this research is carried out not only by computer and information scientists who professionally identify themselves with the 'Social Computing' field, but also researchers in a number of other computer science fields such as Computer Multimedia, Computer Vision, Music Information Retrieval, Natural Language Processing, and Web Science. Therefore, social computing can also be used as an umbrella term for all computer science research that analyses content and activity on social networks. These researchers work with data from after 2004, when social networks and media sharing services started to become popular.[3] The data sets are usually much larger than the ones used in digital humanities. It is not uncommon to find tens or hundreds of millions of posts, photos or other items. Since the great majority of user-generated content is created by regular people rather than professionals, Social Computing studies the non-professional, vernacular culture by default.

2   A branch of computer science focused on the intersection of computational systems and social behaviour. See www.interaction-design.org/literature/book/the-encyclopedia-of-human-computer-interaction-2nd-ed/social-computing.
3   Since it takes 1-2 years to do research and publish a paper, typically a paper published in 2015 will use the data collected in 2012-2014.

The scale of this research may be surprising to humanities and arts practitioners who may not realize how many people are working in computer science and related fields. For example, an October 2015 search on Google Scholar for 'Twitter dataset algorithm' returned 102,000 papers, a search for 'YouTube video dataset' returned 27,800 papers, and a search for 'Flickr images algorithm' returned 17,400 papers. Searching for 'computational aesthetics dataset', I got 14,100 results. Even if the actual numbers are much smaller, this is still impressive. Obviously not all these publications directly ask cultural questions, but many do.

The following table summarizes the differences between the two fields:

Table 3.1. Comparing Social Computing and Digital Humanities.

	Social Computing and various fields of computer science where researchers study social networks and shared media	Digital Humanities (research quantitative analysis using computer science techniques)
Number of publications	Tens of thousands	Few hundred
Period and material studied	Websites and social media content and activity after 2004	Historical artefacts up to the early 20th century
Authors of artefacts studied	Regular people who share content on social networks	Professional writers, artists, composers, etc.
Typical size of data sets	Thousands to hundreds of millions of items, billions of relations	Hundreds to thousands of items

Why do computer scientists rarely work with large historical data sets of any kind? Typically, they justify their research by referencing already existing industrial applications – for example, search or recommendation systems for online content. The general assumption is that computer science will create better algorithms and other computer technologies useful to industry and government organizations. The analysis of historical artefacts falls outside this goal, and, consequently, only a few computer scientists work with historical data (the field of Digital Heritage being one exception).

However, looking at many examples of computer science papers, it becomes clear that they are actually doing Humanities or Communication Studies (in relation to contemporary media) but at a much larger scale. Consider these recent publications: 'Quantifying Visual Preferences Around the

World' (Reinecke & Gajos 2014), and 'What We Instagram: A First Analysis of Instagram Photo Content and User Types' (Hu et al. 2014). The first study analyses worldwide preferences for website design using 2.4 million ratings from 40,000 people from 179 countries. Studies like this of aesthetics and design traditionally belong to the humanities. The second study analysed the most frequent subjects of Instagram photos – a method comparable to art history studies of the genres in the 17th-century Dutch art which would be more appropriately categorized as humanities.

Another example is a paper called 'What is Twitter, a Social Network or a News Media?' (Kwak et al. 2014). First published in 2010, it has since been cited 3,284 times in other computer science publications.[4] It was the first large-scale analysis of Twitter as a social network, using 106 million tweets by 41.7 million users. The study looked in particular at trending topics, showing 'what categories trending topics are classified into, how long they last, and how many users participate'. This is a classic question of Communication Studies, going back to the pioneering work of Paul F. Lazarsfeld and his colleagues in the 1940s who manually counted the topics of radio broadcasts. But I would argue that given that Twitter and other micro-blogging services represent a new form of media, like oil painting, printed books and photography before them, understanding the specificity of Twitter as a medium is also a topic for humanities.

A small number of publications lie at the intersection of Digital Humanities and Social Computing. They take computational methods and algorithms developed by computer scientists for studying contemporary user-generated content and apply them to historical media artefacts created by professionals. The most prominent examples are 'Toward Automated Discovery of Artistic Influence' (Saleh et al. 2014), 'Infectious Texts: modelling Text Reuse in Nineteenth-Century Newspapers' (Smith et al. 2013), 'Measuring the Evolution of Contemporary Western Popular Music' (Serrà et al. 2012) and 'Quicker, faster, darker: Changes in Hollywood film over 75 years' (Cutting et al. 2011).

Until a few years ago, the only project that analysed cultural history on the scale of millions of texts was carried out by scientists rather than by humanists. I refer here to N-Gram Viewer created in 2010 by Google scientists Jon Orwant and Will Brockman following the prototype by two Harvard PhD students in Biology and Applied Mathematics. More recently, however, we see people in Digital Humanities scaling up the data they study. For example, in 'Mapping Mutable Genres in Structurally Complex

4   https://scholar.google.com/citations?user=M6i3Be0AAAAJ&hl=en.

Volumes' literary scholar Ted Underwood (2013) and his collaborators analysed 469,200 volumes from Trust Digital Library. Art historian Maximilian Schich and his colleagues (2014) have analysed the life trajectories of 120,000 notable historical individuals. And even larger historical data sets are becoming available in the areas of literature, photography, film and TV, although they have yet to be analysed. In 2012, The New York City Municipal Archives released 870,000 digitized historic photos of NYC (Taylor 2012). In 2015, HathiTrust made data extracted from 4,801,237 volumes (containing 1.8 billion pages) available for research (2016). In the same year Associated Press and British Movietone uploaded 550,000 digitized news stories covering the period from 1895 to today to YouTube (Associated Press 2015).

What is the importance of having such large cultural data sets? Can't we simply use smaller samples? I believe that there are a number of reasons. First of all, to have a representative sample, we first need to have a much larger set of actual items to draw from or at least a good understanding of what this larger set includes. So, for example, if we want to create a representative sample of 20th-century films, we can use IMDb (2015), which contains information on 3.4 million films and TV shows (including separate episodes). Similarly, we can create a good sample of historical US newspaper pages using the Historical American Newspaper collection of millions of digitized pages from the Library of Congress (2016). However, in many other cultural fields such larger data sets do not exist and without them, it may be impossible to construct representative samples.

The second reason is the following: without a large enough sample, we can only find general trends and patterns, but not local patterns. For example, in the already mentioned paper 'What We Instagram', three computer scientists analysed 1,000 Instagram photos and came up with the eight most frequent categories (selfie, friends, fashion, food, gadget, activity, pet, captioned photos). The sample of 1,000 photos was randomly selected from a larger set of photos shared by 95,343 unique users. It is possible that these eight categories were also most popular among all Instagram photos shared worldwide at the time when the scientists did their study. However, as we at the Software Studies Initiative saw from projects analysing Instagram photos in different cities and their parts (for example, the centre of Kyiv during the 2014 Ukrainian Revolution in *The Exceptional and the Everyday* (Manovich et al. 2014)), people also share many other types of images beyond Hu et al.'s eight categories. Depending on the geographic area and time period, some of these types may replace the top eight in popularity. In other words, while a small sample allows finding the 'typical' or 'most popular,' it does not reveal what I call 'content islands' – types of coherent content with particular semantic and/or aesthetic characteristics shared in moderate numbers.

Cultural Analytics

When I first started thinking about Cultural Analytics in 2005, both Digital Humanities and Social Computing were just getting started as research fields. I felt the need to introduce this new term to signal that our lab's work would not simply be a part of digital humanities or social computing but would cover subject matter studied in both fields. Like digital humanists, we are interested in analysing historical artefacts, but we are also equally interested in contemporary digital visual culture: Instagram as well as professional photography, artefacts created by dedicated non-professionals and artists outside of the art world like those found on deviantart.com,[5] and accidental creators, such as those who occasionally upload their photos to social media networks.

Like computational social scientists and computer scientists, we are also attracted to the study of society using social media and social phenomena specific to social networks. An example of the former would be using social media activity to identify similarities between different city neighbourhoods (Cranshaw et al. 2012). An example of the latter would be analysing patterns of information diffusion online (Cha et al. 2012). However, if Social Computing focuses on the *social* in social networks, Cultural Analytics focuses on the *cultural*. Therefore, the most relevant part of social sciences for Cultural Analytics is sociology of culture, and only after that sociology and economics.

We believe that content and user activities on the Web (on social networks and elsewhere) give us the unprecedented opportunity to describe, model and simulate the global cultural universe while questioning and rethinking basic humanities concepts and tools that were developed to analyse 'small cultural data' (i.e. highly selective and non-representative cultural samples). In the very influential 1869 definition by British cultural critic Matthew Arnold (1869), culture is 'the best that has been thought and said in the world'. The academic institution of humanities has largely followed this definition. And when they started to revolt against their canons and to include the works of previously excluded people (women, non-whites, non-Western authors, queer, etc.), they often included only 'the best' created by those who were previously excluded.

5   'The largest online social network for artists and art enthusiasts', http://about.deviantart.com/, retrieved 22 August 2015.

Cultural Analytics is interested in *everything created by everybody*. In this, we are approaching culture the way linguists study languages or biologists study life on earth. Ideally, we want to look at every cultural manifestation, rather than selective samples, in a systematic perspective not dissimilar to that of cultural anthropology. This larger inclusive scope combining the professional and the vernacular, the historical and the contemporary, is exemplified by the range of projects we have worked on in our lab since 2008. We have analysed historical, professionally created cultural content in all *Time* magazine covers (1923-2009); paintings by Vincent van Gogh, Piet Mondrian and Mark Rothko; 20,000 photographs from the collection of the Museum of Modern Art in New York (MoMA); and one million manga pages from 883 manga series published in the last 30 years. Our analysis of contemporary vernacular content includes *Phototrails* (the comparison of visual signatures of 13 global cities using 2.3 million Instagram photos) (Hochman et al. 2013), *The Exceptional and the Everyday: 144 Hours in Kyiv* (the analysis of Instagram images shared in Kyiv during the 2014 Ukrainian Revolution) (Manovich 2014) and *On Broadway* (the interactive installation exploring Broadway in NYC using 40 million user-generated images and data points) (Goddemeyer et al. 2014). We have also looked at contemporary amateur or semi-professional content using one million artworks shared by 30,000 semi-professional artists on deviantart.com. Currently, we are exploring a data set of 265 million images tweeted worldwide between 2011 and 2014. To summarize, our work doesn't draw a boundary between (smaller) historical professional artefacts and (bigger) online digital content created by non-professionals. Instead, it draws freely from both.

Obviously, online social networks today do not include every human being, and the content shared is sometimes specific to these networks (e.g. Instagram selfies), as opposed to something which existed before. This content is also shaped by the tools and interfaces of technologies used for its creation, capturing, editing and sharing (e.g. Instagram filters, its Layout app, etc.). The kind of cultural actions available are also defined by these technologies. For example, in social networks you can 'like', share or comment on a piece of content. In other words, just as in quantum physics, the instrument can influence the phenomena we want to study. All this needs to be carefully considered when we study user-generated content and user activities. While social network APIs make it easy to access massive amounts of contents, it is not 'everything' by 'everybody'.

The General and the Particular

When the humanities were focused on 'small data' (content created by single authors or small groups), the sociological perspective was only one of many options for interpretation – unless you were a Marxist. But once we started studying online content and the activities of millions of people, this perspective became almost inevitable. In the case of 'big cultural data', the cultural and the social closely overlap. Large groups of people from different countries and socio-economic backgrounds (sociological perspective) share images, video, texts, and make particular aesthetic choices in doing this (humanities perspective). Because of this overlap, the kinds of questions investigated in *sociology of culture* of the 20th century (exemplified by its most influential researcher, Pierre Bourdieu (2010)) are directly relevant for Cultural Analytics.

Given that certain demographic categories have been taken for granted in our thinking about society, it appears natural today to group people into these categories and compare them in relation to social, economic or cultural indicators. For example, Pew Research Center regularly reports the statistics of popular social platform use, breaking up their user sample by demographics such as gender, ethnicity, age, education, income and residence (urban, suburban and rural) (Duggan et al. 2015). So if we are interested in various details of social media activities (such as types of images shared and liked, filters used or selfie poses) it is logical to study the differences between people from different countries, ethnicities, socio-economic backgrounds or levels of technical expertise. The earlier research in social computing did not, and most of the current work still does not consider such differences, treating all users as one undifferentiated pool of 'humanity'. More recently, however, we have started to see publications separating users into demographic groups. While we support this development, we also want to be careful in how far we want to go. Humanistic analysis of cultural phenomena and processes using quantitative methods should not be simply reduced to sociology and only consider common characteristics and behaviours of human groups.

The sociological tradition is concerned with finding and describing the *general* patterns in human behaviour, rather than with analysing or predicting the behaviours of particular individuals. Cultural Analytics, too, is interested in patterns that can be derived from the analysis of large cultural data sets. However, ideally *the analysis of the larger patterns will also lead us to individual cases,* such as individual creators, their particular creations or cultural behaviours. For instance, the computational analysis of all photos made by a photographer during her long career may lead us to the outliers – the photos that are most different from all the rest. Similarly, we may analyse millions of Instagram images shared in multiple cities to discover the types of images unique to each city.

In other words, we may combine the concern of social science, and sciences in general, with the *general* and the *regular*, and the concern of humanities with the *individual* and the *particular*. The just described examples of analysing massive data sets to zoom in on the unique items illustrate one way of doing this, but it is not the only way.

The Science of Culture?

The goal of science is to explain phenomena and develop compact mathematical models for describing how these phenomena work. Newton's three laws of physics are a perfect example of how classical science approached this goal. Since the middle of the 19th century, a number of new scientific fields have adopted a new probabilistic approach. The first example is the statistical distribution describing likely speeds of gas particles presented by Maxwell in 1860, now called the Maxwell-Boltzmann distribution. Throughout the 18th and 19th centuries, many thinkers were expecting that, similar to physics, the quantitative laws governing societies would also be eventually found (Ball 2004), yet this never happened. The closest 19th-century social thought came to postulating objective laws was in the works of Karl Marx. Instead, when positivist social science started to develop in the late 19th and early 20th century, it adopted the probabilistic approach. So instead of looking for deterministic laws of society, social scientists study correlations between measurable characteristics and model the relations between 'dependent' and 'independent' variables using various statistical techniques.

After deterministic and probabilistic paradigms in science, the next paradigm was computational simulation – running models on computers to simulate the behavior of systems. The first large-scale computer simulation was created in the 1940s by the Manhattan Project to model a nuclear explosion. Subsequently, simulation was adapted in many hard sciences, and in the 1990s it was also taken up in the social sciences.

In the early 21st century, the volume of digital online content and user interactions allows us to think of a possible 'science of culture'. For example, by the summer of 2015, Facebook users were sharing 400 million photos and sending 45 billion messages daily (Smith 2015). This scale is still much smaller than that of atoms and molecules.[6] However, it is already bigger than the numbers of neurons in the whole nervous system of an average adult, which is estimated at 86 billion. But since science now includes a few fundamental approaches to studying and understanding the phenomena – deterministic laws, statistical models and simulation – which of them should a 'science of culture' adapt?

Looking at the papers of computer scientists who are studying social media data sets, it is clear that their default approach is statistics.[7] They describe social media data and user behaviour in terms of probabilities. This includes the creation of statistical models – mathematical equations that specify the relations between variables that may be described using probability distributions rather than specific values. A majority of papers today also use supervised machine learning, an automatic creation of models that can classify or predict the values of the new data using already existing examples. In both cases, a model can only account for part of the data, and this is typical of the statistical approach.

Computer scientists studying social media use statistics differently than social scientists. The latter want to *explain* social, economic or political phenomena.[8] Computer scientists are generally not concerned with explaining patterns in social media by referencing some external social, economic or technological factors. Instead, they typically either analyse social media phenomena internally or try to predict the outside phenomena using information extracted from social media data sets. The example of the former is a statistical description of how many favourites a photo on Flickr may receive on average after a certain period of time.[9] The example of the latter is the Google Flu Trends service that predicts flu activity using a combination of Google search data and the US Centers for Disease Control and Prevention's official flu data (Stefansen 2014).

The difference between deterministic laws and non-deterministic models is that the latter describe probabilities, not certainties. The laws of classical mechanics apply to any macroscopic objects. In contrast, a probabilistic model for predicting the number of favorites for a Flickr photo as a function of time since it was uploaded cannot tell us exactly the

---

6   1 cm³ of water contains 3.33 *1022 molecules.

7   Computer scientists also use many recently developed methods including techniques of data mining and machine learning that were not part of 20th-century statistics. I discuss these differences in 'Data Science and Digital Art History,' *International Journal for Digital Art History*, issue 1 (2015), https://journals.ub.uni-heidelberg.de/index.php/dah/article/view/21631.

8   For example, the effect of family background on children's educational performance.

9   See 'Delayed information cascades in Flickr.'

numbers of favourites for any particular photo. It only describes the overall trend. This seems to be the appropriate method for a 'science of culture'. If instead we start postulating deterministic laws of human cultural activity, what happens to the idea of free will? Even in the case of seemingly automatic cultural behaviour (people favouring photos on social networks with certain characteristics such as pretty landscapes, cute pets or posing young females), we don't want to reduce humans to mechanical automata for the passing of memes.

The current focus on probabilistic models in studying online activity leaves out the third scientific paradigm – simulation. As far as I know, simulation has not yet been explored in either Social Computing or Digital Humanities as a tool for studying user-generated content, its topics, types of images, etc. If scientists at IBM's Almaden research centre simulated human visual cortex using 1.6 billion virtual neurons with 9 trillion synapses in 2009 (Fox 2009), why can't we think of simulating, for instance, all content produced yearly by users of Instagram? Or all content shared by all users of major social networks? Or the categories of images people share? The point of such simulations will not be to get everything right or to precisely predict what people will be sharing next year. Instead, we can follow the authors of the influential textbook *Simulation for the Social Scientist* (Gilbert & Troitzsch 2005) when they state that one of the purposes of simulation is 'to obtain a better *understanding* of some features of the social world' and that simulation can be used as 'a method of *theory development*' (emphasis added). Since computer simulation requires developing an explicit and precise model of the phenomena, thinking of how cultural processes can be simulated can help us to develop more explicit and detailed theories than we use normally.[10]

And what about 'big data'? Does it not represent a new paradigm in science with its own new research methods? This is a complex question that deserves its own article.[11] However, as a way of conclusion, I do want to mention one concept interesting for humanities that we can borrow from big data analytics and then push in a new direction.

10   For the example of how agent-based simulation can be used to study the evolution of human societies, see 'War, space, and the evolution of Old World complex societies', http://peterturchin.com/PDF/Turchin_etal_PNAS2013.pdf.

11   If we are talking about research methods and techniques, the developments in computer hardware in the 2000s, including the increasing CPU speed and RAM size, and the use of GPUs and computing clusters, were probably more important than availability of larger data sets. And while use of machine learning with large training data sets achieved remarkable successes, in most cases it does not provide explanations of the phenomena.

The 20th-century social science was working on what we can call 'long data'.[12] That is, the number of cases was typically many times bigger than the number of variables being analysed. For example, imagine that we surveyed 2,000 people asking them about their income, family educational achievement and their years of education. As a result, we have 2000 cases and three variables. We can then examine correlations between these variables, or look for clusters in the data, or perform other types of statistical analysis.

The beginnings of social sciences are characterized by the most extreme asymmetries of this kind. The first positivist sociologist, Karl Marx, divided all humanity into just two classes: people who own means of production and people who don't, i.e. capitalists and the proletariat. Later sociologists added other divisions. Today these divisions are present in numerous surveys, studies and reports in popular media and academic publications – typically, gender, race, ethnicity, age, educational background, income, place of living, religion, and some others. But regardless of details, the data collected, analysed and interpreted is still very 'long'. The full populations or their samples are described using a much smaller number of variables.

But why should this be the case? In the fields of computer media analysis and computer vision, computer scientists use algorithms to extract thousands of features from every image, video, tweet, email, and so on.[13] So while Vincent van Gogh, for example, only created about 900 paintings, these paintings can be described on thousands of separate dimensions. Similarly, we can describe everybody living in a city on millions of separate dimensions by extracting all kinds of characteristics from their social media activity. For another example, consider our own project *On Broadway* where we represent Broadway in Manhattan with 40 million data points and images using messages, images and check-ins shared along this street on Twitter, Instagram and Foursquare, as well as taxi rides data and the US Census indicators for the surrounding areas.[14]

In other words, instead of *long data* we can have *wide data* – very large and potentially endless number of variables describing a set of cases. Note that if we have more variables than cases, such representation would go against the common sense of both social science and data science. The latter refers to the process of making a large number of variables more manageable

12   I am using this term in a different way than Samuel Arbesman in his 'Stop Hyping Big Data and Start Paying Attention to "Long Data"', wired.com, 29 January 2013, www.wired.com/2013/01/forget-big-data-think-long-data/.

13   I explain the reason for using a large number of features in 'Data Science and Digital Art History.' (Manovich 2015).

14   Described at length in the following chapter.

as *dimension reduction*. But for us, 'wide data' offers an opportunity to rethink fundamental assumptions about what society is and how to study it, and similarly, what is culture, an artistic career, a body of images, a group of people with similar aesthetic taste, and so on. Rather than dividing cultural history using one dimension (time), or two (time and geographic location) or a few more (e.g. media, genre), endless dimensions can be put in play. The goal of such 'wide data analysis' will not be only to find new similarities, affinities and clusters in the universe of cultural artefacts, but to question a taken-for-granted view of things, where certain dimensions are taken for granted. This is one example of the general Cultural Analytics method: estrangement (*ostranenie*)[15], making our basic cultural concepts and ways of organizing and understanding cultural data sets foreign to us so that we can approach them anew. In this way, we use data and data-manipulating techniques to question how we think, see and ultimately act on our knowledge.

References

Arnold, Matthew. 1960. *Culture and Anarchy*. Cambridge: Cambridge University Press.

Associated Press. 2015. "AP Makes One Million Minutes of Historical Footage Available on YouTube." 22 July. Accessed 12 February 2016. www.ap.org/content/press-release/2015/ap-makes-one-million-minutes-of-history-available-on-youtube.

Ball, Philip. 2004. *Critical Mass: How One Thing Leads to Another*. New York: Farrar, Straus and Giroux: 69-71.

Bourdieu, Pierre. 2010. *Distinction: A Social Critique of the Judgement of Taste*. London: Routledge.

Cha, Meeyoung, Fabrício Benevenuto, Yong-Yeol Ahn & Krishna P. Gummadi. 2012. "Delayed information cascades in Flickr: Measurement, analysis, and modelling." *Computer Networks* 56: 1066–1076.

Cranshaw, Justin, Raz Schwartz, Jason I. Hong & Norman Sadeh. 2012. "The Livehoods Project: Utilizing Social Media to Understand the Dynamics of a City." The 6th International AAAI Conference on Weblogs and Social Media (Dublin.)

Cutting, James E., Kaitlin L. Brunick, Jordan DeLong, Catalina Iricinschi, Ayse Candan. 2011. "Quicker, faster, darker: Changes in Hollywood film over 75 years." *i-Perception*, vol. 2: 569-576.

Duggan, Maeve, Nicole B. Ellison, Cliff Lampe, Amanda Lenhart & Mary Madden. 2015. "Demographics of Key Social Networking Platforms." Pew Research Center Internet Science Tech RSS. 9 January. www.pewinternet.org/2015/01/09/demographics-of-key-social-networking-platforms-2.

Fox, Douglas. 2009. "IBM Reveals the Biggest Artificial Brain of All Time." *Popular Mechanics*. December 17. www.popularmechanics.com/technology/a4948/4337190/.

Gilbert, Nigel & Klaus G. Troitzsch. 2005. *Simulation for the Social Scientist*, 2nd edition: 3-4.

---

15   The term 'ostranenie' was introduced by Russian literary theorist Viktor Shklovsky in his essay 'Art as a Technique' in 1917. See www.vahidnab.com/defam.htm.

Goddemeyer, Daniel, Moritz Stefaner, Dominikus Baur & Lev Manovich. 2014. "On Broadway."
http://on-broadway.net/.

HathiTrust. 2016. "HTRC Extracted Features Dataset Page-level Features from 4.8 Million Volumes [v.0.2]." HTRC Portal. Accessed 12 February 2016. https://sharc.hathitrust.org/features.

Hochman, Nadav, Lev Manovich & Jay Chow. 2013. "Phototrails." http://phototrails.net/.

Hu, Yuheng, Lydia Manikonda & Subbarao Kambhampati. 2014. "What We Instagram: A First Analysis of Instagram Photo Content and User Types." *Proceedings of the 8th International AAAI Conference on Weblogs and Social Media (ICWSM).*

IMDb. 2015. "IMDb Database Statistics." www.imdb.com/stats. Accessed 10 August 2015.

Kwak, Haewoon, Changhyun Lee, Hosung Park & Sue Moon. 2014. "What is Twitter, a Social Network or a News Media?" *Proceedings of the 19th International World Wide Web (WWW) Conference (ACM)*: 591-600.

Library of Congress. 2016. "About Chronicling America." News about Chronicling America RSS. Accessed 12 February 2016. http://chroniclingamerica.loc.gov/about/.

Manovich, Lev, 2015. "Data Science and Digital Art History." *International Journal of Digital Art History*, issue 1. http://www.dah-journal.org/issue_01.html.

Manovich, Lev, Mehrdad Yazdani, Alise Tifentale & Jay Chow. 2014. "The Exceptional and the Everyday: 144 hours in Kyiv." www.the-everyday.net/.

Reinecke, Katharina & Krzysztof Z. Gajos. 2014. "Quantifying Visual Preferences Around the World. *Proceedings of the SIGCHI Conference on Human Factors in Computing Systems*, CHI '14 (New York: ACM): 11-20.

Saleh, Babak, Kanako Abe, Ravneet Singh & Arora Ahmed Elgammal. 2014. "Toward Automated Discovery of Artistic Influence." *Multimedia Tools and Applications* (Springler, 19 August): 1-27.

Schich, Maximilian, Chaoming Song, Yong-Yeol Ahn, Alexander Mirsky, Mauro Martino, Albert-László Barabási & Dirk Helbing. 2014. "A network framework of cultural history." *Science*, 1 August: 345 (6196): 558-562.

Serrà, Joan, Álvaro Corral, Marián Boguñá, Martín Haro & Josep Ll. Arcos. 2012. "Measuring the Evolution of Contemporary Western Popular Music." *Nature Scientific Reports*. 2, article number: 521.

Smith, Craig. 2015. "By the Numbers: 200 Amazing Facebook Statistics (January 2015)." DMR. 24 January. http://expandedramblings.com/index.php/by-the-numbers-17-amazing-facebook-stats/15.

Smith, David A., Ryan Cordell & Elizabeth Maddock Dillon. 2013. "Infectious texts: modelling text reuse in nineteenth-century newspapers." *Proceedings of the 2013 IEEE Conference on Big Data*: 84-94.

Stefansen, Christian. 2014. "Google Flu Trends Gets a Brand New Engine." Research Blog. 31 October. http://googleresearch.blogspot.com/2014/10/google-flu-trends-gets-brand-new-engine.html.

Taylor, Alan. 2012. "Historic Photos from the NYC Municipal Archives." *The Atlantic*. Accessed 12 February 2016.

Underwood, Ted, Michael L. Black, Loretta Auvil & Boris Capitanu. 2013. "Mapping Mutable Genres in Structurally Complex Volumes." *Proceedings of the 2013 IEEE Conference on Big Data*: n.p.

4.   Case Study

On Broadway

Daniel Goddemeyer, Moritz Stefaner, Dominikus Baur &
Lev Manovich

Modern writers, painters, photographers, filmmakers and digital artists
have created many fascinating representations of city life. Paintings of Paris-
ian boulevards and cafés by Pissarro and Renoir, photomontages by Berlin
Dada artists, *Spider-Man* comics by Stan Lee and Steve Ditko, *Broadway
Boogie-Woogie* by Piet Mondrian and *Playtime* by Jacques Tati are some of
the classic examples of artists encountering the city. Today, a city 'talks' to
us in data. Many cities make data sets available and sponsor hackathons
to encourage the creation of useful apps using their data. For example, the
NYC Open Data website, sponsored by the NYC Mayor's Office, offers over
1,200 data sets covering everything from the trees in the city to bike data.
On top of that, locals and tourists share massive amounts of geo-coded
visual media using Twitter, Instagram and other networks. Services such as
Foursquare tell us where people go and what kind of venues they frequent.
At the start of a new Cultural Analytics project, Daniel Goddemeyer, Moritz
Stefaner, Dominikus Baur and Lev Manovich[1] asked themselves the following questions: How can we represent the 21st century using such rich data
and image sources? Is there a different way to visualize the city besides
graphs, numbers or maps?

The result of their explorations is *On Broadway*: a visually-rich, image-
centric *interface* without maps and where numbers play only a secondary role.

Like a spine in a human body, Broadway runs through the middle of
Manhattan Island curving along its way. In order to capture the activities
nearby, a slightly wider area than the street itself was included. To define
this area, points were selected at 30-metre intervals going through the
centre of Broadway, and 100-metre-wide rectangles centred on every point
were defined (see Figure 4.2). The result is a spin-like shape that is 21,390
metres (13.5 miles) long and 100 metres wide.

This project's attempt to make a combination of a variety of data sets
visible within the same visualization can be seen as an example of 'wide
data'. The data was collected from five main sources: Instagram, Twitter,

---

1   The team's previous work includes Selfiecity: selfiecity.net.

Fig. 4.1:   On Broadway display in the New York Public Library (NYPL)

Fig. 4.2:   Close-up showing the width of the area centred on Broadway that was used as a data filter

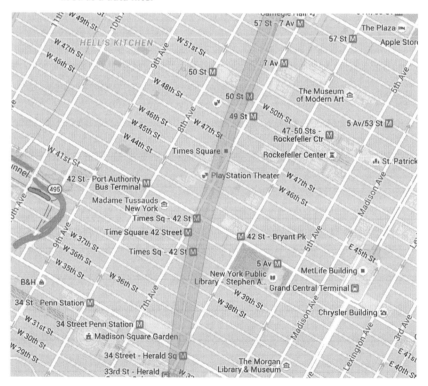

Foursquare, Taxi pick-up and drop-off data and census data from the American Community Service. Using Gnip, a social media monitoring service, all geo-coded Instagram images publicly shared in the New York City area between 26 February and 3 August 2014 were downloaded. This data set contained 10,624,543 images out of which 661,809 are from the Broadway area used for the project. Since the *On Broadway* project is part of the Twitter Data Grant awarded to the Software Studies Initiative, the artists received all publicly shared tweets with images around the world between 2011 and 2014. This data set was filtered, leaving only tweets shared inside the Broadway area during the same time period as was used for Instagram (158 days in 2014). Data from Foursquare could be obtained using its own API. With this service 8,527,198 check-ins along Broadway between March 2009 and March 2014 were downloaded. Chris Whong was able to obtain taxi pick-up and drop-off data from NYC Taxi and Limousine Commission (TLC). Filtering the data set containing the 140 million trips made in Manhattan in 2013 using Broadway coordinates left him with 10,077,789 drop-off and 12,391,809 pick-up locations, a total of 22 million trips. Finally, for the economic indicators, the latest published data from American Community Service (ACS, 2013) was used. It is a yearly survey of the US Census Bureau's sample of the US population. ACS reports the data summarized by census tracks. These are areas that are much larger than the 30 x 100 metre rectangles that are used to define the Broadway area (the 713 selected rectangles cross 73 larger US Census tracks). Given this discrepancy, any Census indicator summarized per track will only approximately apply to the smaller Broadway parts. That is why only a single economic indicator from the estimated average household income is used. This data is shown as one of the layers in the application.

The Visualization

The artwork that directly inspired the project is *Every Building on the Sunset Strip* by Edward Ruscha (1996). It is an artist book that unfolds to 25 feet (8.33 metres) to show continuous photographic views of both sides of a 1.5-mile section of Sunset Boulevard. The interactive installation and Web application represents life in the 21st century city through a compilation of images and data collected along the thirteen miles of Broadway that span Manhattan. The project proposes a new visual metaphor for thinking about the city: a vertical stack of image and data layers created

Fig. 4.3:   A close-up of the installation screen showing a part of Greenwich Village area

from the activities and media shared by hundreds of thousands of people. There are thirteen such layers in the project, all aligned to locations along Broadway. As you move along the street, you see a selection of Instagram photos from each area, left, right and top Google Street View images and extracted top colours from these image sources. In addition, the visualization shows the average numbers of taxi pick-ups and drop-offs, Twitter posts with images, and average family income for the parts of the city crossed by Broadway.

Moritz Stefaner comments on how we were interested in how we could enable seamless navigation between high-level condensed views of the city and zoomed in, anecdotal data. In the exploratory phase of the project, we experimented a lot with different remixes and montages of the many data and image materials we had available. The final application reflects this enormous data diversity and richness: from taxi rides and median income to colour palettes and Twitter messages.

Daniel Goddemeyer draws attention to the fact that we were determined not to use a conventional map view and instead focused on creating a new multi-layered interaction paradigm: 'The use of Google Street View images allows users to quickly look at urban physical context of every data point and Instagram image. In this way we are juxtaposing the digital with the physical.'

Goals

With *On Broadway*, the artists would like to raise awareness of the fact that more and more data about people is produced and collected, not only visibly, but also through subtle and invisible practices. By showing the immense amounts of available data within a single visual interface an experience of estrangement is pursued, hopefully leaving the spectator with food for thought.

During the production of this book the team has continued working on the analysis of all the data assembled for the project. The results of this research will be published as academic articles and also as blog posts on www.softwarestudies.com.

5.   Foundations of Digital Methods

Query Design

Richard Rogers

digital methods and Online Groundedness

Broadly speaking digital methods may be considered the deployment of online tools and data for the purposes of social and medium research. More specifically, they derive from online methods, or methods of the medium, which are reimagined and repurposed for research. The methods to be repurposed are often built into dominant devices for recommending sources or drawing attention to oneself or one's posts. For an example of how to reimagine the inputs and outputs of one such dominant device, consider the difference between studying search engine results to understand in some manner Google's algorithms, or recent algorithmic updates, or treating them, as in the Google Flu Trends project, as indications of societal concerns. Here, there is a shift from studying the medium to using device data to study the societal. That is, akin to the digital methods outlook generally, Google Flu Trends and other anticipatory instruments use online social signals to measure trends not so much in the online realm but rather 'in the wild'.[1]

Once the findings are made the question becomes how to ground them, that is, with conventional offline methods and techniques, such as the Centers for Disease Control's means of studying flu incidence through hospital and doctor reports, as in the Flu Trends project, or through additional, online methods and sources. In digital methods research, online groundedness, as I have called it, asks whether and when it is appropriate to shift the site of 'ground-truthing', to use a geographer's expression. As a case in point, when verifying knowledge claims, Wikipedians check prior art through Google searches, thereby grounding claims via the search engine in online sources.

Digital methods thereby rethink conditions of proof, first by considering the online as a site of grounding, but also in a second sense. One makes social research findings online, and, rather than leaving the medium to harden them, one subsequently inquires into the extent to which the medium

---

1   The US Centers for Disease Control and Prevention (CDC) ran a competition in 2013-14 for instruments that use search and social media data to forecast influenza, and the one employing the data from Google Flu Trends won the award.

is affecting the findings. Medium research thus serves a purpose that is distinct from the study of online culture alone. As I will come to shortly, when reading and interpreting social signals online, the question concerns whether the medium, or media dynamics, is overdetermining the outcomes.

Making Use of Online Data: From the Semantic to the Social

As noted, digital methods make use of online methods, by which I refer to an array of techniques from the computational and information sciences – crawling, scraping, indexing, ranking, and so forth – that have been applied to and redeveloped for the Web. They refer to algorithms that determine relevance and authority and thereby recommend information sources as in Google's famed PageRank, but also boost all manner of items, from songs and 'friends' to potential 'followers'.

Many of the algorithms are referred to as 'social', meaning that they make use of user choices and activity (purposive clicks such as liking), and may be contrasted with the 'semantic', meaning that which is categorized and matched (as in Google's Knowledge Graph). Digital methods seek to take particular advantage of socially derived rankings, that is, users making their preferences known for particular sources, often unobtrusively. Secondarily, the semantic (sources that have been pre-matched or taxonomied) are also of value, for example when Wikipedia furnishes a curated seed list of sources ('climate change sceptics' as a case in point), which have been derived manually by information experts or the proverbial crowd guided by the protocols of the online encyclopaedic community.

The distinction between social and semantic is mentioned so as to emphasize Web-epistemological 'crowdfindings' (as implied by the 'social'), as distinct from 'results' from information retrieval.[2] Thus with digital methods, as I relate below, one seeks to query in order to make findings from socialised Web data (so to speak) rather than query in order to find pre-sorted information or sources, however well annotated or enriched with metadata.

Why Query Google (Still) for Research Purposes?

Over the course of the past decade or more Google arguably has transformed itself from an epistemological machine outputting reputational source

2   Crowdfindings is a term coined by Christian Bröer.

hierarchies to a consumer information appliance providing user-tailored results. Here I would like to take up the question of how and to which ends one might still employ Google as an epistemological machine.

There are largely two research purposes for querying Google: medium and social research. With medium research, one studies (often critically) how and for whom Google works. To which degree does the engine serve a handful of dominant websites such as Google properties themselves in a 'preferred placement' critique, or websites receiving the most attention through links and clicks? One would seek to lay bare the persistence of so-called 'googlearchies' that boost certain websites and bury others in the results, as Matthew Hindman's classic critique of Google's outputs would imply. Here the work being done is an engine results critique, where the question revolves around the extent to which the change in 2009 in Google's algorithmic philosophy, captured in the opening chapter of Eli Pariser's *Filter Bubble,* from universal to personalized outputs, dislodges or upholds the pole positions of dominant sites on the Web. Indeed, another critical inroad in engine results critique is the so-called filter bubble itself, where one would examine the effects of personalization, investigating Pariser's claim that Google furnishes increasingly personalized and localised results. In this enquiry, one may reinvigorate Nicholas Negroponte's 'Daily Me' argument and Cass Sunstein's response concerning the undesirable effects of homophily, polarization and the end of the shared public exposure to media which leaves societies without common frames of reference. In this line of reasoning, personalization leads to social atomisation and severe niching, otherwise known as 'markets of one', as described by Joseph Turow in *Niche Envy.* It also would imply the demise of the mass media audience.

In the second research strategy, there is a mode switch in how one views the work of the search engine (and for whom it could work). Google's queries, together with its outputted site rankings, are considered as indicators of social trends. That is, instead of beginning from the democratizing and socializing potential of the Web and subsequently critiquing Google for its reintroduction of hierarchies, one focuses on how examining engine queries and results allows for the study of social sorting. How to study the hierarchies Google offers? Which terms have been queried most significantly (at which time and from which location)? Do places have preferred searches? May we geo-locate temporal pockets of anxiety? The capacity to indicate general and localisable trends makes Google results of interest to the social researcher.[3]

---

3   Not only Google Trends but also Google Related Search provides means for studying keyword salience as well as the association between keywords, including co-occurrence.

Fig. 5.1:   **Greenpeace campaigns, 1996-2012, ranked and arrayed as word cloud according to frequency of appearances on Greenpeace.org front page. Source: Data from the Internet Archive, archive.org. Analysis by Anne Laurine Stadermann.**

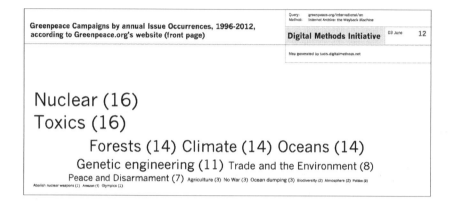

Greenpeace Campaigns by annual Issue Occurrences, 1996-2012, according to Greenpeace.org's website (front page)	Query: greenpeace.org/international/en Method: Internet Archive: the Wayback Machine **Digital Methods Initiative** 03 June 12
	Map generated by tools.digitalmethods.net

Nuclear (16)
Toxics (16)
   Forests (14) Climate (14) Oceans (14)
   Genetic engineering (11) Trade and the Environment (8)
      Peace and Disarmament (7) Agriculture (3) No War (3) Ocean dumping (3) Biodiversity (2) Atmosphere (2) Politics (2)
Abolish nuclear weapons (1) Amazon (1) Olympics (1)

Fig. 5.2:   **Greenpeace campaigns mentioned on Greenpeace.org as ranked word cloud, 2012. Source: Data from Greenpeace.org gathered by the Lippmannian Device, Digital Methods Initiative. Analysis by Anne Laurine Stadermann.**

Greenpeace Campaigns mentioned on Greenpeace International website	Query:site: http://www.greenpeace.org/ Method: Query Google Scraper for campaign terms **Digital Methods Initiative** 09 May 12
	Map generated by tools.digitalmethods.net

Nuclear (11300)
Climate change (9860) Oceans (9390) Forests (9370) Agriculture (8790) Peace & Disarmament (8720) Toxic pollution (8540)

Apart from trends one may also study dominant voice, commitment and concern. One may ask in the first instance, when and for which keywords do certain actors appear high on the list and others marginal? Which actors are given the opportunity to dominate and drive the meaning of terms and their discussion and debate? Here the engine is considered as serving social epistemologies for any keyword (or social issue) through what is collectively queried and returned.

The engine also can be employed to the study of commitment in terms of the continued use of keywords by individual actors, be they governments, non-governmental organizations, radical group formations or individuals.

Fig. 5.3: **Greenpeace with numerous mentions of Fukushima and World Wildlife Fund with few, November 2016. Source: Data and visualization by the Lippmannian Device, Digital Methods Initiative.**

Fukushima nuclear disaster as environmental and species concern?	**Digital Methods Initiative**	
Query:	site:greenpeace.org Fukushima site:worldwildlife.org Fukushima	
Method:	Query leading environmental and species NGOs for Fukushima	24 November

Map generated by tools.digitalmethods.net

environment (26400) species (3)

Here the researcher takes advantage not of the hierarchies inputted and outputted (socio-epistemological sorting) but of the massive and recent indexing of individual websites. For example, non-governmental organization Greenpeace once had the dual agenda of environmentalism and disarmament (hence the fusion of 'green' and 'peace'). Querying Greenpeace websites lately for issue keywords would show that their commitment to campaigning for peace has significantly waned in comparison to that for environmental causes, for green words resonate far more than disarmament ones. Here one counts incidences of keywords on Web pages for the study of issue commitment (see Figures 5.1 and 5.2).

One also may query sets of actors for keywords in order to have an indication of the levels of concern for an issue. For example, querying a representative environmental group and a species group (respectively) for Fukushima would show that the environmental group is highly active in the issue space whilst the species NGO is largely absent, showing a lack of concern for the matter (see Figure 5.3).

In all, for the social researcher, Google is of interest for its capacity to rank actors (websites) per social issue (keyword), thereby providing source hierarchies, and allowing for the study of dominant voice. It is also pertinent for its ability to count the incidence of issue words per actor or sets of actors, thereby allowing for the study of commitment through continued use of keywords.

Clean Google Results to Remove 'Artefacts'?

One might distinguish between the two research types above by viewing one as primarily doing media studies and the other social research. Yet in practice, the two are entangled with one another. As mentioned in the introduction, here the entanglement assumes a particular form. Medium research is in service of social research in the sense of concentrating on the extent to which the findings made have been overdetermined by media effects.

It is important to stress from the outset that it not assumed that engine effects can be removed *in toto*, thus enabling a researcher to study 'organic' results, the industry term for editorial content untouched by advertising or preferred placement. Rather there should be awareness of a variety of types of routinely befouling artefacts ('media effects') that nevertheless are returned by the engine. Google properties (e.g. YouTube videos), Google user aids (e.g. 'equivalent results' for queried terms), and SEO'd products (whether through white or black hat techniques) are all considered media effects, and in principle could be removed or footnoted. There are software settings (e.g. remove Google properties from results), query design (use quotation marks for exact matches) and also strategies for detecting at least obviously SEO'd results.

The more problematic issue arises with any desired detection of the effects of personalization. The point here is that users now co-author engine results. The search engine thereby produces artefacts that are of the user's making. The search engine, once critiqued for its social sorting and Matthew effect in the results, leans towards inculpability, since users have set preferences (and had preferences set for them) and some results are affected. There is the question of detecting how many and which results are personalized in one form or another, according to one's location (country as well as locality), language, personal search history as well as adult and violent content filter.

Certain queries would likely have no organic results in the top ten, thus making any content cleaning exercise into an artificial act of removal, given that most users: a) click the top results, b) have the results set to the default of ten, and c) do not venture beyond one page of results. There are also special cases to consider for removal, such as Wikipedia, which is delivered in the top results for nearly all substantive queries, making it appear to be at once an authoritative source (for its persistent presence) and an engine artefact (for its uncannily persistent presence). Wikipedia's supra-presence, so to speak, provides a conundrum for the researcher who may wish to clean content of Google artefacts and media effects, and is perhaps the best case for retaining them at least in the first instance.

One way forward would be to remove the user, so to speak, and strive to have the engine work as unaffected as possible. Removing the user is a means of re-conjuring the pre-2009 distinction between universal results (served to all) and personalized results (served to an individual user). A research browser would be set up, where one is logged out of Google, and no cookies are set. The ncr (no country redirect) version of Google is used, or one would query from a non-location, or obfuscated one.

Studying Media Effects or the Societal 'in the Wild'?

The question of whether Google merely outputs Google artefacts and medium effects or reveals social trends has been raised in connection with the flagship big data project, Google Flu Trends (Lazer et al. 2014). As mentioned at the outset, the project, run by Google's non-profit Google.org, monitors user queries for flu and flu-related symptoms, geolocates their incidence and outputs the timing and locations of heightened flu activity; it is a tool for tracking where the virus is most prevalent. Yet does the increased incidence of queries for flu and flu-related symptoms indicate a rise in the number of influenza cases 'in the wild', or does it mean that TV and other news of the coming flu season prompt heightened query activity? TV viewers may be using a 'second screen' and fact checking or enhancing their knowledge through search engine queries. Given that Flu Trends was over reporting for a period of time, compared to its baseline at the US Centers for Disease Control (and its equivalents internationally), the project seemed to be overly imbued with media effects.

Thus one may seek research strategies to study medium effects, formulating queries that in a sense put on display or amplify the effects. For which types of queries do more Google properties appear? How can Google be made to output user aids that are telling? How to detect egregiously SEO'd results?

When using Google as a social research machine, the task at hand, however, is to reduce Google effects, albeit without the pretension of completely removing them. This is the main preparatory work, conceptually as well as practically, prior to query design.

When Words are Keywords: A Query Design Strategy

The question of what constitutes a keyword is the starting point for query design, for that is what makes querying and query design practically part of a research strategy. When formulating a query, one often begins with keywords so as to ascertain who is using them, in which contexts and with which spread or distribution over time. In the following a particular keyword query strategy or design is put forward, whereby one queries competing keywords, asking whether a particular term is winning favour and amongst whom.

The keyword has its origins in the notion of a 'hint' or 'clue'. The *New Oxford American Dictionary* (built into Apple OS's dictionary) calls it 'a word which acts as the key to a cipher or code'. In this rendering keywords do not so much have hidden but rather purposive meaning so as to enable an unlocking or an opening up. Relatedly, Raymond Williams, in his book *Keywords*, discusses them in at least two senses: 'the available and developing meanings of known words' and 'the explicit but as often implicit connections which people are making' (1976: 13). Thus behind keywords are both well-known words (elucidated by Williams's elaborations on the changing meaning of 'culture' over longer periods of time, beyond the high/low distinction) or neologistic phrases such as recent concerns surrounding 'blood minerals' or the more defused 'conflict minerals' mined and built into mobile phones. The one has readily available yet developing meanings and the other are new phraseologies that position. For the query design I am proposing, the purposive meaning of keywords is captured by Williams most readily in his second type (the new language). The first type may apply as well, such as in the case of a new use or mobilization of a phrase, such as 'new economic order' or 'land reform'. The question then becomes what is meant by it *this time*.

Concerning how deploying a keyword implies a side-taking politics, I refer to the work of Madeleine Akrich, Bruno Latour and others, who have discussed the idea that, far from having stable meanings (as Williams also related), keywords can be part of programmes or anti-programmes. Programmes refer to efforts made at putting forward and promoting a particular proposal, campaign or project. Conversely, anti-programmes oppose these efforts or projects through keywords. Following this reading, keywords can be thought of as furthering a programme or an anti-programme. There is, however, also a third type of keyword I would like to add, which refers to efforts made at being neutral. These are specific undertakings made *not* to join a programme or an anti-programme. News outlets such as the BBC, *The New York Times* and *The Guardian* often have dedicated style guides that advise their reporters to employ particular language and avoid other. For example, the BBC instructs reporters to use generic wording for the obstacle separating Israel and the Palestinian Territories:

> The BBC uses the term 'barrier', 'separation barrier' or 'West Bank barrier' as an acceptable generic description to avoid the political connotations of 'security fence' (preferred by the Israeli government) or 'apartheid wall' (preferred by the Palestinians) (BBC Academy, 2013).

When formulating queries, it is pertinent to consider keywords as being parts of programmes, anti-programmes or efforts at neutrality, as this outlook allows the researcher to study trends, commitments and alignments between actors. To this end (and in contrast to discourse analysis), one does not wish to have equivalents or substitutes for the specific issue language being employed by the programmes, anti-programmes and the neutral programmes. For example, there is a difference between using the term 'blood minerals' or the term 'conflict minerals', or using 'blood diamonds' or 'conflict diamonds', because the terms are employed (and repeated) by particular actors to issuefy, or to make into a social issue forced and often brutal mining practices that fuel war (blood diamonds or minerals) or to have industry recognize a sensitive issue and their corporate social responsibility (conflict diamonds or minerals). Therefore, they should not be treated as equivalent and grouped together. (Here it is useful to return to the point that one should use quotation marks around keywords when querying, because without quotation marks and thus specific key word queries, Google returns equivalents.) Indeed, one should treat 'conflict minerals' and 'blood minerals' as separate, because as parts of specific programmes they show distinctive commitments and they can help to draw alignments. If someone (often a journalist) begins using a third term, such as 'conflict resources', it likely constitutes a conscious effort at being neutral and not joining the programmes using the other terms. Those who then enter the fray and knowledgeably employ *what have become keywords* (in Williams's second sense) can be said to be taking up a position and a side, or avoiding one.

To demonstrate the notion of programmes, anti-programmes and efforts at neutrality further, the Palestinian-Israeli conflict, alluded to above, presents a compelling case for studying positioning as well as (temporary) alignment. There are two famous, recorded exchanges that took place at the White House in the US between then President George W. Bush and the leader of the Palestinian Authority, Mahmoud Abbas; and, secondly, between President Bush and the then Prime Minister of Israel, Ariel Sharon (see Figure 5.4). These exchanges, from the time when the barrier was under construction, show the kinds of positioning efforts that are made through the use of particular terms and thus the kind of specific terminology that one should be aware of when formulating queries. They also reveal temporary alignments that put on display diplomacy, with the US President using the Palestinian and then the Israeli preferred terminology in the company of the respective leaders, but only partly, thereby never fully taking sides.

The first exchange between President Bush and the Palestinian leader, Abbas, begins with a discussion in which Bush refers to the barrier as a 'security fence', which is the official Israeli term. Abbas then makes an attempt to correct this keyword by replying with the term 'separation wall', thereby using a very different adjective – separation instead of security – to allude to the interpretation of the purpose of the barrier as separating peoples and not securing Israel. Abbas also uses a poignant noun, wall. The word 'fence', as in the Israeli 'security fence', connotes a lightweight, neighbourly fence. By calling it a 'wall', however, Abbas connotes the Berlin Wall. The third person in this exchange, the journalist, then steps in with the term 'barrier wall' in an effort not to take sides, though at the moment 'wall' actually gives the Palestinian position some weight. Following this exchange, Bush, being diplomatic, realizes when talking to Abbas that the word 'wall' is being used, so he switches terms and concludes by using the term, albeit without an adjective that would validate Abbas and clash with the official Israeli term.

Four days later, the Israeli Prime Minister, Sharon, visits the White House to talk to President Bush, and he begins by using 'security fence', the official Israeli term. A journalist steps in and seems not to have read any newspaper

Fig. 5.4: **The use of keywords by US, Palestinian and Israeli leaders, showing (temporary) terminological alignments and diplomacy. Exchanges between the leaders at the Rose Garden, US White House, 2003.**

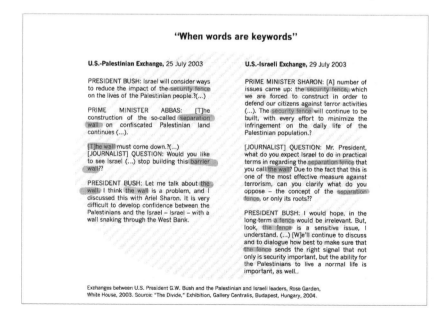

"When words are keywords"

U.S.-Palestinian Exchange, 25 July 2003

PRESIDENT BUSH: Israel will consider ways to reduce the impact of the security fence on the lives of the Palestinian people.?(...)

PRIME MINISTER ABBAS: [T]he construction of the so-called separation wall on confiscated Palestinian land continues (...).

[T]he wall must come down.?(...)
[JOURNALIST] QUESTION: Would you like to see Israel (...) stop building this barrier wall??

PRESIDENT BUSH: Let me talk about the wall. I think the wall is a problem, and I discussed this with Ariel Sharon. It is very difficult to develop confidence between the Palestinians and the Israel – Israel – with a wall snaking through the West Bank.

U.S.-Israeli Exchange, 29 July 2003

PRIME MINISTER SHARON: [A] number of issues came up: the security fence, which we are forced to construct in order to defend our citizens against terror activities (...). The security fence will continue to be built, with every effort to minimize the infringement on the daily life of the Palestinian population.?

[JOURNALIST] QUESTION: Mr. President, what do you expect Israel to do in practical terms in regarding the separation fence that you call the wall? Due to the fact that this is one of the most effective measure against terrorism, can you clarify what do you oppose – the concept of the separation fence, or only its roots??

PRESIDENT BUSH: I would hope, in the long-term a fence would be irrelevant. But, look, the fence is a sensitive issue, I understand. (...) [W]e'll continue to discuss and to dialogue how best to make sure that the fence sends the right signal that not only is security important, but the ability for the Palestinians to live a normal life is important, as well..

Exchanges between U.S. President G.W. Bush and the Palestinian and Israeli leaders, Rose Garden, White House, 2003. Source: "The Divide," Exhibition, Gallery Centralis, Budapest, Hungary, 2004.

style guides on the matter, because he first says 'separation fence' and then 'wall'. The journalist, moreover, does not use 'security fence' and, therefore, the question he poses, whilst critical, also seems one-sided for it was preceded by quite some Palestinian language (separation, wall). Bush concludes by being diplomatic once again to both parties involved: he is tactful to Sharon by just using the word 'fence', but he does not use any adjective so as to be wary of Abbas, his recent visitor.

Wall and fence talk in the Middle East, of course, is very specific conflict terminology, but it does highlight a particular programme ('security fence'), an anti-programme ('separation wall') as well as an effort at being neutral ('barrier wall'). It also shows how temporary alignments, often only partial ones, are made with great tact, providing something of a performative definition of diplomacy.

Issue spaces can be analysed with this sort of keyword specificity in mind. A related example in this regard concerns the United Nations (UN) Security Council's debates on the barrier between Israel and the Palestinian Territories, which took place in 2003 and 2005 when it was first being constructed (Rogers & Ben-David 2010). The terms used by each country participating in the debates were lifted directly from the Security Council transcripts. The resultant issue maps, or network graphs, contain nodes that represent countries, clustered by the term(s) that each country uses when referring to the barrier (see Figures 5.5 and 5.6). The network clearly demonstrates the specificity of the terminology put into play by the respective countries at the table as well as the terminological alignments that emerge. When countries utter the same term, groupings or blocs form, to speak in the language of international relations. For example, the largest surrounds 'separation wall', and mention of other terms ('expansionist wall', 'racist wall', 'security wall', 'the barrier', 'the fence', 'the wall', 'the structure', 'separation barrier', and so forth) make for smaller groupings or even isolation.

In 2003 a majority of countries came to terms around 'separation wall' or 'the wall', both Palestinian side-taking terms, and there was a smattering of more extreme terms, e.g. 'racist wall'. On the other side of the divide, the term 'security fence', the official Israeli nomenclature, is only spoken by Israel and Germany, showing terminological alignment between the two countries. Two years later, in 2005, the next UN Security Council debate on the barrier took place, and a similar pattern of terminology use emerged, albeit with two distinct differences. Neutral language had found its way into the debate, with 'the barrier' enjoying support. And this time, Israel was alone in using the term 'security fence', and is thereby isolated.

**Fig. 5.5:   Cluster graph showing co-occurring country uses of terminology for
the structure between Israel and the Palestinian Territories, UN Security
Council meeting, 2003. Visualization by ReseauLu.**

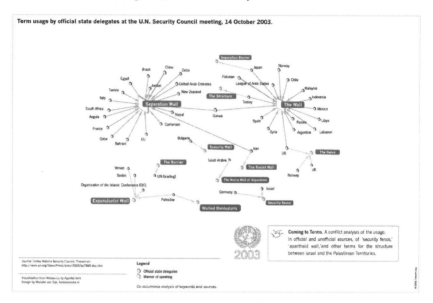

**Fig. 5.6:   Cluster graph showing co-occurring country uses of terminology for
thestructurebetweenIsraelandthePalestinianTerritories,UNSecurityCouncil
meeting, 2005. Visualization by ReseauLu.**

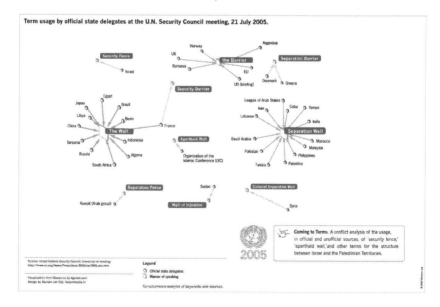

Countries are 'linked' or isolated by terminology. They settle into a debate by subscribing to programmes, anti-programmes and efforts at neutrality, together with light gestures towards the one side or another (e.g. by using just wall or fence). In some cases, there are evident language blocs. Each bloc shows alignment in that countries (over time) come to terms with other countries by means of using the same language. It is precisely this alignment of actors to programmes, anti-programmes or efforts at neutrality that one seeks to build into query design from the outset.

Unambiguous and Ambiguous Queries

If you peruse the search engine literature, there are mentions of navigational queries, transactional queries and substantive queries, among other types. Yet, on a meta-level, we can broadly speak of two kinds of queries: unambiguous and ambiguous. The original strength of Google and its PageRank algorithms lay in how they dealt with an ambiguous query that matches more than one potential result and thereby is in need of some form of 'disambiguation'. An example that was often used in the early search engine literature is for the query 'Harvard'. This could refer to the university, a city (in Illinois, USA) or perhaps businesses near the university or in the city. By looking at which sites receive the most links from the most influential sites, PageRank would return Harvard University as the top result because it would presumably receive more links from reputable sources than a dry-cleaning business near the university, for example, called Harvard Cleaners. Therefore, without unambiguous matching of keyword to result, the outputs depend on a disambiguating mechanism (Google's PageRank) that places Harvard University at the top. The ability to disambiguate is also thereby socio-epistemological or one that reveals social hierarchies. Harvard University is at the top because it has been placed there through establishment linking practices.

The social researcher may take advantage of how the search engine treats ambiguous queries. In the example, the ambiguous keyword, 'rights', is queried in a variety of local domain Googles (e.g. google.co.jp, google.co.uk etc.), in order to create hierarchies of concerns (rights types) per country, thereby employing Google as a socio-epistemological machine.

Contrariwise, an unambiguous query is one in which it is clear which results one is after. If we return to the cluster maps of countries using particular terms for the barrier between Israel and the Palestinian Territories, precise terms were used. By putting these terms in quotation marks and querying them, Google would return an ordered list of sources that use those specific terms. If one forgoes the use of quotation marks in the query, Google, as mentioned, 'helpfully' provides the engine user with synonyms or equivalents of sorts. For example, if one does not wish to make a distinction between mobile phones (British English) and cell phones (North American English), you can simply search for [mobile phones] without quotation marks and Google will furnish results for both of them. If one places a term in quotation marks, however, Google will provide results specific to that one term.

It is instructive to point out a particular form of annotation when writing about queries. When noting down the specific query used, the recommendation is to use square brackets as markers. Therefore, a query could be ["apartheid wall"], where the query has square brackets around it and the query is made as unambiguous as possible (for the engine) by using quotation marks. Oftentimes, when a query is mentioned in the literature, it will have only quotation marks without the square brackets. A reader is often left wondering whether the query was in fact made with quotation marks or whether the quotation marks are used in the text merely to distinguish the term as a query. To solve this problem, the square brackets annotation is employed. If one's query does not have quotation marks they are dropped but the square brackets remain.

Doing Search as Research

There are two preparatory steps to take prior to doing search as research. The first one is to install a research browser. This means installing a separate instance of your browser, such as Firefox, or creating a new profile in which you have cleaned the cookies and otherwise disentangled yourself from Google. The second preparatory step is to take a moment to set up one's Google result settings. If saving results for further scrutiny later (including manual interpretation as in the Rights Types project discussed below), set the results from the default 10 to 20, 50 or 100. If one is interested in researching a societal concern, one should set geography in Google to the national level – that is, to the country level setting and not to the default city setting. If one is interested in universal results only, consider obfuscating one's location. In all cases one is not logged into Google.[4]

---

4   It is also important to note that simply using private browsing tools, such as the incognito tool on Google Chrome, does not suffice as a disentanglement strategy, as this only prevents the saving of one's search history to one's own machine. It is still being saved at headquarters so to speak. When in incognito mode, one is still served personalized results.

I would like to present, first, an example of research conducted using unambiguous queries. The project in question concerns the Google image results of the query for two different terms for the same barrier: ["apartheid wall"], which is the official Palestinian term for the Israeli-Palestinian barrier mentioned previously, versus the Israeli term, ["security fence"] (see Figure 5.7). The results from these two queries present images of objects distinctive from one another. The image results for ["apartheid wall"] contain graffitied, wall-like structures, barbed wire, protests, and people being somehow excluded, whereas with ["security fence"] there is another narrative, one derived through lightweight, high-tech structures. Furthermore, there is a series of images of bomb attacks in Israel, presented as justification for the building of the wall. There are also information graphics, presenting such figures as the number of attempted bombings and the number of bombings that met their targets before and after the building of the wall. In the image results we are thus presented with the argumentation behind the building of the fence. The two narratives resulting from the two separate queries are evidently at odds, and these are the sorts of findings one is able to tease out with a query design in the programme/anti-programme vein. Adding neutral terminology to the query design would enrich the findings by showing, for example, which side's images (so to speak) have become the neutral ones.

When doing search as research as above, the question is often raised whether to remove Google artefacts and Google properties in the results, and under which circumstances. Wikipedia, towards the top of the results for substantive queries, is ranked highly in the results for the query ["apartheid wall"] yet has as the title of its article in the English-language version an effort at neutrality in 'West Bank barrier', however much it includes a discussion of the various names given to it. Whilst a Google artefact, Wikipedia's efforts at neutrality should be highlighted as such rather than removed. A more difficult case relates to a Google artefact in the results for an ambiguous query [rights] in google.com, discussed in more detail below. The R.I.G.H.T.S. organization is returned highly in the results, owing more to its name than to its significance in the rights issue space. Here again the result was retained, and footnoted (or highlighted) as a Google artefact, which in a sense answers questions regarding the extent or breadth of artefacts in the findings. Here the research strategy is chosen to highlight rather than remove an artefact, so as to anticipate critique and make known media effects.

As the last example, I would like to present a project using an ambiguous query that takes advantage of Google's social sorting. In this

Fig. 5.7: **Contrasting images for ["Apartheid Wall"] and ["Security Fence"] in Google Images query results, July 2005.**

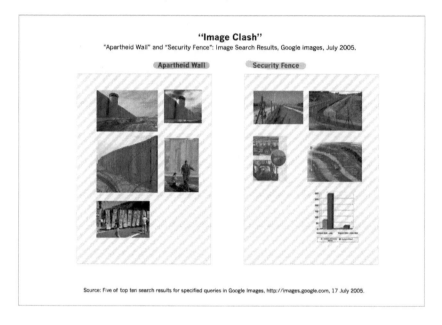

case we undertook a project about rights, conducted by a large group of researchers who spoke some 30 languages amongst them. Using this abundance of diverse language skill, we set about to determine which sorts of rights are held dear to particular cultures relative to others. In the local languages we formulated the query for [rights], and we ran the query in all the various local domain Googles per language spoken, interpreting the results from google.se as Swedish concerns, .fi for Finnish, .ee for Estonian, .lv for Latvian, .co.uk for British, and so forth. With the results pages saved as HTML (for others to check), the researchers were instructed to work with an editorial process where they manually extracted the first 10 unique rights from the search results of each local domain Google.[5] Information designers visualized the results by creating an icon for each right type and a colour scheme whereby unique rights and shared rights across the languages were differentiated. The resultant

5   According to Google's terms of service, one is not allowed to save results, or make derivative works from them. The research thus could be considered to break the terms of service, however much the spirit of those terms is to prevent commercial gain through redistribution rather than to thwart academic research. The results pages are saved as HTML, with a uniform naming convention so that one could return to them, and they, in recognition of the terms of service, were not shared to a data repository.

Fig. 5.8: **Rights types in particular countries, ranked from Google results of the query [rights] in the local languages and local domain name Googles (Google.se, Google.fi, Google.ee and Google.it), July 2009.**

infographic graphically shows rights hierarchies per country as well as those rights that are unique to a country and those shared amongst two or more countries. One example of a unique right is the case of Finland, in which the 'freedom to roam' is high on the list (see Figure 5.8). Far from being a trivial issue, what this freedom means is that one can walk through someone's backyard, whereas in other countries (e.g. the UK) it is not a right, and organizations are lobbying for the right to ramble and walk the ancient pathways. Another example is in Latvia, where pension rights for non-citizens are of particular importance.

Conclusions

Digital methods have been developed as a distinctive strategy for internet-related research where the Web is considered an object of study for more than online or digital culture only. As a part of the computational turn in social research, digital methods were developed as a counterpart to virtual methods, or the importation of the social scientific instrumentarium into the Web, such as online surveys. Digital methods, as an alternative, strive to employ the methods of the medium, imagining the research affordances of engines and platforms, and repurposing their methods and outputs for social (and medium) research.

The contribution here is foundational is the sense of outlining certain premises of digital methods but also the nitty-gritty of doing online analysis. In conclusion, I would like to return to the premises of doing digital methods with Google Web Search in particular as well as to the finer points of query design, which underpins 'search as research' as an approach distinctive from other analytical traditions, such as discourse and content analysis.

First, in the digital method, search as research, Google is repurposed from its increasing use as a consumer information appliance, with personalized results that evermore seek to anticipate consumer information needs (such as with autosuggest as well as the Google Instant service). Rather, Google is relied upon as an epistemological machine, yielding source hierarchies and dominant voice studies (through its ranked results for a keyword query) as well as individual actor commitment (through its quantitative counts for a single or multiple site query). Transforming Google back into a research machine (as its founders asserted in the early papers on its algorithms) these days requires disentangling oneself from the engine through the installation of a clean research browser and logging out. Once in use, the research browser is not expected to remove all Google artefacts from the output (e.g. Google properties, SEO'd results, etc.), but in the event they become less obfuscated and an object of further scrutiny (medium research) together with the social research one is undertaking with repurposed online methods.

Query design is the practice behind search as research. One formulates queries whose results will allow for the study of trends, dominant voice, positioning, commitment, concern and alignment. The technique is sensitive to keywords, which are understood as the connections people are currently making of a word or phrase, whether established or neologistic, leaning on Raymond Williams's second definition of a keyword. Indeed, in the query design put forward above, the keywords used could be said to take sides, and are furthermore conceptualized as forming part of a programme or anti-programme, as developed by Madeleine Akrich and Bruno Latour. I have added a third means by which keywords are put into play. Journalists, and others conspicuously not taking sides, develop and employ terms as efforts at neutrality. ["West Bank barrier"] is one term preferred by BBC journalists (and the English-language Wikipedia) over ["security fence"] (Israeli) or ["apartheid wall"]. Querying a set of sources (e.g. country speeches at the UN Security Council debates) for each of the terms and noting use as well as common use (co-occurrence) would show positioning and alignment, respectively.

Secondly, for digital methods practice, I would like to emphasize that for query design in the conceptual framework of programme/anti-programme/efforts at neutrality, one retains the specific language (instead of grouping terms together), because the exact matches are likely to show alignment and non-alignment. Furthermore, language may also change over time. Therefore, if one conducts an overtime analysis, one can determine whether or not certain actors have, for example, left a certain programme and joined an anti-programme by changing the language and terms they use. Some countries may have become neutral, as was noted when contrasting term use in the 2003 versus the 2005 Security Council debates on the barrier. As another example, one could ask, has there been an alignment shift signified through actors leaving the 'blood minerals' programme and joining the 'conflict minerals' programme?

Thirdly, whilst the discussion has focused mainly on unambiguous queries, search as research also may take advantage of ambiguous ones. As has been noted, if we are interested in researching dominant voice, commitment and showing alignment and non-alignment, an unambiguous query is in order. Through an ambiguous query, such as [rights], one can tease out differences and distinct hierarchies of societal concerns across cultures. Here a cross-cultural approach is taken which for search as research with Google implies a comparison of the results of the same query (albeit in each of the native languages) of local domain Google results.

Finally, query design may be viewed as an alternative to forms of discourse and content analysis that construct labelled category bins and toss keywords (and associated items) into them. That is, in query design specificity of the language matters for it differentiates as opposed to groups. More generally, it allows one to cast an eye onto the entire data set, making as a part of the analysis so-called long tail entities that previously would not have made the threshold. One studies it all without categorizing and without sampling, which (following Akrich and Latour) allows not only for the actors to speak for themselves and for the purposes of their programme, anti-programme or efforts at neutrality, but (following Lev Manovich's Cultural Analytics) provides opportunities for new interpretive strategies. That there arises a new hermeneutics (one that combines close and distant reading) could also be seen as the work ahead for the analytical approach.[6]

6   At the lecture delivered at the digital methods Winter School, January 2015, Lev Manovich proposed work on a 'new hermeneutics' after the study and visualization of 'all data', substituting continuous change for periodization and continuous description for categorization.

Acknowledgments

The author would like to thank Anat Ben-David for her work on query design, and Becky Cachia for editorial assistance. Michael Stevenson, Erik Borra and researchers at the Digital Methods Initiative, University of Amsterdam, provided crucial input.

References

Akrich, Madeleine & Bruno Latour. 1992. "The De-Scription of Technical Objects." *Shaping Technology / Building Society: Studies in Sociotechnical Change*, ed. Wiebe Bijker & John Law, 205-224. Cambridge, MA: MIT Press.

BBC Academy. 2013. "Israel and the Palestinians." *Journalism Subject Guide*. London: BBC, www.bbc.co.uk/academy/journalism/article/art20130702112133696.

Ginsberg, Jeremy, Matthew H. Mohebbi, Rajan S. Patel, Lynnette Brammer, Mark S. Smolinski & Larry Brilliant. 2009. "Detecting influenza epidemics using search engine query data." *Nature* 457: 1012-1014.

Hindman, Matthew. 2008, *The Myth of Digital Democracy*. Princeton: Princeton University Press.

Lazer, David, Ryan Kennedy, Gary King and Alessandro Vespignani. 2014. "The Parable of Google Flu: Traps in Big Data." *Science* 343 (6176): 1203-1205.

Pariser, Eli. 2011. *The Filter Bubble*. New York: Penguin Press.

Negroponte, Nicholas. 1995. *Being Digital*. London: Hodder and Stoughton.

Rogers, Richard & Anat Ben-David. 2010. "Coming to Terms: A conflict analysis of the usage, in official and unofficial sources, of 'security fence,' 'apartheid wall,' and other terms for the structure between Israel and the Palestinian Territories." *Media, Conflict & War* 2 (3): 202-229.

Sunstein, Cass. 2001. *Republic.com*. Princeton: Princeton University Press.

Turow, Joseph. 2006. *Niche Envy*. Cambridge, MA: MIT Press.

US Centers for Disease Control. 2014. "CDC Announces Winner of the 'Predict the Influenza Season Challenge'." Press release, 18 June, www.cdc.gov/flu/news/predict-flu-challenge-winner.htm.

Williams, Raymond. 1975. *Keywords: A Vocabulary of Culture and Society*. London: Fontana.

6. Case Study

Webs and Streams – Mapping Issue Networks Using
Hyperlinks, Hashtags and (Potentially) Embedded Content

Natalia Sánchez-Querubín

Political scientist Hugo Heclo first employs the term 'issue networks' in
The New American System, a book published by the conservative think
tank, The American Enterprise Institute, in 1978. The term describes the
emergence of groups of loosely associated NGOs, funders, academics, policy-
watchers and activists working to influence policy in Washington, D.C.
during the 1970s. These webs of actors, with 'issues as their interest, rather
than interests defining positions on issues' (Heclo: 102), represented a new,
and for Heclo concerning, mode of political organization. The activities of
these 'issue-people', he argued, preceded the involvement of government
officials, politicians and the general public, and thus they carried with them
a threat to democratic legitimacy: 'We tend to overlook the many whose
webs of influence provoke and guide the exercise of power. These webs
are what I will call "issue networks"' (*ibid.*). The opaqueness of the issue
network became, indeed, substantial to Heclo's argument. He admonishes,
for example, about the difficulties of knowing where a 'network leaves off
and its environment begins' (*ibid.*) and who the dominant participants are
in groups in constant state of flux.

Four decades later the term figures without the alarming connotations
for the most part and instead describes issue politics experienced as part of
liberal democracy. The details of this transition are beyond the scope of this
paper and have already been developed at length by Marres (2006). Nevertheless, visiting the origins of the term helps remind one of the labour-intensive
and strategic nature of issue making and the methodological challenges for
rendering these groups legible through issue network mapping. Regarding
the latter, academics and practitioners have found epistemological and
methodological opportunities on the Web. The practice of mapping issue
networks, when taken to online environments, involves repurposing public
displays of connection between Web entities (most commonly by employing
webs of hyperlinks) and reading them through a 'politics of association'
(Rogers 2012). With that being said, the aim of this paper is to contribute
to this tradition by proposing a framework for using not hyperlinks but
streams of hashtags as a way of redoing issue network analysis for social

media. To do this, I characterize issue networks as research objects on the internet, suggest how the hashtag stream can be read through a 'politics of association', and follow by reviewing three leading techniques for working with it. I conclude with a suggestion for further study: repurposing traces left by social media content embedded on external platforms could offer yet another technique for mapping networks, located somewhere within webs and streams.

Three Premises on What Are (and Are Not) Issue Networks

The first premise states that issue networks are assemblages of actors whose ties emerge around issues and are maintained through issue labour. This is to say, that associations do not depend on shared positions, previous alliances or common goals, as in the community or policy-network, but rather they are brought together by public entanglement with an affair, and thus potentially, with each other. For example, when turning to the Web to study the issuefication of engineered foods, the remarks made by Marres and Rogers (2005) did not meet expectations about finding debates or conversations taking place in digital public spheres. Instead, the activity encountered was described as 'issues being done in networks by a variety of techniques' that serve to present 'the issue, what it was about, and what should be done about it' (923). Tracing how actors do particular issues is what ultimately enabled the deployment of ties and the location of issue networks.

The second premise adds to the first: actors in issue networks are heterogeneous and their labour is time-sensitive and occasionally opposi-tional. Hence, they differ from 'the friendly networks of the social and the noncommittal networks of information sharing', and instead 'direct our attention to antagonistic configurations of actors from the governmental, non-governmental and for-profit sectors, and the contestation over issue framings that occurs in them' (Marres 2006: 15). For instance, returning to the study referenced above, organizations from different sectors both opposing and supporting engineered foods participate in defining the risks associated with them, and if studied over time, the realignments of their commitments would potentially be observable. The third premise describes issue networks as hierarchical assemblages, in which some actors are better connected, enjoy more resources and have better platforms. Consequently, when looking at the promises made by networks one might find that they differ from the actual structuring of actor relationships. This makes the ren-dering of the distribution of agency into an activity of political importance.

The three premises not only delineate what issue networks are, they also inform their mapping practice, which is to locate and make them legible. For example, one may ask, who is in the business of 'doing' a particular issue and are they acting as a network? For instance, are they intertwined with clusters of actors and sub-issues, or particular events and slogans? And if so, do they change over time and is agency fairly distributed among them? For answering these questions the techniques put forward by contemporary issue network mappers involve taking advantage of the traceability, agreeability and networkness of online interactions, as well as studying issue labour by repurposing info-actions and data transfers. In fact, the internet can be regarded as a 'particularly fruitful site of research for empirical inquiry into distributed processes of issue formation', for example, by attending to 'the minutes of a meeting of an expert committee, the plans of an activist group, fresh scientific data, that is, many of the snippets of information' (Rogers & Marres 2004: 134). Translated into method, in order to map an issue network, one can begin with an issue, follow up by designing trials to repurpose info-traces in order to locate actors and draw associations between them (thus fleshing out networks), and then proceed to unflatten and annotate them.

Lastly, the capture and analysis of these traces is enabled by digital methods, as with the ones reviewed in the coming section – which 'strive to follow the evolving methods of the medium' (Rogers 2013: 2-3) – in order to perform issue network mapping with hyperlinks and hashtags. Before moving forward, a critical outlook is recommended: when mapping one must move beyond aspirations of finding objects 'cleaned' from the biases of digital devices and instead approach 'noise' assertively. Or better said, 'the investigation of how digital settings influence the public articulation of contested affairs must then become part of our empirical inquiry' (Marres 2015: 19). Thus a platform's definition of what counts as relevant or connected cannot be assumed innocently, but rather must be devised to both include and critique how digital objects participate and shape the public making of issues.

Webs of Hyperlinks

Reading link-making through a 'politics of association' becomes a way of thinking critically through the medium and operationalising the study of issue networks using co-link analysis, a well-documented technique for locating issue networks on the Web. Rogers introduces the 'politics of association' as an alternate way to think about and map the Web, separate from notions of Web spaces as pathways navigated by users who freely authored info-stories. Instead, he conceives the selectivity, directionality and intentionality involved in hyperlinking as epistemologically valuable, indicative of discursive connection and an opportunity for the exploration not of hyper-textuality but of information politics. Consequently, 'making a link to another site, not making a link, or removing a link may be viewed as acts of association, non-association or disassociation, respectively.' In turn, hyperlinking becomes an activity through which one can learn about professional and public political culture, through so-called 'hyperlink diplomacies' (Rogers 2010: 117). For example, governmental pages tend to link amongst each other, while corporate pages rarely do so.

The *modus operandi* is to follow hyperlinks between Web entities (rather than, for example, digging scandalous secret data transfers on the back end) and use them in order to detect entangled actors in the business of doing an issue: '[it is these] sets of inter-linked pages which treated the affair in question, which we dubbed issue-networks' (Marres & Rogers 2005: 1). To facilitate this form of research the now well-known network locator software, Issue Crawler, was developed by Rogers and his colleagues at govcom. org. Users can input URLs relevant for an issue area (compiled with expert lists or search engine queries) for the crawler to fetch shared hyperlinks, expanding the known network and visualizing it as a directed graph. Here directness is fundamental. Two-way links are read differently than those that go unreciprocated: for example, in the first instance entities may be said to acknowledge each other, while the latter can be indicative of aspirational relationships. Lastly, in order to unflatten and annotate the issue network, inbuilt functions in the crawler and qualitative analysis become available and help profile actors according to their linking behaviour. Edge degree locates clusters and isolated concerns, domain names aid grouping entities by sectors, actors are pinpointed on maps using IP-addresses, agenda points are used to label nodes and edges, and reading into the framing of hyperlinks helps characterize relationships. For example, one can inquire if a hyperlink is found 'under a particular heading, or as part of an overview of the issue' (*ibid.*). Formats matter and, if found in PowerPoint or PDF files instead of directly on the site, one's issue might suffer.

The Hashtag Stream as Issue Space

If tracing hyperlinked webs deployed issue spaces demarcated by acts of associations, following hashtags now produces the stream as a new type of issue space. Broadly defined, the stream is a live thematic flow of tweets containing the same hashtag, created when users place the # symbol before a string of characters, and that one assumes enjoys topical affinity. In order to capture a hashtag stream the researcher may use dedicated software and, in negotiations with API and query, fetch samples of tweets along with their metadata over a period of time. For example, in a number of case studies referenced below, the T-CAT tool developed by the Digital Methods Initiative was used to capture tweets posted between 23 November 2012 and 30 May 2013 that included hashtags related to climate change, such as #climatechange and #globalwarming.

Fortunately for the issue researcher, hashtags are as amicable as the hyperlink. They have, for instance, already been theorized with relation to publics, topical formations, public time and liveness (Bruns & Burgess 2011; Highfield 2012; Marres & Weltevrede 2013). What this section then aims to demonstrate is that they too can be read through a 'politics of association' and streams repurposed for locating issue networks. Regarding the latter, a first point to be made is that similar to hyperlinked webs, hashtag streams are not easily described as conversation or debate spaces. Unless one traces threads of replies and mentions between users and reconstructs the ebb and flow of their interactions, what is most accurately found are actors in the business of formatting, framing and circulating issues in tweets. For instance, hashtags formalize policy ideas (Jeffares 2014), enable the circulation of campaigns and contextualize statements by means of association to recognizable areas of concern and vocabularies. To illustrate this, when studying the #Ferguson stream, Bonilla and Rosa (2015) describe the uprisings as increasingly framed as part of larger global affairs through hashtags pairing: '#Egypt #Palestine #Ferguson #Turkey, U.S. made tear gas, sold on the almighty free market represses democracy' (n.p). On a similar note, Moyer (2015) of *The Washington Post*, reflects on the political implications of having the hashtag #baltimoreriots, instead of more neutral terminology such as 'protest', trending as the events unfold. Moyer frames the situation with a reminder: 'naming is a political act' (n.p). In all, employing hashtags can be described as intentional and somewhat strategic association with topical streams and with those that participate in them. Consequently, the co-occurrence of hashtags can be read as discourse and capturing the vocabularies, actors and URLs attached to them can help deploy networks of entangled actors and objects.

A second point is that, as with hyperlinks, hashtag association also allows topical mobility between contested positions. While in the Web, users follow one-way links amongst Web entities and now the social media user journeys between streams using hashtags. This is used tactically, allowing users to infiltrate, for example, ideologically demarcated streams, and thus, it is not uncommon to find 'politically motivated individuals annotating tweets with multiple hashtags whose primary audiences consist of ideologically-opposed users' (Conover et al. 2011: 1). The intention is to expose them to different points of views, bounding together heterogeneous and oppositional actors. Lastly, because hashtags can be traced back to their users, a third point to be made is that they provide researchers with the means to profile and group actors based on their tagging labour, and thus deploy issue networks using (but not limited to) three techniques presented below.

Profiling Tweet Collections, Hashtags Publics and Issue Tweets

The first technique involves profiling a tweet collection by repurposing the metrics and metadata associated with the captured tweets in order to answer research questions. For example, in the mentioned climate change collection, the following inquiry underlined the research: Within the larger issue of climate change, do sub-issues of adaption, mitigation, scepticism and conflict bring together different assemblages of actors and things? And do their interests overlap? An answer was produced by filtering the stream using the keywords [adaption], [mitigation], [scepticism] and [conflict], resulting in four sub-collections along with their metrics, including most active and mentioned users, shared URLs, retweets and second-tier hashtags (see Figure 6.1). To uptake platform relevance, the organizational principle singled out entities that laboured most efficiently and travelled better, and thus are assumed key to the issue network. Intensity and frequency in Twitter, it is argued, can replace features such as centrality when dealing with actors as success is often 'a function of the message frequency instead of the network structure' (Toledo & Galdini 2013: 263). Ultimately, the exercise revealed that in each subarea of the climate change issue, different types of actors excelled. For adaptation NGOs working on food security dominated, while eco-friendly lifestyle blogs and academics ranked highly within mitigation, and hashtags related to scepticism were co-opted to raise climate awareness.

The second technique invites profile users involved with a hashtag (or hashtag publics) based on who they are and what it is that they like to tweet about. For instance, by looking at account profiles one can group users based on field, domain or discipline, as was done by Marres and Gerlitz (2015) in their study of hashtags related to climate change events which

Fig. 6.1: Profiling adaptation and its place in climate change debates with Twitter (I). Hashtag profile poster. Liliana Bounegru, Sabine Niederer (University of Amsterdam); Alex Williams, Noel Wimmer, San Yin Kan, Carlo De Gaetano, Stefania Guerra (DensityDesign). Twitter data ranges from 23 November 2012 to 30 May 2013 and was analysed during the digital methods Summer School, 24 June – 5 July 2013. http://climaps. org/#!/narrative/reading-the-state-of-climate-change-from-digital-media. Visualization is licensed under a Creative Commons Attribution-ShareAlike 4.0 International License.

included dividing account holders as human and non-human (more on this below) and characterized them as individuals, news sources or politics. In their study they found that event hashtags are mainly pushed by the politically inclined. One can also perform content analysis and focus with more detail on the tweets produced by selected users in the stream, and determine if ties emerge amongst them based on, for example, political affiliation if coded as conservative or liberal. The technique can be extended by visiting the accounts, coding tweets that were produced before the stream was captured, and testing the consistency of their tweeting when the hashtags were not trending (for an example see Conover et al. 2011). Lastly, if keeping close to the logics of hyperlinking, the researcher can use an expert list of accounts run by NGOs, activists and politicians as a starting point and test if they follow, retweet or reply to each other, extend the network, and see if their publics overlap. All in all, the outcomes use different levels of detail to describe who is in the business of doing a particular issue on Twitter and what ties they enjoy beyond their thematic entanglement.

The last technique deploys ties between actors based on tweeting styles. A first operationalization involves mapping networks made of co-occurring hashtags (i.e. topical clusters), made of associated areas of concern and emerging actor-object formations. With this in mind, Niederer and Waterloo visualize climate-related hashtags as nodes and trace edges between them when they are used together, with proximity describing the likelihood of their co-occurrence (see Figure 6.2). The criterion here is no longer platform relevance, as in the previous example, but instead co-occurrence. Thus most active actors make way for the most active issues (Marres & Gerlitz 2015). In their graph, the associations of drought and conflict describe the increasing public uptake of this overlap.

A second example, this time around the hashtag #openaccess, takes the process a step further by profiling not only hashtags occurring together but also deploying users that tend to combine hashtags in similar ways. The results of this particular mapping indicate how big publishers have taken over an issue space once dominated by activists by means of combining open access with publicizing hashtags (Gray et al. 2016). A final operationalization is reminiscent of the unflattening of hyperlink networks: ties among actors using hashtags can be described based also on directionality and rhythm. For example, 'users who rarely post tweets but have many followers tend to be information seekers, while users who often post URLs in their tweets are most likely information providers' (Pennacchiotti & Popescu 2011: 282).

Fig. 6.2: **Co-hashtag map in climate Twitter collection. Sabine Niederer, Sophie Waterloo (University of Amsterdam), Gabriele Colombo (Density Design). http://climaps.org/#!/map/profiling-adaptation-and-its-place-in-climate-change-debates-with-twitter-ii. Twitter data ranges from 18 September 2012 to 23 November 2013 and was analysed during the Digital Methods Initiative Fall Data Sprint, 21-25 October 2013. Visualization is licensed under a Creative Commons Attribution-ShareAlike 4.0 International License.**

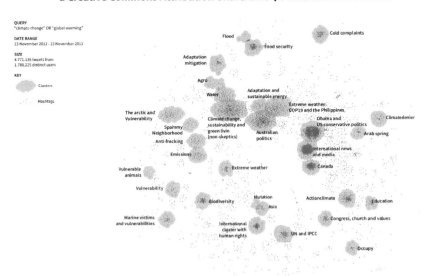

Tracing Embedded Issue Networks

Journalists and other actors involved in issue labour online currently employ embedded tweets as a mode of digital referencing (somewhat similar to in-text hyperlinking) that enables statements to be included in the body of articles and blog posts while retaining a link that can be followed back to their authors and the platforms in which they were originally produced. Embedding, if one takes as example Twitter's media guidelines, is 'one way to add additional context [...] often employed by journalists and publications to enhance their stories' (Twitter 2015). This type of usage is encountered when embedded tweets are used as eye witness testimonies to breaking news, narratives are built around tweets produced by politicians and celebrities about matters of public concern, and when hashtags created by activists are detected by the mainstream media, tweets containing them are fetched in order to populate articles and produced curated lists. An inventory published by *The Times* containing the most powerful tweets with the hashtag #yesallwomen, a grassroots feminist 'meme event' (Thrift 2014) used to raise awareness about everyday experiences of misogyny, and a list of recommended accounts run by journalists, activists, politicians and researchers engaged in tweeting about climate change published by *The Guardian*, serve as examples. This paper's concluding suggestion is that embedding can also be, as was done with hyperlinks and hashtags, repurposed for studying issue labour and locating issue networks, by means of tracing the displacement of social media content across platforms. Since it is beyond the scope of this last section to produce a technique or an accompanying case study, what will instead be provided are avenues for thinking about how this research might be done and interpreted elsewhere. What kinds of issue networks are embedded issue networks? And how can embedding be rendered epistemologically valuable for the issue researcher and be read through a 'politics of associations'?

From the user's perspective, embedding tweets is quite simple, pressing a button included on the tweet makes the code available to be copied and pasted on a website's template, a request is sent, and the tweet can be seen in a non-native space, so to speak. Consequently, embedded issue networks can be thought of as being composed of Web entities such as websites, blogs and news media platforms and the tweets that become embedded in them. These 'data pours' (Liu 2004) occurring, especially through 'social buttons', have been studied at length both theoretically and empirically by Helmond (2015). The phenomenon, which she describes as platformisation, describes the media ecologies that emerge as a result of the modular and programmable qualities of Web platforms, to which embedded content and the code that animates them are part of. What is proposed here is that these 'data pours' can be studied for the benefit of issue research by applying techniques that would enable one to follow the links created by those that embed and those that become embedded, and go on to annotate these connections with respect to their substance, directionality and selectivity. For example, what assemblages of actors emerge as entangled with a given topic if the accounts attached to the embedded tweets are profiled? Could comparing lists of embedded tweets from various news sources lead to finding biases and omissions? Do account holders endorse their inclusion on a list and, if not, how can they resist, for example, by deleting their statement on the platform? And if settings and plug-ins could be tweaked, could politics be read into them?

With respect to the latter, work that looks critically at the practice of embedding both in terms of the framing and settings chosen by journalists might help the issue researcher design mapping trials. For example, in their

study about how The Lede uses embedded citizen journalist videos, Wall
and El Zahed (2014) argue that a transformation takes place when videos
are relocated from social media. In their analysis they describe not only
the qualities of these user-generated videos in terms of their length and
aesthetic qualities, but they also take note of how the video was framed
by the media platform. They discover that, even though one can in fact
determine when a video will start and end playing when embedding it, the
news organization was inclined to show them in their entirety. However, in
the tags and text used to label and introduce the video the term 'clip' was
mostly used, while professional videos were associated instead with the
word 'report'. A similar question might be asked of how tweets are embedded and framed by journalists. A second author who touches on the topic
is Chouliaraki (2010). In her description of the intersections between digital
technologist and citizen journalism, she highlights issues that inherently
arise when journalists embed not single tweets but streams of tweets in
their platforms. These streams are usually composed of tweets sharing a
hashtag and are updated as new tweets are produced. 'The key implication
of this multi-mediated textually' – she argues – 'is that it dislocates ordinary
voice from a coherent news narrative of "dramatic action", condenses it in
"sound-bite" form and places it in a temporally cohesive but narratively
incoherent sequence' (2010: 12). Then when the embedding is automatic, the
critique can then be done at the level of the platform and one can attend
in more detail to how processes of calculation and organization of social
media platforms participate in the creation of topical assemblages around
issues, in and beyond Twitter.

References

Bonilla, Yarimar & Jonathan Rosa. 2015. "#Ferguson: Digital protest, hashtag ethnography, and
    the racial politics of social media in the United States." *American Ethnologist* 42 (1): 4-17.
Bruns, Axel & Jean E. Burgess. 2011. "The use of Twitter hashtags in the formation of ad hoc
    publics." *Proceedings of the 6th European Consortium for Political Research (ECPR) General
    Conference* (August).
Chouliaraki, Lilie. 2010. "Ordinary witnessing in post-television news: towards a new moral
    imagination." *Critical Discourse Studies* 7 (4): 305-319.
Conover, Michael, Jacob Ratkiewicz, Matthew R. Francisco, Bruno Gonçalves, Filippo Menczer
    & Alessandro Flammini. 2011. "Political polarization on Twitter." *ICWSM* 133: 89-96.
Francis, Maya K. 2014. "10 Ferguson Twitter Accounts You Need to Follow." *Philadelphia Magazine*:
    19 August. http://www.phillymag.com/news/2014/08/19/10-ferguson-twitter-accounts-follow/.
Friedman, Ann. 2014. "Hashtag journalism The pros and cons to covering Twitter's trending
    topics." *Columbia Journalism Review.* 29 May.

Gerlitz, Carolin & Anne Helmond. 2011. "Hit, Link, Like and Share. Organizing the social and the fabric of the web." *digital methods Winter Conference Proceedings:* 1-29. Goldsmiths Research Online.

Gray, Jonathan, Liliana Bounegru, Natalia Sanchez-Querubin, Richard Rogers. 2016. *The New Republic of Letters? Studying Open Access as a Sociotechnical Controversy on Digital Media.*

Highfield, Tim. 2012. Talking of many things: using topical networks to study discussions in social media. *Journal of Technology in Human Services, 30* (3-4): 204-218.

Jeffares, Stephen. 2014. *Interpreting hashtag politics: Policy ideas in an era of social media.* Palgrave Macmillan.

Leuven, Sarah Van, Ansgard Heinrich & Annelore Deprez. 2013. "Foreign reporting and sourcing practices in the network sphere: A quantitative content analysis of the Arab Spring in Belgian news media." *New Media & Society*: 1461444813506973.

Liu, Alan. 2004. "Transcendental data: Toward a cultural history and aesthetics of the new encoded discourse." *Critical Inquiry* 31 (1): 49-84.

Marres, Noortje. 2004. "Tracing the trajectories of issues, and their democratic deficits, on the Web: The case of the Development Gateway and its doubles." *Information Technology & People* 17 (2): 124-149.

Marres, Noortje & Richard Rogers. 2005. "Recipe for tracing the fate of issues and their publics on the Web." In *Making Things Public: Atmospheres of Democracy*, ed. Bruno Latour & Peter Weibel, 922-935. Cambridge, MA: The MIT Press.

Marres, Noortje. 2006. "Net-work is format work: issue networks and the sites of civil society." In *Reformatting Politics: Networked Communications and Global Civil Society*, ed. Jodi Dean, John Asherson & Geert Lovink. Routledge.

Marres, Noortje & Esther Weltevrede. 2013. "Scraping the Social? Issues in live social research." *Journal of Cultural Economy* 6 (3): 313-335.

Marres, Noortje. 2015. "Why Map Issues? On Controversy Analysis as a Digital Method." *Science, Technology & Human Values* 40 (5): 1-32.

Marres, Noortje & Carolin Gerlitz. 2015. "Interface Methods: Renegotiating relations between digital social research in STS and sociology." *Sociological Review* 64 (1): 21-46.

Moyer, Justin. 2015. "'Baltimore riots' transform into 'Baltimore uprising'." *The Washington Post*, 29 April.

Pennacchiotti, Marco & Ana-Maria Popescu. 2011. "A Machine Learning Approach to Twitter User Classification." *ICWSM* (11) 1: 281-288.

Puschmann, Cornelius. 2015. "The form and function of quoting in digital media." *Discourse, Context & Media* 7 (March): 28-36.

Rogers, Richard. 2010. "Internet Research: The Question of Method." *Journal of Information Technology and Politics* 7 (2/3): 241-260.

—. 2010. "Mapping Public Web Space with the Issuecrawler." In *Digital Cognitive Technologies: Epistemology and Knowledge Society*, ed. Claire Brossard & Bernard Reber, 115-126. London: Wiley.

—. 2013. *Digital Methods*. Cambridge, MA: MIT Press.

Thrift, Samantha C. 2014. "# YesAllWomen as Feminist Meme Event. *Feminist Media Studies*." 14 (6): 1090-1092.

Toledo, Marco & Rafael Galdini. 2013. "Gatekeeping Twitter: message diffusion in political hashtags." *Media Culture Society* 35 (2) (March): 260-270.

Section 2
Data Practices in Digital Data Analysis

7.   Digital Methods

From Challenges to *Bildung*

Bernhard Rieder & Theo Röhle

In a previous text (Rieder & Röhle 2012) we argued that the existing traditions of the humanities and social sciences, including their particularities, interests and methods, are currently encountering an object – the computer – that is characterized by its own logics, logistics, styles of reasoning (Hacking 1992), habits, (best) practices, modes of valorisation, actor-networks and institutions. The computer may well be a contained technical object, but its accumulated history and therefore its substance is full of heterogeneous elements that constitute a type of *a priori* that cannot be easily ignored. Now that various attempts are being made to build 'digital' versions or extensions of long-established disciplines, this encounter marks a moment of destabilization and deterritorialization, a moment that implies significant contingency and different possible outcomes. Although it remains doubtful that even Kuhn's 'normal science' (1962) was ever truly settled, this is a moment that provokes and requires far-reaching debate and inquiry into the practice, meaning and purpose of our academic disciplines.

The encounter between the humanities and computing plays out in different ways in different arenas, but needs to be addressed in principle as well as in relation to particular settings. The fact that after 50 years of experimentation many of the fundamental questions remain deeply controversial can be seen as an indicator for how close these questions come to core debates about the means and purposes of scholarly work. While terms like 'digital humanities', 'Cultural Analytics', 'digital methods' or 'web science' can play the role of buzzwords, their proliferation can be seen as indicator for a 'computational turn' (Berry 2011a) that runs deeper than a simple rise of quantitative or 'scientific' modes of analysis. Large and often unusual data sets, advanced visualization techniques and fuzzy processing have led some of those who have held numbers, calculations and computers at a safe distance for a long time to warm up to new computational possibilities. Our core question was therefore: If these new methods are more than just another set of tools in our arsenal, how do we deal with the fundamental transformations that challenge established epistemological practices and paradigms?

The starting point for our previous investigation was the concept of 'method'. Defined by the Oxford English Dictionary as 'pursuit of knowledge, mode of investigation', we are also reminded that this pursuit is both systematic and orderly. Additionally, method is directed and purposeful: specific decisions are tied to specific goals. Like a blueprint or recipe, research methods guide behaviour and even if some of our approaches are only moderately explicit, their commonality allows us to share experience and establish reference points that provide orientation – even when there is little agreement on utility and validity.

Although we are wary of Tom Scheinfeldt's assessment of ours as a 'post-theoretical age' (Cohen 2010), his diagnosis of a 'methodological moment' is certainly appropriate. Coming from German academic tradition, we developed our perspective against a backdrop of decades of *Methodenstreit* ('methods dispute'), beginning with Weber's endorsement of sociology as an 'understanding' (*verstehend*) rather than an 'explaining' (*erklärend*) discipline, which later morphed into the famous *Positivismusstreit* ('positivism dispute') between Adorno and Popper. Part of this was the sometimes profoundly paralysing and sterile opposition between quantitative and qualitative research methods in empirical social science. While not truly analogue to Snow's 'two cultures' problem (1959), there are certainly parallels here that point towards different ways of knowing and thinking – styles of reasoning – caught up in larger normative horizons, as seen in the altercations between 'critical' and 'administrative' types of research, epitomized by the clash between Adorno and Lazarsfeld.

Our refusal to cede to simple oppositions is built on an anti-essentialist approach to many of the concepts that appear in these debates. Computation, quantification, algorithm, visualization, graph, data analysis, statistics, software, and so forth, are terms that point to concepts – but also to objects, practices and skill sets – that we consider to have considerable internal heterogeneity and variation. That does not mean that they are not caught up in particular configurations and constellations that are productive in very specific ways in terms of knowledge and power; but it means that the spaces of design and 'appropriation' (Akrich 1998) of computational methods afford considerable leeway and do not translate into or perform singular logics. Even if 'the digital' has become a dominant passage point, it works like a meat grinder: the shredded material does not come out as a single thread, but as many.[1] To connect back to the *Methodenstreit*: compu-

---

[1]   For a detailed investigation into different types of digital processing, see Winkler (2015) (where the meat grinder is actually used metaphorically on the cover).

tational methods can be both deductive and inductive (see e.g. Tukey's (1962) concept of exploratory data analysis), both quantitative and qualitative in outlook, both critical and administrative. But these spaces of movement, of epistemic freedom have to be constructed and defended, sometimes by forging alliances, sometimes by demarcation; certainly through a better understanding of what computers can actually contribute to knowledge production and of the ways they produce this epistemic 'surplus'.

If digital technology is set to change the way scholars work with their material, how they 'see' it and interact with it, a pressing question is how these methods affect the way we generate, present and legitimize knowledge in the humanities and social sciences. In what way are the technical properties of these tools constitutive of the knowledge generated? What are the technical and intellectual skills we need to master? What does it mean to be a scholar in a digital age? To a large extent, the answers to these questions depend on how well we are able to critically assess the methodological transformations we are currently witnessing.

As a growing range of investigations into the status of (big) data (e.g. Gitelman 2013; Elmer, Langlois & Redden 2015; Amoore & Piotukh 2015), as well as ongoing discussions in the digital humanities (Gold 2012; Arthur & Bode 2014; Svensson & Goldberg 2015) suggest, there is something deeply complicated about this methodological moment. We argue that, if some of the criticism being phrased towards the wider field of digital humanities and social sciences is indeed justified, this should not be seen as discouragement, but as a challenge, in the most engaging sense of the term.

In this chapter, we want to shortly summarize what we consider to be five central challenges before interrogating Berry's concept of 'digital *Bildung*' (Berry 2011a) as a means of facing these challenges. Our goal in this discussion is, maybe paradoxically, to move the spotlight from 'the digital' and the associated über-skill, programming, to the plethora of concepts and *knowledges* mobilized in digital tools. To this end, we discuss three examples that allow us to both concretise and complicate the debate.

Five Challenges

In our previous paper (Rieder & Röhle 2012), we presented a non-exhaustive list of broad issue clusters that we believe have to be addressed if we want to productively integrate the new methods without surrendering control over the conceptual infrastructure of our work. Our question was not how to conduct 'good' digital research in the narrow sense: we were not concerned with specific methodological pitfalls or 'errors' in data collection, or with the choices and applications of methodological tools, but with the larger ramifications of digital research inside the field of the humanities and social sciences. In that sense, we wanted to tackle the challenges faced by even the 'best' work in the field.

A first challenge, which we called 'The Lure of Objectivity', raised the question why computational tools have sparked such a tremendous amount of interest when it comes to studying social or cultural matters. One explanation might be the notion that the computer is able to reach beyond human particularities and into the realm of objectivity. We discussed the fascination that the ideal of detached, mechanical reasoning was able to induce historically and asked whether this fascination might keep us from laying bare the many explicit and implicit decisions that went into our tools and instruments. Questions of bias and subjectivity, which the computer was thought to do away with, enter anew on a less tangible plane – through the choices concerning modes of formalization and algorithmic procedures, as well as through the various ways data processing can mask partiality (see Barocas & Selbst 2015). This becomes an especially pressing problem when studying commercial social media platforms. Considering the 'politics of circulation' (Beer 2013) that these platforms are embedded in and the resulting elaborate ecosystems of API regulations (Bucher 2013; Puschmann & Burgess 2014; Rieder et al. 2015), issues of preselection constitute a major methodological dilemma. The challenge is thus to accept the fact that, on an epistemological level, computational methods often create complications rather than resolve them.

Under the heading 'The Power of Visual Evidence', we discussed the role of visual output, such as depictions of network topologies, timelines or enriched cartographies. Since these visualizations possess spectacular aesthetic – and thus rhetorical – qualities, we asked how the argumentative power of images could (or should) be criticized. We stressed the tradition of critical inquiry into the use of images that the humanities have fostered over the years, but remarked that the situation now has indeed changed, since digital humanists themselves produce and rely on images as evidence and heuristic devices. The challenge is thus to maintain a productive self-reflexive inquiry into our own visual practices, i.e. to acknowledge how analysis and cognition are both partial and interwoven with power relations – both currently and historically (Halpern 2015) – without abandoning the promise of gaining insights via visual forms (Drucker 2014: 130-137).

'Black-boxing' referred to our ability to understand the method, to see how it works, which assumptions it is built on, to reproduce and criticize it. Despite the fact that writing software forces us to make procedures explicit by laying them out in computer code, 'readability' is by no means guaranteed. However, an open process of scrutiny is one of the pillars of scholarship and, in the end, of scholarship's claim to social legitimacy. We argued that this problem presents itself on at least three different levels: a) concerning the practical possibility to access the most obvious layer of functional specification, i.e. a tool's source code; b) concerning the ability to understand the code and, even more importantly, the ability to grasp its epistemological ramifications, and c) concerning methods that become opaque despite being fully explicit, such as techniques issued from the field of machine learning, where the connections made between inputs and outputs can no longer be easily retraced by human observers. This point really concerns the question how the epistemological surplus that is provided by computation can be specified, controlled and relayed to others without falling victim to the sometimes deceptive simplicity of graphical user interfaces and shiny visualizations.

We identified 'Institutional Perturbations' as a fourth set of challenges. We saw a chance that, given the growing need for computational expertise, the humanities may increasingly hire researchers from computer-adept disciplines. Also, computational methods may have advantages in settings where even humanistic research is increasingly financed on a project basis – which implies very particular pragmatics based on structured time frames, planned expectations and identifiable 'deliverables'. The challenge, we argued, is to develop a sensibility for such wider repercussions of methodological innovation. In many areas there is an argument to be made for the confident defense of methods that are based on principles other than mechanized 'persistent plodding' (Wang 1963: 93).

The fifth issue we highlighted was 'The Quest for Universalism'. Here, we argued that the establishing of pervasive concepts and principles becomes increasingly common whenever computers come into play. When reality is perceived to adhere to a specifiable system of rules, the computer appears to be the quintessential tool to represent this system and to calculate its dynamics. The epistemological commitments and reductive nature of the underlying models are often 'forgotten' when it comes to the explanations derived from them. Instead, the scope of the explanations is extended indefinitely, reminiscent of the universalist aspirations running through historical discourses on computation. Concepts from network science are a case in point. The challenge is, thus, to arrive at a more adequate demarcation of the explanatory reach of formal models, e.g. by combining different methodological configurations, both digital and non-digital.

In terms of a conclusion, we continue to advocate involvement with the new methods. By involvement, we mean both the actual application of these methods and a critical reflection of such uses. We thus argue for a transfer of the concept of 'critical technical practice', proposed by Agre (1997a), to the scholarly domain: a practice that oscillates between concrete technical work and methodological reflexivity. Current approaches that draw on Agre's concept hold a lot of promise in this regard. As Matt Ratto, Sara Ann Wylie and Krik Jalbert (2014) argue, actual engagement with materiality – what they call 'critical making' – can be a productive complement to the traditional linguistic forms of knowledge production, also in fields such as STS and media studies. Rather than developing methods with a clear goal in mind, the design process can be a means to advance a more inquisitive attitude towards our digital environments – 'bringing unconscious aspects of experience to conscious awareness, thereby making them available for conscious choice', as Sengers et al. state in their outline of 'reflective design' (2005: 50).

In what follows, we want to focus specifically on the challenge of black boxing and, more generally, on the role of digital tools in emergent research constellations. All of these challenges, however, connect more or less directly to the question what we need to know in order to make this critical, reflective, inquisitive and nuanced practice a reality. We thus turn to the matter of knowledge and skill, which has been discussed with particular vigor in the digital humanities, often with a focus on programming as the watershed expertise that separates 'who's in and who's out' (Ramsay 2011). We consider this emphasis to encode a somewhat reductive understanding of computing and suggest a deeper appreciation of both conceptual and technical knowledge and practice in the face of an ever increasing arsenal of digital methods.

From Challenges to *Bildung*

In this section, we approach the question of the challenges for and to (digital) humanities and social sciences through the lens of Berry's notion of 'digital *Bildung*', 'a liberal arts that is "for all humans"' (2011b: 20), although we will focus on digital humanists and social scientists rather than a general public.[2] Our question is what we need to know to become digital

---

2   Berry's description of digital Bildung as 'a rolling process of reflexive thinking and collaborative rethinking' (2011b: 22) seems to share many characteristics with design traditions that invoke Donald Schön's notion of 'reflection-in-action' (1983), as Agre (1997b: 10) also does.

scholars able to 'examine, theorise, criticise and imagine' (*ibid.*: 169) research methodology – the systematic and reasoned pursuit of knowledge – that is caught up in computation. Ultimately, we believe that this debate remains vague and superficial without a concrete set of references. We will therefore discuss three examples, which we hope will contribute to a more in-depth discussion of how the challenges we identified can be related to a broader notion of digital *Bildung*.

A key question in this discussion is whether it is possible (or desirable) to train 'computationally enlightened' humanists who will themselves actually write the computational methods they will apply in their analyses. We hold that this notion is tempting, but ultimately unrealistic and even potentially problematic: while anybody can learn to write a bit of code in a couple of days, the practice of programming or software development requires far-reaching acculturation and many, many hours of practice. If we consider disposable time as a limited resource, the priority given to programming may actually come to the detriment of other technical and conceptual skills that facilitate the critical understanding of computational procedures. The singular focus on code may detract from what is actually coded.

Because for any experienced programmer, code may well be the medium of expression but, just like a writer attempts to say something through language, the meaning expressed through programming is functionality; and while the two cannot be fully separated, programmers and computer scientists generally reason on a conceptual level that is certainly circum-scribed by the requirements of mechanical computation – what one of us has called the 'shadow of computation' (Rieder 2012) – but express-ible in various forms, from systematized vocabulary and conversation to flowcharts and, more often than not, mathematical notation. While implementation is certainly not irrelevant, the methodological core, the very definition of what computation adds resides in what the program does. This functional level can be of daunting complexity, even if many sophisticated techniques can be boiled down to a small number of cen-tral ideas. Subsuming these ideas under the broad notion of 'the digital' locks the analysis to a surface view that risks hiding the methodological substance or rationale of the work performed by methods rendered in software. Facing the challenges outlined above depends, at least in part, on whether we are able to get to the conceptual core of the computa-tional techniques we are using. Only then can we assess the potentials, limitations and styles of reasoning held by the tools we integrate into our research configurations.

To flesh out this argument in more depth, we turn to three examples that allow for a nuanced approach and highlight the difficulty of setting overarching principles. In all of these examples, we ask what 'understanding' a computational technique would mean.

Statistics

Since the empirical social sciences have been using digital tools as integral part of their work for decades, applied statistics is a good place to start. One of the most widely used software packages in the Social Sciences is SPSS (formerly Statistical Package for the Social Sciences) and the significant reliance by researchers on this program begs the questions to what extent these scholars are capable of 'understanding' – or even seek to understand – the considerable methodological and epistemological choices and commitments made by the various analytical techniques provided. If we consider, for example, regression analysis, a technique that is extremely productive (literally, no endorsement implied) in academic research as well as in business and government, as a means to produce an epistemic surplus, how would we go about understanding more precisely what the technique and its intellectual contribution consists of?

The source code of SPSS is not available, but the way the software calculates its analytical measures is well documented in mathematical notation and relies on established and much discussed constructs such as the Pearson coefficient for correlation (r) or established regression techniques. Looking at an open-source alternative such as PSPP (no acronymic expansion), what would we actually gain from reading the source code instead of simply consulting the documentation and checking the research papers it refers to?

While a critique of the standardization and streamlining of research through widely available software packages is important and raises many concerns,[3] it does not tell us how epistemological agency can be wrestled back from tools that make exceedingly complex methodological procedures available through simple graphical interfaces. A critique of digital tools is incomplete without a critique of their *users* and the wider settings they are embedded in. As banal as it may sound, what is required to understand and use SPSS reflectively – or any statistics package for that matter – is a robust understanding of statistics and probability theory, not a crash

---

3   See Uprichard et al. 2008 for an in-depth discussion of the significance of SPSS for sociology.

course in Java. What is black boxed in such a tool is not merely a set of calculative procedures, which are, in the end, sufficiently well documented, but statistics as a field that has not only its own epistemological substance, but many internal debates, contradictions and divergences. The 'thirteen ways to look at the correlation coefficient' identified by Rodgers and Nicewander (1988) and the debates around null hypothesis testing, which Gigerenzer, Krauss and Vitouch (2004) refer to as the 'null ritual', are just two of many examples for the quite fundamental disagreements in the practice of applied statistics. While software can be designed in a way that highlights these divergences, it is too much to ask of a program to carry the weight of providing an education in the field it is mechanizing. This raises and complicates the question of the educational embedding of digital tools. If students and researchers are trained in using these tools without considerable attention being paid to the conceptual spaces they mobilize, the outcomes can be highly problematic. Digital *Bildung* thus requires attentiveness not just to the software form, but to the actual concepts and methods expressed and made operational through computational procedures.

Network Analysis

A very similar argument can be made for the popular field of network visualization. It is again important to notice that the point and line form comes with its own epistemic commitments and implications, and graph analysis and visualization tools like Gephi (Bastian et al. 2009) further structure the research process. But where do we go from there? If we consider that graph theory still provides powerful and interesting means to analyse a data set, what would critical analytical practice look like? For example, how can we consider the layout algorithms that transform n-dimensional adjacency matrices[4] into two-dimensional network diagrams? These artefacts interpose themselves as mediators because each algorithm reveals the graph differently, highlighting specific aspects of its structure, thus producing a specific *interpretation*.

There are different families of algorithms – most approaches are based on force simulations, but other strategies such as simulated annealing exist as well – but even the same algorithm, fed with different parameters, can

4   An adjacency matrix is a way of representing a graph as a special kind of table (a square matrix) that specifies which nodes are connected to each other.

produce quite different outcomes. If we apply the ForceAtlas2 algorithm (Jacomy et al. 2014) to a graph file, should we go to Gephi's source repository on Github and search for the ForceAtlas2.java file and try to make sense of it? What would we find there? A few hundred lines of Java code that implement a highly iterative simulation of attracting and repulsing forces that makes ample use of the notion of 'swinging' (in a very literal sense) to find an 'optimal' position for nodes on the canvas without getting stuck in local optima.[5] It is very naive to believe that anybody who has not had considerable training in both programming and simulation modelling can say anything meaningful about how ForceAtlas2 is implementing the force-direction concept differently from its historical and conceptual ancestor, the work of Fruchterman and Reingold; and much less how these differences affect spatialisation in concrete circumstances. How will properties of nodes and topological structure affect positions on the map? Which aspects of the latent structures in the data does the diagram reveal?

Even with the required training, testing and running the algorithm on different data sets with different parameters is a necessity to begin to understand how outcomes relate to instances of computation because no human brain can anticipate the result space of even simple functions iterated thousands of times. The problem, again, comes from the fact that tools such as Gephi have made network analysis accessible to broad audiences that happily produce network diagrams without having acquired robust understanding of the concepts and techniques the software mobilizes. This more often than not leads to a lack of awareness of the layers of mediation network analysis implies and thus to limited or essentialist readings of the produced outputs that miss its artificial, *analytical* character. A network visualization is closer to a correlation coefficient than to a geographical map and needs to be treated accordingly.

We would again argue that the critical mastery of the methodological substance introduced by the software would be best served by studying material on graph theory, graph spatialisation and, in particular, literature on concrete analytical applications. Looking into the history and state of the art of sociometrics and network science would be helpful to acquire 'graph literacy'. To be even more concrete, an in-depth study of Linton Freeman's The *Development of Social Network Analysis* (2004) would be a good start. Inevitably, spending considerable amounts of time trying

---

5   Consider an analogue problem: a simple algorithm for hill climbing consisting of 'always go up' will end up on top of a hill (a local optimum), but not necessarily on the highest one (the global optimum). Swinging counteracts a similar problem of getting 'stuck' in a local optimum.

out different algorithms on different data sets to build understanding
of the specific ways they interpret a graph is crucial. Reflective practice
requires much more than a critical attitude, it requires *deeper* involvement
with the associated knowledge spaces to make sense of possibilities and
limitations.

Thousands of Images

These two examples are certainly not fully representative of the tools used
in the field, but the argument can be extended beyond the more complex
software packages just discussed. The work that Lev Manovich (2012) has
done under the label 'Cultural Analytics' can serve as an example: to order
black and white manga images on a scatter plot, Manovich uses 'entropy
calculated over greyscale values of all pixels in a page' for the y-axis, and
after pointing to the history of the entropy concept explains what this
measure expresses in terms of the images in question: 'If an image consists
of a few monochrome areas, its entropy will be low. In contrast, if an image
has lots of texture and details and its colours [...] vary significantly from
place to place, its entropy will be high.' (Manovich 2012: 266).

   Independently of what we think about what Manovich is doing with
these images in intellectual terms (Art history? Image science?), it is his
considerable training and experience in working with digital images that
allows him to confidently relate a mathematical measure to actual visual
properties of the images in question. We are not qualified to say whether the
results Manovich gets from this operation are truly useful for his analytical goals, but this is not the question here. What matters is that the skill
applied in this example is the capacity to reason on images in formal or
mathematical terms, to connect these terms to visual properties of the
image as it is perceived by humans, and to derive an epistemic surplus from
the whole operation. What would we gain from looking at the source code
of Manovich's script? Perhaps we would find an error. Perhaps we could
come up with a more efficient implementation. But although Manovich
does not provide the used measure in mathematical notation (why not?),
his reference to Claude Shannon is a good reason to believe that the entropy
measure in question is something like -sum(p * log2(p)), where p contains
the image's histogram in 256 bins if the image is encoded in 8-bit.

   Now, just like Anscombe's famous four data sets (1973) that are quite different in structure but have the same statistical properties, a very synthetic
measure like entropy, which expresses something about a complex object

Fig. 7.1: **The four scatter plots from Anscombe (1973). They have identical values for number of observations, mean of the x's, mean of the y's, regression coefficient of y on x, equation of regression line, sum of squares of x, regression sum of squares, residual sum of squares of y, estimated standard error of bi, and multiple r2. Anscombe uses them in an argument for the usefulness of visualization in statistics.**

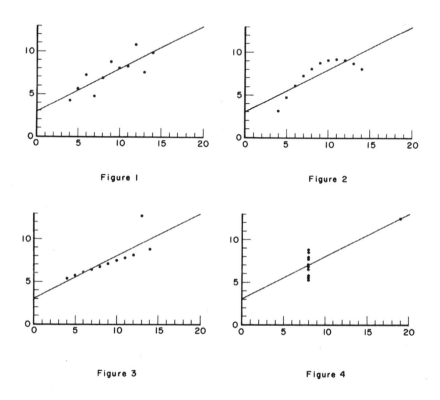

such as an image in a single number, can label a very large number of very different images with the same value. Thus, Manovich not only had to commit to the entropy measure as such, but also to the entropy measure as it reacts to the data set in question. From what we understand, a greyscale gradient would have a very high entropy value since the histogram does not contain any information on how the colours are spatially distributed; it's a simple occurrence count for every colour. Would a certain colouring style in a manga thus 'break' the measure? For certain data sets – Barnett Newman or Piet Mondrian maybe? – the measure could be completely useless because the salient element would be the arrangement of surfaces rather than the probability distribution of colours.

There is no doubt that programming skills are useful in this context. But entropy is not a 'programming' concept; it is, like most statistical measures, a means to summarize data, a means to speak about data from a very particular vantage point. It is reductive, certainly, but reductive in a *specific way* and therein lies its epistemic character. As a concept, entropy ties into the complex histories of information theory and statistics[6], and reflective use will have to attend to these connections.

This is the work digital humanists and social scientists have to do and they cannot easily delegate it to computer science collaborators or hired programmers. Notice that this is a complex technical discussion that does not contain a single question about programming. Any somewhat capable programmer could produce a script from the specification 'calculate entropy from greyscale histogram' and in environments like MATLAB there are even predefined functions that do all the work for us. The actual methodological 'content' and commitment is simply not a question of 'software', first and foremost. Certainly, we can only do this because there is software in the first place, and interfaces hide and cement our commitments, but the knowledge required to judge the method in question is only in very small part related to the question of code; rather, it spans a space from information theory to art history and visual studies in a way that certainly involves abstraction, but of a different kind than programming implies.

Conclusions

While our three examples might be considered very specific, we think that similar arguments could be made for a wide variety of cases where software performs a *method*. While methodological concepts and techniques enter in negotiation with implementation, the 'content' of software is a procedure *expressed* in code, not simply code. We can certainly find cases where the mathematical dimension of a tool is completely trivial, but we would argue that in most of the tools that are used by digital scholars, significant methodological work is performed by techniques that have their origins in the conceptual substance of disciplines such as statistics, information science, sociometrics, computer science and – quite often – mathematics.

---

6   For an account of these histories that is accessible to and interesting for humanists, see for example Christian Kassung's (2001) contextualization of Robert Musil's 'Man Without Qualities' within modern physics, esp. pp. 132-260.

And this is the crux, here. Although we fully agree with Berry (2012) that digital *Bildung* – in particular for the digital humanist, but also beyond – would benefit from 'iteracy [...] defined broadly as communicative competence in reading, writing and executing computer code', the focus on programming as 'writing code' rather than 'implementing a technique' runs the risk of missing this more conceptual level that is, in our view, both epistemologically more relevant to scholarship relying on digital tools and, in many cases, more accessible in terms of skills to acquire.

While our evidence is only anecdotal, we notice in much of the humanities a desire to explain technology as quickly as possible through something else. Instrumental rationality, cybernetic utopias, neoliberalism, phantasies of perfect control, positivism, revenue maximization, and so forth. These assessments may ultimately be enlightening and meaningful at a very broad level of analysis. But if we want to meet the challenges of computational methods, we have to encounter technology as technology for at least a little while. Paradoxically, the one-sided focus on the 'digital' aspect of computational methods and, in conjunction, on programming as the *Via Regia* to digital enlightenment implies a reductionism that, again, serves to keep technology 'small'. There is no doubt that programming skills and 'iteracy' are extremely valuable and a way to ease into some of the harsher complexities involved in computational methods. But we hope to have demonstrated through our examples that the tools we have come to use mobilize wide arrays of knowledge that we should only grudgingly compress into the supposedly coherent category of 'the digital'. The problem of black boxing does not begin with the opacity of computer code, but with the desire to banish technology from the 'world of signification' (Simondon 1958: 10).[7] Behind the laudable efforts to increase levels of technical capacity lies the dangerous phantasm that technology's epistemologies are ultimately 'thin' and that once programming skill has been acquired, mastery and control return.

We believe, on the contrary, that any nontrivial software tool implies thick layers of mediation that connect to computation as such, certainly, but in most cases also imply concepts, methods and styles of reasoning adapted from various other domains. We can critique the standardization of research through software all we want, but, to put it bluntly, there is no critical practice of statistics without considerable knowledge of statistics,

---

7   'Culture is out of balance because it recognizes certain objects, such as the aesthetic object, and grants them the right of residence in the world of meaning, while it relegates other objects, and in particular technical objects, to the world without structure of those things that do not have a meaning, only a use.' (Simondon 1958: 10, authors' translation).

independently of the question which tools are used. The problem of *Bildung* cannot be reduced to the acquisition of a set of skills. What Simondon (1958) calls 'culture technique' (technical acculturation) should not be limited to technical training, but needs to start with the recognition that technology constitutes a fundamental way of relating to the world and human diversity goes hand in hand with technological pluralism (cf. p. 218).

We have to be able to think *with* and *in* technology as a medium of expressing a will and a means to know. This is not only necessary to decide when to apply what techniques and to interpret the results they produce; it is also necessary to decide where the computational is superfluous, deceptive or simply sucking up to some funding agency's idea of 'innovative' research. Digital methods are here to stay and to go beyond the simplistic reflexes of enthusiasm and rejection we need to engage in critical practice that is aware of the shocking amounts of knowledge we have stuffed into our tools.

References

Agre, Philip. 1997a. "Toward a Critical Technical Practice: Lessons Learned in Trying to Reform AI." *Social Science, Technical Systems, and Cooperative Work: Beyond the Great Divide*, ed. G.C. Bowker et al., 131-157. Mahwah, NJ: Lawrence Erlbaum Associates.

—. 1997b. *Computation and Human Experience*. Cambridge; New York: Cambridge University Press.

Akrich, Madeleine. 1998. "Les utilisateurs, acteurs de l'innovation." *Education Permanente* 134: 79-90.

Amoore, Louise & Volha Piotukh. 2015. *Algorithmic Life. Calculative Devices in the Age of Big Data*. London: Routledge.

Anscombe, Francis John. 1973. "Graphs in Statistical Analysis." *The American Statistician* 27 (1): 17-23.

Arthur, Paul L. and Katherine Bode, eds. 2014. *Advancing Digital Humanities. Research, Methods, Theories*. Houndsmills, New York: Palgrave Macmillan.

Barocas, Solon & Andrew D. Selbst. 2016. "Big Data's Disparate Impact." *California Law Review* 104. http://papers.ssrn.com/sol3/papers.cfm?abstract_id=2477899.

Bastian, Mathieu, Sebastien Heymann & Mathieu Jacomy. 2009. "Gephi: an open source software for exploring and manipulating networks." *ICWSM* 8: 361-362.

Beer, David. 2013. *Popular Culture and New Media. The Politics of Circulation*. New York: Palgrave Macmillan.

Berry, David M. 2011a. "The computational turn: Thinking about the digital humanities." *Culture Machine* 12 (2).

—. 2011b. *Philosophy of Software. Code and Mediation in the Digital Age*. New York: Palgrave Macmillan.

—. 2012. "Iteracy: Reading, Writing and Running Code." http://stunlaw.blogspot.nl/2011/09/iteracy-reading-writing-and-running.html.

Cohen, Jacob. 1988. *Statistical Power Analysis for the Behavioural Sciences*. 2nd edition. Hillsdale: Lawrence Erlbaum Associates.

Cohen, Patricia. 2010. "Digital keys for unlocking the humanities' riches." *New York Times*, November 17, http://www.nytimes.com/2010/11/17/arts/17digital.html.

Drucker, Johanna. 2014. *Graphesis. Visual Forms of Knowledge Production*. Cambridge, MA: Harvard University Press.

Freeman, Linton. 2004. *The Development of Social Network Analysis: A Study in the Sociology of Science*. Vancouver: Empirical Press.

Gigerenzer, Gerd, Stefan Krauss & Oliver Vitouch. 2004. "The Null Ritual. What You Always Wanted to Know About Significance Testing but Were Afraid to Ask." In *The Sage Handbook of Quantitative Methodology for the Social Sciences*, ed. David Kaplan, 391–408. Thousand Oaks, CA: Sage.

Hacking, Ian. 1992. "Statistical language, statistical truth and statistical reason: The self-authentication of a style of scientific reasoning." In *The social dimensions of science*, ed. E. McMullin, 130-157. Notre Dame: University of Notre Dame Press.

Halpern, Orit. 2014. *Beautiful Data. A History of Vision and Reason since 1945*. Durham; London: Duke University Press.

Jacomy, Mathieu, Tommaso Venturini, Sebastien Heymann & Mathieu Bastian. 2014. "ForceAtlas2, a continuous graph layout algorithm for handy network visualization designed for the Gephi software." *PLoS one* 9 (6): e98679.

Kassung, Christian. 2001. *EntropieGeschichten. Robert Musils "Der Mann ohne Eigenschaften" im Diskurs der modernen Physik*. Munich/Paderborn: Fink.

Kuhn, Thomas S. 1962. *The Structure of Scientific Revolutions*. Chicago: University of Chicago Press.

Manovich, Lev. 2012. "How to Compare One Million Images." In *Understanding Digital Humanities*, ed. David M. Berry, 248-278. New York: Palgrave Macmillan.

Ramsay, Stephen. 2011. "Who's In and Who's Out." Stephen Ramsay (blog), 8 January. http://stephenramsay.us/text/2011/01/08/whos-in-and-whos-out/.

Ratto, Matt, Sara Ann Wylie & Kirk Jalbert. 2014. "Introduction to the Special Forum on Critical Making as Research Program." *The Information Society* 30 (2): 85-95.

Rieder, Bernhard. 2012. "What is in PageRank? A Historical and Conceptual Investigation of a Recursive Status Index." *Computational Culture* 2, http://computationalculture.net/article/what_is_in_pagerank.

Rieder, Bernhard & Theo Röhle. 2012. "Digital Methods: Five Challenges." In *Understanding Digital Humanities,* ed. David M. Berry, 67-85. New York: Palgrave Macmillan.

Rieder, Bernhard, Rasha Abdulla, Thomas Poell, Robbert Woltering & Liesbeth Zack. 2015. "Data critique and analytical opportunities for very large Facebook Pages: Lessons learned from exploring 'We are all Khaled Said'." *Big Data & Society* 2 (2): 2053951715614980.

Rodgers, Joseph Lee & W. Alan Nicewander. 1988. "Thirteen Ways to Look at the Correlation Coefficient." *The American Statistician* 42 (1): 59–66.

Schön, Donald A. 1983. *The Reflective Practitioner. How Professionals Think in Action*. New York: Basic Books.

Simondon, Gilbert. 1958. *Du mode d'existence des objets techniques*. Paris: Aubier.

Snow, C.P. 1959. *The Two Cultures*. Cambridge, MA: Cambridge University Press.

Svensson, Patrik & David T. Goldberg, eds. 2015. *Between Humanities and the Digital*. Cambridge, Mass.: MIT Press.

Tukey, John W. 1962. "The Future of Data Analysis." *The Annals of Mathematical Statistics* 33: 11–67.

Uprichard, Emma, Roger Burrows & David Byrne. 2008. "SPSS as an 'inscription device': from causality to description?" *The Sociological Review* 56 (4): 606-622.

Wang, Hao. 1963. "Toward Mechanical Mathematics." In *The modelling of Mind*, ed. K.M. Sayre & F.J. Crosson. South Bend, IN: Notre Dame University Press.

Winkler, Hartmut. 2015. *Prozessieren. Die dritte, vernachlässigte Medienfunktion*. Munich/Paderborn: Fink.

8.   Data, Culture and the Ambivalence of Algorithms

William Uricchio

Humans have long defined, assessed, analysed and calculated data as factors in how they navigate reality. Indeed, the rules for what constitute data, together with the logics of their assembly, make up a core component of culture. Whether they be omens or numbers, whether they are qualitative or quantitative, whether they involve heuristics, hermeneutics or the rules of mathematics, the dyad of data and their organizing schemes give cultural eras their specificity. Considering developments ranging from Mayan astronomical calendars to Copernicus's heliocentric observations, from seventeenth-century navigational charts to twentieth-century actuarial tables, one might say that this dyad underpins cultural possibility itself.[1]

Data have never been more abundant than they are today. Their unprecedented quantity owes as much to the digital encoding of most traceable phenomena as to the production of data by actors beyond our species. Whereas in the past, human observation translated events in the world into data, today, networked non-human actors are capable of directly generating machine-readable data. But as in the past, all that data would be meaningless without an organizing scheme. Behind the quintillions of bytes, behind our computers' ever-growing processing power, is an organizing scheme in the form of the algorithm. Like data, algorithms can be human- or machine-generated. And although an ancient idea, the algorithm has – or so I will argue – reached a tipping point in terms of its cultural operations: it is now being deployed in ways that redefine long-held subject-object relationships and, in so doing, it poses some rather fundamental epistemological questions.

This change in the balance of things has produced its share of anxieties, as familiar ways of doing things seem superseded by 'the algorithm'. The recent explosion of headlines where the term 'algorithm' figures prominently and often apocalyptically suggests that we are re-enacting a familiar ritual in which 'new' technologies appear in the regalia of disruption. But the emerging algorithmic regime is more than 'just another' temporarily unruly

---

1   Portions of this essay first appeared as William Uricchio, 'Recommended for You: Prediction, Creation and the Cultural Work of Algorithms,' *The Berlin Journal* 28 (Spring 2015): 6–9.

new technology. My thesis is that the algorithm, an approach to problem solving that goes back at least to Euclid's *Elements* (ca. 300 BC) and that enjoyed significant development in the hands of Leibniz and Pascal, has achieved new force as a cultural technology thanks to a confluence of factors that include the emergence of big data, intensive processing power and high-speed networks. It alters the subject-object relationship hard-wired in the project of the modern and visible in technologies like the printing press and three-point perspective, both of which amplify individual agency. Yet, like these technologies, the algorithm, combined with data, can be read as defining an emerging epistemic era. If we are indeed like those in the early fifteenth century who were poised on the edge of a new order of things, will we, like some of them, be inclined to embrace their potential for a new vision of ourselves in the world, a new social order? Or will we miss the radical potential of a new technology, retrofitting it to serve the still-dominant interests of the old?

Technologies do not, in themselves, change anything, but rather are socially constructed and deployed. So as we watch the possibilities of a new technology take shape in the hands of those with the greatest economic power, we have good reason to be anxious. The dyad of big data and algorithms can enable new cultural and social forms, or they can be made to reinforce the most egregious aspects of our present social order. That is a political choice, of course. But what is truly new about this configuration is that we have a choice at all, of a magnitude not seen since the fifteenth century. The pages ahead will chart these new enablements: first, by considering the definitional dynamics of algorithms; second, by looking at their newly acquired place particularly as a condition of cultural production; and finally, by raising some questions regarding the larger epistemic implications of this new order and how we as a society will grasp it.

Definitional Dynamics

The term 'algorithm' seems to conjure up responses disproportionate to the simplicity of its meaning. Formally speaking, an algorithm is simply a recipe, a process or set of rules usually expressed in algebraic notation. The actual values plugged into the algorithm are less the point than the step-by-step formulations that govern their processing. They scale easily, whether working with the relatively meager data of the pre-computer era or the more than 2.5 quintillion bytes of data generated daily at the time of this writing. Yet despite their relative simplicity, algorithms today pose some significant definitional problems, mostly because of a series of misapprehensions. Tarleton Gillespie (2014) has noted three broad uses of the term that obscure its meaning. Algorithms are invoked as synecdoche when the term stands in for a sociotechnical assemblage that includes the algorithm, model, data set, application and so on. They reveal a commitment to procedure, formalizing social facts into measurable data and clarifying problems into models for solution. And they function as talismans when the term implies an 'objectifying' scientific claim. Indeed, one might step back and note that these three uses say much more about social anxieties and aspirations than they do about algorithms. How, for example, can one make a claim to 'objectivity' with an authored protocol whose operations depend on the highly variable character and structure of a particular data set? And yet a glance at any newspaper will confirm the accuracy of Gillespie's insights about the term's ambiguity. The definition of the algorithm is also complicated by more insistent epistemological problems. Nick Seaver (2013) finds that most discussions of algorithms get caught up with issues of access and expertise. Access is an issue because many commercial algorithms, Google's for instance, are closely guarded secrets. 'If only we had access...' the mantra goes. But even if we had access, we would immediately face the expertise problem, for most individual algorithms inhabit vast interdependent algorithmic systems (not to mention models, goals, data profiles, testing protocols, etc.), and disaggregating and making sense of them typically require large teams of experts. But even more troublesome is the fact that any given process usually has many possible algorithmic combinations (circa 10 million in the case of a Bing search), some of which might be uniquely deployed or used for purposes of personalization or even testing. Individual algorithms and algorithmic clusters are recycled and appear in different settings, with some dating from before World War II still in circulation today. This means that we can never be sure precisely which set of algorithmic elements we are examining, and even if we were, the work of personalization would limit our ability to compare findings. A further twist appears in the form of disciplinary specificity. The valences of the term 'algorithm' differ in mathematics, computer science, governance, predictive analytics, law and in the culture at large, complicating cross-disciplinary discussion.

Finally, unlike earlier technologies, developments in machine learning have enabled algorithms to self-optimize and generate their own improvements. They can now self-author and self-create. This greatly complicates notions of authorship, agency and even algorithms' status as tools, which imply an end user.

Together, the various factors described by Gillespie and Seaver, which are embedded in our tradition of study and even our inherited notions of agency and authorship, all combine to render the simple definition of an algorithm as a 'rule set' or 'recipe' into something quite... loaded. And they fundamentally challenge our inherited notions of culture and cultural production. The humanities research agenda not only has to deal with the implications of radically reconfigured notions of the author, agency and textual stability, but also has to embrace radically expanded corpora. Data, the structure of the data set, models, software systems and interfaces all play determining roles in cultural production and, as such, are not only appropriate but increasingly important sites for humanistic inquiry. Their analysis requires not only new literacies but evaluative paradigms that in many cases have yet to be created. Lev Manovich (2001) made an early appeal to meet these needs in his *The Language of New Media*, and this essay extends that call to include the algorithms underlying these operational systems.

Culture

Given the role that the dyad of algorithms and data currently plays in shaping our access to information (Google) and the social world (Facebook), and their centrality to finance (algorithmic trading) and governance (from predictive policing to NSA-style parsing of vast troves of data), looking at their cultural work might seem a low priority. Each of these sectors reveals some affordances of the pairing, and their most visible – and disturbing – applications reflect the interests of the prevailing power structure. However, the abusive deployment of algorithmically enabled data says more about the contradictions of our social order than the algorithm or data per se. Blaming 'the algorithm' or 'big data' puts us in the position of a bull fixated on the matador's cape: we fail to see the real source of malice.

We can sidestep the easy conflation of algorithms and data in the explicit service of power by turning to the cultural sector in order to throw into relief the dyad's capacities to re-order the subject-object relationships at the heart of the new representational order. This re-ordering has far more profound implications than the retrofitting of algorithms and data in the service of twentieth-century notions of power (though doing the latter may wind up killing us if we aren't alert). With art it is generally easier to see through the representation process and find traces of the underlying production system. The arts help us to see more clearly.

Just as algorithms have a deep history but have also recently achieved new power thanks to their changing circumstances (big data and dramatic improvements in processing and transmission), their use in the arts also has a long history as well as a fast-evolving present. The historically oldest applications deploy algorithms to organize data for purposes of textual production, basically using the algorithm like a traditional artistic tool, though with an important twist. More recent applications go further, using algorithmic configurations of data for purposes of textual selection and customization, combing through large data sets to establish correlations regarding taste and likely matches between users and texts. Brief disambiguations of these different applications follow:

Algorithms as Tools in Traditional Artistic Production

The canon form in music, essentially an algorithm, goes back at least to the Middle Ages; and algorithms have appeared in works ranging from the *Musikalisches Würfelspiel* attributed to Mozart to Lejaren Hiller's compositions using the ILLIAC computer in the 1950s. Brian Eno (1975) put his finger on the aesthetic twist of this application when he said:

> Since I have always preferred making plans to executing them, I have gravitated towards situations and systems that, once set into operation, could create music with little or no intervention on my part. That is to say, I tend towards the roles of planner and programmer, and then become an audience to the results. (n.p.)

This disaggregation of artistic process from execution is nothing new (Rodin famously relied on it for his major sculptural works) but it has served as a persistent characteristic in the long history of algorithmic art. Tradition enters the picture when artists make a claim for 'their' authorship, rendering the algorithm a tool. The 1968 exhibition Cybernetic Serendipity, with its display of algorithmically generated music, painting, choreography, film and graphics, demonstrated the powers of this new toolkit across the arts to audiences in London and Washington. By the mid-1990s, artists such as Roman Verostko and Jean-Pierre Hébert proclaimed the tool as the basis of a movement: the Algorists.[2] Today, the integration of algorithms into everyday textual production is so fundamental as to be quotidian (algorithms enable colour

2   See www.algorists.org/.

correction, editing and the very existence of image in film and video (Hoelzl & Marie 2015); recording, mixing and the creation of sound elements in music; the word processing program that I am using to craft this text, and so forth).

But paired with big data, the algorithm has grown far more powerful. According to *The New York Times*, the company Automated Insights alone created more than one billion algorithmically generated stories in 2014, mostly routine sports and financial market reporting (Podolny 2015). These two domains are made up of well-structured data sets, with timelines and data points that enable easy characterization and serve as low-hanging fruit for an emergent industry. But *The Times* story gave a sense of the ambitions for storytelling algorithms produced by companies such as Narrative Science, and they go far beyond 'translating' simple data trails to generating creative prose and poetry.

Textual Recommendation Systems

A very different and relatively recent cultural use of algorithms paired with large data sets takes the form of selecting and pushing *which* texts we have access to, that is, of recommendation systems. Consider Echo-Nest's prediction algorithms that comb through data derived from millions of users' behaviours as well as data drawn from musical texts, seeking correlations by extrapolating from past behaviours into future desires or by searching for other users' patterns that might offer a basis for suggestions. To the extent that users play along and offer consistent feedback, Pandora, Spotify and other streaming music services that use EchoNest's algorithms demonstrate an uncanny ability to identify and provide access to the desired, the familiar and the reassuring. As users of Amazon's book recommendation services or Netflix's film and video suggestions know, the same principles apply on these platforms as well. Indeed, one of the often referenced developments in this space was the 2009 Netflix Prize, a $1,000,000 bounty for creating the greatest improvements to Netflix's own collaborative filtering algorithm for predicting user ratings of films (the winner, Bellkor, achieved a 10.09% improvement on predictions).[3] In these

3   The Netflix competition began in 2006 and ended with the 2009 award to the Bellkor team. The terms of the prize required that winners publish a description of the winning algorithm. Throughout the multi-year process, critics claimed that Netflix's release of data sets violated US Fair Trade laws as well as the Video Privacy Protection Act. The Netflix Prize website has archived much of the process: www.netflixprize.com/.

predictive systems, the past is prologue, as the data generated through our earlier interactions shape the textual world selected for us. No 'surprises' or 'unwanted' encounters, just uncannily familiar themes and variations. This logic extends into the informational domain as well, where it has been the subject of sharper critique, mostly focused on the argument that such predictive systems create an echo chamber in which our existing views of the world are reinforced but rarely challenged.[4]

Prediction as a Gatekeeper for Textual Production

Taste prediction has another rapidly growing dimension: in some settings the combination of data and algorithms serves as gatekeepers for cultural production, and in the process has displaced the embodied knowledge of established tastemakers. Epagogix, a company that specializes in risk mitigation, has found a niche in advising investors in the film and television industry about the likely success of a given project. Data from the script as well as various casting configurations are analysed by Epagogix's proprietary algorithms, along with a financial assessment that may (or may not) serve as an incentive for investment. Needless to say, long-time industry specialists view such developments with suspicion if not outright contempt, but investors, convinced by the seeming objectivity of numbers and the system's more-often-than-not accurate predictions, think otherwise. Such investor response is understandable at a moment when most stock trading is algorithmically determined: the algorithm is a vernacular of sorts. But it also confirms Gillespie's observation that the algorithm is a talisman, radiating an aura of computer-confirmed objectivity, even though the programming parameters and data construction reveal deeply human prejudices. The bottom line here is that decisions regarding what will and will not be produced are now often based on data of unknown

---

4   The 'echo chamber' effect is widely used in journalism and mass communications to refer to the closed circle of media utterances and audience beliefs, as in Kathleen Hall Jamieson & Joseph N. Cappella, *Echo Chamber: Rush Limbaugh and the Conservative Media Establishment* (New York: Oxford University Press, 2008). The concept has been extended to social media such as Facebook, where algorithms filter and sequence the posts that users see, effectively creating an echo chamber. See for example Eli Pariser, *The Filter Bubble: What the Internet Is Hiding from You* (London: Penguin Press, 2011). Facebook researchers Eytan Bakshy, Solomon Messing and Lada Adamic argue, however, that the data do not support this view ('Exposure to Diverse Information on Facebook' 7 May 2015: https://research.facebook.com/blog/exposure-to-diverse-information-on-facebook/).

quality (What do they actually represent? How were they gathered?) that are fed into algorithms modelled in unknown ways (What constitutes success?).

'Live' Textual Production

Another relatively recent application of algorithms and textual data sets regards what might be termed 'live' or dynamic 'on-demand' textual production. Whereas we saw that one of the oldest continuing cultural uses of algorithms was as a tool to streamline what we might term the production of traditional texts (from an occasional Mozart composition to Narrative Science's articles for *Forbes*), here the texts are dynamic (in the sense of being interactive), responsive (in the sense of being tailored to individual preferences) and inherently unstable (that is, no two texts are identical). Interactive documentaries, often in the form of textual environments (i.e. databases) permit the user to follow his or her interests, with the resulting navigational trail as text. This approach requires the user's active interaction and choice; however, we are fast moving towards a situation where choices regarding text selection (i.e. data selection) will be made on the fly by algorithms armed with data about our preferences. Here, personalization algorithms meet textual production algorithms to create what seems like a seamless, traditional text, even though it will be a unique, real-time data ensemble for our eyes only.

The hundreds of reader responses to the *Times* article amply demonstrated the provocative nature of these developments: text-generating algorithms force us to ask what it means to be human and how that relates to artistic production; production filters force us to reflect on the nature of our automated cultural gatekeepers; personalized texts force us to consider the future of shared experiences. For most commenters, the answer was clear-cut: algorithmic creativity and content-as-data in the traditional cultural sectors seem oxymoronic. Culture is precisely about human expression, and anything else is either trickery or parody. But to designers of algorithms and data sets, such discourse – to the extent that it articulates a human *je ne sais quoi* – is useful in pinning down precisely the gap between human and algorithmic expressions, enabling engineers to define and to chip away at the problem. Much like the issue of intelligence, long-held assumptions regarding man-the-measure are undergoing a Copernican-like decentring, and in this sense, the coincidental appearance of developments such as post-humanism, actor network theory, object-oriented ontology and the rest suggests that sectors of the academy are indeed thinking seriously about a paradigm shift and alternatives to a human-centric culture.[5] All this is to say that the cultural deployments of algorithms and data have different valances. An early and continuing strand of creativity has harnessed algorithms and data to the work of familiar artistic paradigms, where things like authorship and attribution are still relevant (Eno and Verostko still sign their computer-generated works). But as just noted, a rapidly emerging set of developments has seen algorithms used as filters, shaping our access to the cultural repertoire; as gatekeepers, helping to determine what will and will not be produced; and as semi-autonomous forces of production, writing texts, composing music and constructing films – all dynamically personalized and assembled on the fly. Of course, these are still early days and results can sometimes be erratic (Microsoft's Tay AI neural net chatbot was abruptly terminated shortly after her public release in 2016 when 'she' spouted Nazi rhetoric (Bright 2016)). But generally, so long as Moore's Law holds, these developments are growing more intensive, driven by the ever more pervasive place of computational systems in our lives, the ability of algorithms to self-improve without active human intervention, and the ever-increasing depth of our data sets. They raise crucial questions regarding agency and attribution (how to negotiate the space between human designers and machine learning? What is the nature of authorship and the creative act?), point of view (whose values, experiences and perceptions are bound up in this new order and the underlying definition of data?) and cultural access (what notion of 'personalization' enables – or delimits – our encounters with texts, and with what implications?).

The Bigger Picture

Why do these questions, and the increasing insistence with which they are posed, matter? What are the stakes involved? Heidegger (1938) used an image, the 'world picture' (*Weltbild*), to mark the birth of the modern, saying that the moment at which the world becomes picture is the same moment that the human emerges as the subject in a characteristically

5   These terms entail a vast and growing body of literature, including Graham Harman, *The Quadruple Object* (London: Zero Books, 2011); Levi Bryant, Graham Harman & Nick Srnicek, *The Speculative Turn: Continental Materialism and Realism* (Melbourne: re.press, 2011); Katherine N. Hayles, *How We Became Posthuman: Virtual Bodies in Cybernetics, Literature, and Informatics* (Chicago: University of Chicago Press, 1999); Bruno Latour, *Reassembling the Social: An Introduction to Actor-Network-Theory* (New York: Oxford University Press, 2005).

modern subject-object relationship. He argues that the modern social order can be defined through a representational system characterized by precisely defined subject-object relations (the world as picture), a metaphysics of exactitude and an underlying spatiotemporal grid – all qualities that we can see materialized in Gutenberg's printing press and Brunelleschi's notion of perspective, technologies that amplified the subject and her viewing position.[6]

In the hundreds of years between these early-fifteenth-century developments and Heidegger's twentieth century, despite countless historical undulations and discoveries, we encounter a consistent logic of attribution, of a stable self and relationship to the world, a notion of mathematics as a language of precision, calculability and predictability. By contrast, the algorithm enabled by big data – as shown in the cultural deployments just discussed – stands between the calculating subject and the object calculated; it refracts the subject-centred world. Together algorithms and data filter what we have access to, produce our texts with unseen hands and unknown logics, and reshape our texts, rendering them contingent, mutable and 'personalized'.

The implications of this change, if we take thinkers like Heidegger seriously, are profound. Consider the contrast between Diderot's *Encyclopédie* and the crowdsourced Wikipedia, or between Canaletto's painting of Piazza San Marco and the hundreds of differently authored photos that in the aggregate constitute Photosynth's 'synth' of the same locale. With Diderot's compendium and Canaletto, the editor and the painter are known, their point of view embodied, their relationship to the object clear, and their text stable. With texts such as Photosynth, the author is potentially collective, diffused and anonymous; the points of view multiple; the relationship to the object both data-based and algorithmically mediated; and the text ever-changing and mutable. These differences, *grosso modo*, distinguish the project of the modern, Heidegger's 'age of the world picture', from the enablements of the data-powered algorithmic era.

Authorship, in the algorithmic context, is both pluriform and problematic. It turns on the algorithmic re-ordering of data (textual elements), informed and shaped by algorithmic assessments of data (reliability and preference correlations), all algorithmically calculated to achieve certain data markers (user rates). This is not to ignore human agency: humans

6   For a developed version of this argument, particularly as it regards visualization technologies such as augmented reality and Photosynth, see William Uricchio, 'The Algorithmic Turn: Photosynth, Augmented Reality and the State of the Image' in *Visual Studies* 26:1 (2011): 25–35.

take the photographs or shoot the video clips that make up a Photosynth 'synth' or an interactive documentary (even if these processes also reveal fundamental partnerships between the human creator and light-as-data and algorithms-as-image-stabilizers built into our cameras).[7] But when those human-created images are re-rendered into the abstraction of data sets, when those data are algorithmically deployed and stitched back into an image, then categories such as authorship, agency and motive are fundamentally blurred. Descartes' triumphant subject and the *Ich* implied in Heidegger's *Weltbild* are not eradicated, for their traces remain abundant in the individual images and clips. Rather, they are fundamentally repositioned by the algorithmic and data regimes that now stand between the subject and object.

If we understand this, we can think through the opportunities that await us rather than panic at the loss of the old certainties. We can explore the affordances of algorithmically-enabled collaboration and the new forms of collective creativity that might emerge from a world re-articulated as data, rather than tolerating the crude use of algorithmic systems and data sets to exploit and oppress. We can try to understand the implications of widespread personalization, the challenges of a predictive economy in which data trails become constitutive and the impact of a culture of radical contingency. How? We can first comprehend that conditions have changed, that we need to shift our focus from the simple causalities of the subject-object binary to a far less decipherable algorithmic intermediary. To do so requires a new literacy, not in the sense of making composited algorithms legible, for that is beyond comprehension, but rather by attending to their operations, noting their defaults, critiquing their judgements and the definitions of the data they are processing. And particularly at this moment of transition, we must carefully assess the ends to which these new tools are put – whether they are being bent to the whims of the old subject (aggregating power and control) or facilitate new collectivities.

In framing these issues, I've gone back several times to the fifteenth century and the emergence of modern technologies such as the printing press and three-point perspective. These technologies amplify the position of the individual human subject and resonate through the six centuries of the modern that followed. That they are taken for granted even today, when they are increasingly displaced by a radically different representational regime and set of technologies, shows us that old habits die hard. Not

---

7   And conversely, algorithms and data sets are in the majority of cases human-authored and assembled, even if they can go on to self-generate, further complicating the situation.

surprisingly for a moment of transition, today's dominant deployments of algorithmically enabled systems emulate the representational traditions of the past: they often look ordinary and familiar. And we respond accordingly, reading a Narrative Science-authored newspaper article as we would a human-authored story or viewing a Photosynth image as we would a photograph. It's easy to miss the radical reworking of cultural logics *in media res*, easy to re-inscribe the new and uncertain into the familiar categories of the past… or to reject them as threats to the status quo.

We can probably learn something from our predecessors in the late Middle Ages, poised on the cusp of the modern, encountering the printing press and three-point perspective. What did people make of new and, in retrospect, era-defining technologies *before* that era was defined? Scholars such as Elizabeth Eisenstein (1979) have tended to see the printing press as a trigger for the modern (knowledge stabilization, spread, etc.), while others such as Adrian Johns (1988) have more recently chronicled the disparate and unruly practices that attended its initial decades. In Eisenstein's story, emerging technologies exerted an impact, making a splash as harbingers of the new; and in Johns's, they were taken up by a late-medieval populace and used in aberrant and contradictory ways. I would argue that we are in a similar position with our new era-defining technologies of algorithms enabled by big data and massive processing power.

The new era has yet to be defined, and it is impossible to know how future historians will inscribe our trajectory. Of course, the 'newness' of this regime comes with the danger that it will be retrofitted to sustain the excesses and contradictions of the fast-aging modern, to empower particular individual points of view, to control and stabilize a master narrative. But it also offers an opportunity for critical thinking and an imaginative embrace of the era's new affordances. And for these opportunities to be realized, we need to develop critical perspectives, to develop analytical categories relevant to these developments and our place in them.

Much of what we today call the humanities harkens back to traditions developed during the long span of the modern, traditions predicated upon the stable subject-object relationship noted earlier and captured by Heidegger's concept of the *Weltbild*. But although the term 'humanities' was coined in the Renaissance of the fifteenth century (*studia humanitatis*), its texts and values go back to the pre-modern world of classical Greece and Rome, where the humanities involved practice more than study. The question is whether we can draw on this era-spanning tradition to anchor, critically assess and navigate the 'age of the algorithm' (to put the new era in terms equivalent to Heidegger's 'age of the world picture'). Can we disentangle the centrality of the individual subject from the humanity at the core of the humanities agenda? Can we rethink our inherited categories of authorship and agency in ways that stimulate a critical discourse of collaborative and algorithmically-enabled work? Can we shift from familiar conditions such as precision, calculability and predictability and learn to grapple with the contingent, mutable and personalized? Is a poetics of data within our reach or even desirable?

To even begin to answer these questions, we need to develop new literacies capable of assessing various data forms and organizing schemes such as algorithms. We have to understand how they are deployed and develop a critical sense of their limits, capacities, implications and possibilities. How do they operate, not so much as technological ensembles but as patterning activities, as enablers of collaboration and creativity, as potentially critical practices? The humanities – the questions their texts and values pose, the critical stance they espouse, the comparative and historical framings they deploy, the analytic attention that they expend – have never been more important. Yes, modernist assumptions need fundamental revision, and their corpora need to be radically expanded to include categories like data and algorithms. And yes, poised as we are on the cusp of a new era, we have much to learn from similar transitions in the past, particularly regarding the predictable rear-guard actions of those who seek to exploit the potentials of the new to extend the power dynamics of the old.

References

Bright, Peter. 2016. "Microsoft terminates its Tay AI chatbot after she turns into a Nazi." *Ars Technica*. 24 March. http://arstechnica.com/information-technology/2016/03/microsoft-terminates-its-tay-ai-chatbot-after-she-turns-into-a-nazi/.

Eisenstein, Elizabeth L. 1979. *The Printing Press as an Agent of Change*. Cambridge UK: Cambridge University Press.

Eno, Brian. 1975. *Discreet Music* (liner Notes). Audio CD. EG Music.

Gillespie, Tarleton. 2014. "Algorithm [draft][# Digitalkeywords]." *Culture Digitally*, June. http://culturedigitally.org/2014/06/algorithm-draft-digitalkeyword/.

Heidegger, Martin. 1938. "Die Zeit Des Weltbildes." *Holzwege*. Frankfurt a.M.

Hoelzl, Ingrid & Rémi Marie. 2015. *Softimage: Towards a New Theory of the Digital Image*. Bristol: Intellect.

Johns, Adrian. 1998. *The Nature of the Book: Print and Knowledge in the Making*. Chicago: University of Chicago Press.

Manovich, Lev. 2001. *The Language of New Media*. Cambridge, MA: The MIT Press.

Podolny, Shelley. 2015. "If an Algorithm Wrote This, How Would You Even Know?" *The New York Times*. 7 March.

Seaver, Nick. 2013. "Knowing Algorithms." *Media in Transition* 8: 1–12. Cambridge, MA: MIT.

9. Unknowing Algorithms

On Transparency of Unopenable Black Boxes

Johannes Paßmann & Asher Boersma

Algorithmic Black Boxes as a Challenge for Media Studies

The primary source for the suspicion with which the rise of and subsequent dependency on software as research instrument in the humanities is met, is that one does not know what *the machine* does. In many cases 'machine' means algorithm. *Algorithmic black boxes* have become so widespread that this objection could already be voiced as soon as a researcher uses Google. In *digital methods* and beyond, there is a dominant tendency for research processes to be dependent upon algorithmic black boxes, which even theoretically cannot be 'opened' (Bucher 2012). Kate Crawford speaks in this context of the 'disappointingly limited calls for algorithmic "transparency", which seem doomed to fail' (2016: 11).

The dependency on algorithmic black boxes has been addressed as a problem for research practices by Bernhard Rieder and Theo Röhle (2012). They have called 'black-boxing' one of the major challenges for digital methods, and continue their pursuit for a solution along the same lines in this volume. They delineate this technical black-boxing as a matter of accessibility (such as in the case of 'the' Google algorithm or countless other proprietary algorithms) and code literacy (cf. *ibid.*: 76), but also as not-understandable on a 'more abstract' level, as 'the results they produce cannot be easily mapped back to the algorithms and the data they process' (*ibid.*). Still, Rieder and Röhle propose this should not keep us from using them, as there is a workaround to this, which is 'to use different tools from the same category whenever possible in order to avoid limiting ourselves to a specific perspective' (*ibid.*: 77). Different algorithms would bring different aspects of a data set to the fore when one experiments with them, switches between different ones, etc.. Thus what Rieder and Röhle have proposed – and continue to seek for in this volume with their focus on the 'bizarre amount of knowledge we have stuffed into our tools' (Rieder & Röhle in this book) – are ways to minimise the size of black boxes by enlightening formerly black parts.

With this article however, we would like to draw attention to an approach from a different direction. Instead of focusing on how to gain positive knowledge in order to make these black boxes 'more transparent', we would like to outline a concept of transparency that is not so much concerned with positive knowledge, but that deals with skills which help dealing with those parts of an artefact that one still does not know. In that sense our proposal comes in after Rieder and Röhle have left the scene successfully: we ask how to behave towards what remains black after all. We consider this important, as we assume that the minimising strategy will be decreasingly helpful in the future. The conjuncture of algorithmic black boxes is so huge and encompassing that questions of how to minimise the unknown will increasingly be replaced by questions of how to behave towards the unknowable. What appears debatable may thus be not how to make a given black box more transparent so much as the concept of transparency itself.

What we found is that different authors have given significantly different meanings to the term transparency. We would like to differentiate between two notions here. On the one hand, there is what we call *formalized transparency*, which largely tries to obtain 'more positive knowledge' on 'the content' of a black box. On the other hand, we see *practical transparency*, which does not try to open black boxes, but to develop skills without raising the issue of openability. These two concepts of transparency do not exclude each other. Rather, they outline two different sets of practices dealing with black boxes which can complement each other.

Don't Open Every Black Box!

When Sociology of Science and the movement that was later termed *Laboratory Studies* adopted the term *black box* in the 1970s, its function was somewhat different from today. Richard D. Whitley stated at the time: 'The view of scientific knowledge maintained by much of the sociology of science had led to an ideology of "black boxism" which restricts research to the study of currently observable inputs to, and outputs from, a system. Any study of the internal processes, which may be unobservable at the moment, is declared taboo.' (1972: 63)

The problem that he points out here is not that in research practice there are too many intransparent material black boxes, but that the 'site of scientific action offers a unique opportunity to investigate the process of knowledge production, which continues to be a "black box" to social studies of science', as Karin Knorr Cetina put it ten years later (1982: 102).

Latour and Woolgar also talk critically about black boxing, stating that with the help of 'money, authority, confidence' certain kinds of knowledge are prevented from being questioned, making it almost improbable to raise alternatives (1979: 242). This is quite similar to the concept of black boxing that Gregory Bateson uses some years earlier:

> A 'black box' is a conventional agreement between scientists to stop trying to explain things at a certain point [...] It's a word that comes from the engineers. When they draw a diagram of a complicated machine, they use a sort of shorthand. Instead of drawing all the details they put a box to stand for a whole bunch of parts and label the box with what that bunch of parts is supposed to do. (Bateson 1972: 39)

What all these black boxes (Whitley; Knorr Cetina; Latour & Woolgar; Bateson) have in common is the normative implication that they should actually be opened. In her later work, however, Knorr Cetina stresses that certain black boxes in scientific research processes cannot and should not be opened. She mentions the example of heart surgeons who want to be present when a donor heart is removed from a body, to see and feel the organ they will have to transplant later. Nobody can explicitly say what the use of this is, or what kind of information the surgeon gets or processes when he or she is present at the removal, but everybody agrees this is necessary:

> The scientist's body as an information-processing tool is a black-boxed instrument. The absence of discourse concerning embodied behavior corresponds to the use of embodied information processing as a substitute for conscious reflection and communication. The acting body works best when it is a silent part of the empirical machinery of research. (Knorr Cetina 1999: 99)

This means that in research practices we find black boxes that should not be opened. These black boxes remain intransparent in a conventional, formalized sense, but that is in no way problematic for the scientist in the practice of research. She (and none of her colleagues or the ethnographers researching laboratory life) sees, hears, etc. what is happening, but this produces no deficit for her. Quite on the contrary, an explication of 'what is actually happening' may deprive her of these kinds of 'knowledge'. This is quite similar to when somebody starts thinking about their PIN code when typing it at the supermarket register: the fingers 'know' the code, but as soon as 'the brain' tries to think about it explicitly, the fingers will 'forget' it. This raises the question whether the calls for transparency in discourses around algorithms actually have to point to what Knorr Cetina called 'conscious reflection and communication' when conscious reflection is impossible anyway, or if here transparency may mean to embody the functioning and dysfunction of a certain artefact: if we cannot 'know' (in an explicit sense) what algorithms do and which inaccuracies they have, can we at least embody them to such a degree that we know when to rely on their results and when to become distrustful? This would mean that they become transparent, not insofar as 'one sees what is happening', but rather in such a way that they withdraw in practice.

Practical Transparency: Knowing When and How to Be Careful

The notion that we call practical transparency has already been applied in the realm of digital media research. Susan Star, Geoffrey Bowker and Laura Neumann write that at the 'individual level of scale', transparency means a user 'does not have to be bothered with the underlying machinery or software. In this sense, an automobile is transparent when a driver sits down, turns the key, and drives off, all without the foggiest notion of how internal combustion works' (2003: 242). This means, and this is crucial, that black boxing is not an obstacle for transparency here, but the primary condition for its very possibility.

Applying this notion of transparency to algorithmic black boxes would only be half the solution as it does not provide means to position oneself critically towards what is inside the black box. This concept however has a long tradition in the philosophy of technology, and has actually always been an ideal of media and media practices. It is here that we find an understanding of transparency and its limits that allows for the critical position we seek.

Most prominently, we find this idea in Marx's *Maschinenfragment*. Originally however – although Marx does not mention this – the idea comes from Hegel. Loosely speaking, Hegel differentiates *Maschine* (machine) and *Werkzeug* (almost translatable as *tool*). The tool follows the hand, whereas the hand has to follow the machine. The tool mediates between man and the environment, as an inert but still rather passive thing in the producer's hand – the German word *Werkzeug* expresses this hierarchical relation, *Zeug* is the stuff, the unimportant, the heteronomous. That the tool is inert means that it forces its user to discipline himself, as Axel Honneth comments, with the result that on the one hand, the user 'transforms himself into a thing'. But at the same time he experiences that in this self-disciplining, the subjective *Geist* acquires the ability to realize itself in the product of tool-using work (cf. Honneth 2014 [1994]: 61). This would mean that for the ideally disciplined Hegelian tool-user the tool is practically transparent.

The machine on the other hand requires a different type of disciplining. At first it seems that the 'user' lets the machine work for himself, 'but his own activity thereby becomes more formalised. His dull work constricts him to a single point [...] shrinking [his] skills" (Hegel 1983 [1805/6]: 139). At the end of this process, even this formal work is *aufgehoben* (sublated, abolished, suspended, superseded, but also preserved). The machine working for you ultimately inverts your relation to it: you work for the machine, doing only machine work. Hegel considers machine usage as a fraud against nature, which in turn takes revenge: the more man subjugates nature using machines, the lower he himself sinks (cf. Hegel 1974 [1803/4]: 332). The tool thus appears in that respect as the opposite of the machine, as it follows the intentional activity of its users and can be made transparent as they learn to master it with certain skills, whereas the machine on the other hand makes its users transparent by mastering them.

Our differentiation between Hegel's concepts of *Maschine* and *Werkzeug* is, as mentioned, relatively rough. The German philosopher Hans-Christoph Schmidt am Busch is a bit more precise here; he differentiates between tool as a means of labour ('Werkzeug als Arbeitsmittel') and tool as a thing ('Werkzeug als Ding'), and the actual tool is always both (2002: 48ff). Similar to the algorithm that allows you to make certain parts practically transparent (one can 'know' what they do) and others not (one can 'know' their inaccuracies), the Hegelian tool also has a dual character as *means* and *thing* at the same time. The ideal however is a practical transparency that can be achieved through acquisition of skills.

This process of appropriating a technical artefact in such a way that it becomes transparent through acquired skills may actually be one of Maurice Merleau-Ponty's most prominent considerations. Certain artefacts can become transparent in such a way that they become part of one's body schema, they are incorporated or, as he writes, *embodied*. Merleau-Ponty names several examples of embodiment, one of them being the blind man's stick, which withdraws when used. At the end of a learning process, for its user, the stick is no longer an object, as he does not perceive it as anything distinct from his body: the stick's ending is the beginning of its user's perceptual field, and the stick's measurable length no longer matters (1962

---

1   This quote is from Leo Rauch's translation and refers to *Jenaer Realphilosophie* (1805-06), chapter II 'Wirklicher Geist', subchapter b 'Vertrag'.

[1945]: 167)[2]. The world of tactually perceived objects then does not begin with his skin, but with his stick's ending. Thus he does not *interpret* the pressures the stick makes towards the hand. On the contrary, embodiment means that explicit interpretation is no longer necessary, just like it is not necessary to interpret contact with one's skin (cf. *ibid.*: 178).

For Merleau-Ponty, the same principle works for other artefacts like typewriters and pipe organs. Two examples that he gives are particularly interesting for us. The first is a woman with a plume hat, who can keep a safe distance between the feather in her hat and everything that may break it off without calculating the distance between the top of her feather and the respective objects. The same goes for the second example, a car that one wants to drive through a tunnel. Car and hat do not function as objects with measurable volumes, but have become demands for a certain amount of free space (*ibid.*: 167)[3].

The feather and the stick are both 'extensions of man', but they bring quite different aspects of these extensions to the fore. The stick appears as a transparent mediator to perceive *and* act upon the environment. The feather on the other hand does not appear as a mediator here (which does not mean it could not be used as such, but it's just not as suited for that kind of task as the stick is). It does not so much produce practical transparency, but forces you to learn when and how to be careful. As already mentioned, for practices involving algorithmic black boxes, both appear important: to embody what they can do, that is Merleau-Ponty's stick (which corresponds to Hegel's notion of *Werkzeug als Arbeitsmittel*) and to embody its inaccuracies as well, which is represented by Merleau-Ponty's feather (and corresponds to Hegel's notion of *Werkzeug als Ding*).

Thus the feather highlights the known unknown that you need to embody in a particular way if you want to produce knowledge with algorithms, whereas the blind man's stick highlights the embodied known or not explicitly known known. When both kinds of knowledge about algorithms, the positive 'stick knowledge' and the negative 'feather knowledge', are taken together, it appears possible to act towards unopenable black boxes.

---

2   'Le bâton de l'aveugle a cessé d'être un objet pour lui, il n'est plus perçu pour lui-même, son extrémité s'est transformée en zone sensible.'
3   'Le chapeau et l'automobile ont cessé d'être des objets dont la grandeur et le volume se détermineraient par comparaison avec les autres objets. Ils sont devenus des puissances volumineuses, l'exigence d'un certain espace libre.'

In one of our earlier articles, a case was presented where two researchers used Gephi algorithms to visualize Twitter data (Paßmann 2013). There, exactly, this difference became apparent: the researchers differentiated between certain activities of an algorithm that they would undoubtedly consider solid results and for which they would take responsibility – this was for example the case when the distance between two nodes in a network visualization was 20 cm. On the other hand, there were results on the map which they did not 'dare to say anything about' (*ibid.*) – in this case when the distance between two nodes was only two cm. The latter would be this 'feather knowledge' telling its users when and how to be careful (demanding a certain amount of free space, i.e. the known unknown), whereas the 20 cm, after sufficient experience, would be in the realm of the 'stick knowledge'. When approached through the lens of formalized transparency, the whole algorithm would appear as a black box here, which with the help of Rieder and Röhle can be cut down to a significantly smaller size. In terms of practical transparency, the remaining part that we formally cannot know can be practically transparent either through embodiment, as with the stick, or through a carefully paced out unknowing, as with the feather.

One result of such 'feather knowledge' would then be to realize which other sources, external to software and database, are necessary to work around the known unknowns, like ethnographic data for example. Regularly these other sources will be some kind of everyday knowledge, which has not been optimized as much as, for example, knowledge about software and databases. That means that, at best, practical transparency turns unknown unknowns in to known unknowns. Finding ways to deal with these new known unknowns needs more attention, we would argue, than the inner workings of black boxes. We know they will be increasingly unopenable.

References

Bateson, Gregory. 1972. *Steps to an Ecology of Mind*. Chicago: University of Chicago Press.

Bucher, Taina. 2012. "Want to be on the top? Algorithmic power and the threat of invisibility on Facebook." *New Media & Society* 14 (7): 1164-1180.

Crawford, Kate. 2016. "Can an Algorithm be Agonistic? Ten Scenes from Life in Calculated Publics." *Science, Technology & Human Values* 41 (1): 77-92.

Hegel, Georg Wilhelm Friedrich. 1974 [1803/1804]. "Anhang zur Jenaer Realphilosophie, Ausarbeitung zur Geistesphilosophie von 1803/4." In *Frühe politische Systeme*, ed. Gerhard Göhler, 293-335. Frankfurt a.M./Berlin/Wien.

—. 1983 [1805/6]. *Hegel and the Human Spirit. A translation of the Jena Lectures on the Philosophy of Spirit (1805-6) with commentary.* transl. Leo Rauch. Detroit [i.o.: idem (1976 [1805/6]): Gesammelte Werke. Bd. 8: Jenaer Systementwürfe III. Hamburg].

Honneth, Axel. 2014 [1994]. *Kampf um Anerkennung. Zur moralischen Grammatik sozialer Konflikte*. Frankfurt a.M.

Knorr Cetina, Karin. 1982. "Scientific Communities or Transepistemic Arenas of Research? A Critique of Quasi-Economic Models of Science." *Social Studies of Science* 12 (1): 101-130.

—. 1999. *Epistemic Cultures. How the Sciences Make Knowledge*. Cambridge, MA.

Latour, Bruno and Steve Woolgar. 1979. *Laboratory Life: The Construction of Scientific Facts*. Princeton, NJ.

Merleau-Ponty, Maurice. 1962 [1945]. *Phenomenology of Perception*. transl. Colin Smith. New York/London [i.o.: idem: Phénoménologie de la Perception, Paris].

Paßmann, Johannes. 2013. "Forschungsmedien erforschen. Zur Praxis mit der Daten-Mapping-Software Gephi." In *Vom Feld zum Labor und zurück*, ed. Raphaela Knipp, Johannes Paßmann & Nadine Taha (Hrsg.): 113-130. Siegen.

Rieder, Bernhard & Theo Röhle. 2012. "Digital Methods, Five Challenges." In *Understanding Digital Humanities*, ed. David M. Berry, 67-84. Houndsmills.

Schmidt am Busch, Hans Christoph (2002). *Hegels Begriff der Arbeit*. Berlin.

Star, Susan Leigh, Geoffrey C. Bowker & Laura J. Neumann. 2003. "Transparency beyond the individual level of scale: Convergence between information artifacts and communities of practice." In *Digital library use: Social practice in design and evaluation*, ed. Ann Peterson, Nancy A. Van House & Barbara P. Buttenfield, 241-269. Cambridge, MA, London.

Whitley, Richard D. 1972. "Black Boxism and the Sociology of Science. A Discussion of the Major Developments in the Field." *The Sociology of Sciences*, ed. Paul Halmos, 61-92. Keele.

10. Social Data APIs

Origin, Types, Issues

Cornelius Puschmann & Julian Ausserhofer

Introduction

Application programming interfaces (APIs) represent an increasingly relevant form of data access in both academic research and beyond. Many popular social media services provide APIs to developers, which can also be used to collect information relevant to social scientists, industry researchers and journalists, as do some more traditional data providers, such as archives and databases. In science and scholarship, fields that study digital media, and some which are concerned with other areas of inquiry (economics, climatology, medicine), have taken up the use of APIs. As more and more information becomes available online, providing access in a standardized way is a convenient and efficient way for turning data that is generated by users (Facebook, Twitter), routinely collected by organizations (public research institutes, national statistics offices), and generated and enriched by cultural institutions (GLAM: galleries, libraries, archives, museums) and news organizations into information that can be used in a number of ways both for academic and applied research, as well as for tackling real-world problems.

In this chapter, we discuss different aspects of APIs from the perspectives of social scientists who use APIs for data collection. We describe (1) the origin of APIs in software development, (2) conduct a survey of popular Web APIs by type, and (3) discuss issues with regard to the reliability, validity and representativeness of data retrieved from APIs. We close by pointing to future developments in this area.

API Origins

The Oxford English Dictionary defines an API as 'the interface between the operating system and an application program; the protocol to be observed by the writer of an application program designed to run under a particular operating system'. Beal (2016) similarly speaks of 'a set of routines, proto-cols, and tools for building software applications' and goes on to say that it 'specifies how software components should interact'. APIs have a long history in computer programming. They stand in contrast to application binary interfaces (ABIs) which are based on binary, rather than interpreted, code. An API can make it easier to extend existing applications with new features by providing a framework that relies on pre-established functions. APIs also facilitate access to data, usually in order to provide new functions, which translates into greater utility of the service or application. Data access through Web APIs, in contrast to the broader understanding of an API as a programming framework that implements a set of standard behaviours (for languages such as C or Java), will be our focus in this chapter. APIs are often provided in the form of a package or library that includes specifications for data structures, functions and object classes. In the case of Web-based SOAP and REST services which underpin many popular social media services, a Web API is simply a specification of remote calls available to users of the API. SOAP and REST are the two most widely used exchange standards for doing this on the Web, with REST much more popular. REST is able to return results in different formats, most notably JSON, while SOAP supports only XML. JSON has proven particularly popular, being both able to represent complex data structures and being (relatively) readable to humans, while XML is comparatively less easy to learn. Web APIs based on SOAP or REST afford essential CRUD operations (create, read, update and delete) that underpin most data interactions. In other words, they are much narrower in their ability but also in their complexity, than are general purpose programming APIs.

Popular Web APIs

Web APIs are a fairly recent innovation in comparison to programming APIs in a broader sense. Still more recent is their adoption in social science research. The number of REST-based Web APIs listed by ProgrammableWeb, a global directory for APIs, surpassed 14,000 in 2015. The list of APIs tracked by ProgrammableWeb includes areas such as finance, science, education, mapping, games and messaging.

In addition to private companies, public institutions such as cultural heritage organizations and statistics offices increasingly offer APIs. In these organizations, APIs are usually part of larger open data strategies. Important providers include the UN[1], the WHO and the World Bank. Also, many federal

---

1   http://data.un.org/Host.aspx?Content=API. The other APIs mentioned below can be found through ProgrammableWeb's directory or the search engine of your choice, using 'API' and the organization's name as search terms.

and regional governments have implemented Web APIs. Many of these can be accessed through open data portals that have been implemented in the past years (e.g. data.gov, data.gov.uk, open-data.europa.eu, etc.). CKAN, the open-source system behind many open data portals, provides the framework for most of these APIs.

A handful of influential global news organizations such as the BBC, The New York Times, The Guardian, NPR, USA Today and ZEIT Online have also started to offer parts of their content through APIs. The biggest beneficiaries of this step seem to be the organizations themselves though, since the offerings of APIs make internal R&D efforts more efficient, help to further commercialize the news content, and facilitate external networks of open innovation (Aitamurto & Lewis 2013). Nevertheless, some content and (meta)data can also be used fruitfully for research.

Areas with high volumes of data creation, such as the (life) sciences, are particularly open to APIs to facilitate data exchange and enable new forms of information reuse. The rOpenSci collection offers a number of API libraries for the R programming language. Platforms for publishing and storing research data such as Dryad or figshare can be queried, as can be archives of scientific articles such as arXiv and PLoS. Countless sources of scientific data, but also cultural heritage material from Europeana, countless museums and the Internet Archive are available.

In addition to the above-mentioned APIs provided in different sectors, the APIs of large social media companies have been of great importance for the social sciences and humanities in the past years. Some of the most popular services, not only for research, include the APIs offered by Facebook, Twitter, Reddit and Instagram in the social network category, Google Maps and Yelp in the geolocation category, and Spotify and Soundcloud in the music category (Brennan 2015).

While these APIs 'provide new ways of sharing and participating, they also provide a means [...] to achieve market dominance, as well as undermine privacy, data security, contextual integrity, user autonomy and freedom' (Bodle 2011: 320). Therefore, Web APIs cannot be seen solely as support software systems. Because they shape the organizations that provide them and format the rules under which external software developers can make use of them, APIs can be seen as powerful mediators in a datafied society (Ausserhofer [forthcoming]; Bucher 2013).

Through the establishment of social data APIs, social media companies seek to set up an open innovation ecosystem that draws application developers to the platform. The companies invest considerable resources to keep external programmers engaged with the API because they believe that this improves their internal innovation capacity. Some companies even argue that by giving third parties such as researchers access to social trace data, they contribute to the public good. While this may be true for some cases, often this can be seen as measures for PR purposes, a form of 'open washing' (Villum 2014).

Social media platforms process billions of API requests annually. The central function of such requests is to provide derivative services or functionalities that increase the usefulness of the social media platform. However, as company policies change, a company's data management regime may become stricter. Twitter is an example of this approach. Initially offering broad access to data in the first years of its operation in order to encourage development of derivate services, such as software clients for unsupported platforms, the company reasserted its control by making access to data more restrictive in several successive steps over recent years (Puschmann & Burgess 2014). This shift took place alongside acquisitions (Tweetdeck, Gnip) and a number of derivate service providers going out of business, merging or changing their business model.

Strategic reasons are not the only motivators behind such changes. Facebook has greatly restricted access to user data through the API out of privacy concerns, as have other platforms. When dubious actors acquire large amounts of data that are clearly not used for the API's intended purpose, this often leads to a tightening of policies by the API's operators, if only because providing and sustaining the performance of an API is not trivial computationally. When Twitter greatly enhanced the ability of its search API, it was largely because the engineering feat of making historical Twitter data indexable was very difficult to resolve (Zhuang 2014). APIs, in other words, incur significant costs to businesses which may be invisible to users, who may be under the impression that data sits in the company archive like books on a shelf, ready to be picked up. Social media data, in addition to being available directly from platforms such as Facebook, Twitter and Instagram, are also stored, indexed and repackaged by dedicated social analytics providers such as Gnip (owned by Twitter) or Datasift (partnered with Facebook).

Reliability, Validity and Representativeness of API Data

We have so far argued that APIs are a useful data source for scientific research. There is, however, also reason for scepticism. Commercial platforms such as Facebook and Twitter do not provide their APIs as a service to researchers, but have other uses which inhibit reproducible sampling and frequently render data sets incomplete (González-Bailón et al. 2014;

Gerlitz & Rieder 2013). Capturing data from such platforms is also computationally resource-intensive, imposing limitations on research. Below, we pose a list of questions for scholars who engage in research that is based on data from an API. These questions are intended to highlight issues that typically arise in research designs that draw upon digital data sources. While these are very similar to standard social science tenants of research design, it is worthwhile to reiterate some of these issues in the context of data API.

'How purposeful is the sampling strategy?'

By purposeful we mean, 'What is the impact of technical constraints on sampling?' How do language implementations of the API, content fields for data and metadata, rate limitations and the availability of APIs for certain types of content all shape the sampling strategy? Consider this in the context of Twitter. The streaming and search APIs are well-supported in different languages. Content is provided in the form of tweets which are the preferred unit of analysis over discussion turns, topical frames or other, more conceptually-grounded units of analysis. Rate limitations for Twitter have become stricter over time, but are still quite lenient. Extracting and analysing Twitter data is easier and more popular than Facebook data, even though Facebook is far more popular than Twitter (Tufekci 2014).

'How clear is the sampling procedure?'

By clarity we mean, 'How clear is it what steps were undertaken to arrive at the sample?' Random stratified sampling is traditionally a pillar of empirical analysis, but this fails in many instances when sampling from social media sources. As Ruths and Pfeffer (2014) have pointed out, random Twitter samples are non-random in the sense that the server collecting the data and fluctuations in message volume both have an impact on the randomness of a sample. Since randomness is difficult to achieve for Twitter researchers who do not have access to a large volume (or ideally the entirety) of tweets, much sampling relies on snowball sampling or other convenience strategies. This is both bad for the reliability of results and raises complexity issues.

'How reliable is the sampling?'

By this we mean, 'Would the same query to the API at different times or from different people return similar results?' This is much more straightforward in some APIs than in others, depending on the overall volume of content. APIs for archives, online news or public records will be much more reliable than commercial APIs for social media content.

'How valid is the operationalization undertaken in the research?'

By this we mean, 'Is it analytically sound to operationalize a data variable in a particular way?' Examples would be to characterize the number of followers a Twitter user has as a measure of her influence or the number of reads that an article receives as a measure of its popularity. The issue hardly ends there, but research that is based on digital data faces particularly complex questions of operationalization because in contrast to data sources such as surveys or interviews, the data comes in a highly suggestive pre-packaged form. Many social media metrics lead a dual life of meaning for users and platform providers with both parties influencing them deliberately or unintentionally.

'How representative is the sample of the population?'

By this we mean both, 'How well does the sample represent that platform from which it was drawn?' and, 'How well does the platform represent other platforms, users or sources of information?' In the case of Twitter and Facebook, it is a nontrivial problem to draw samples that are representative of either platform. Secondly, it is equally challenging to formulate valid assumptions about how well these samples represent groups of people more broadly.

'How reproducible is the research in total?'

By this we mean, 'How hard would it be to conduct similar research that tests the findings of the study?' In the case of exclusively big data samples, it is quite hard, just as it would be with smaller but historical samples of social media data. APIs as such do much to greatly improve reproducibility, by providing a common source of access to researchers. Proprietary data sets on CD-ROM or with strict access protection do much to effectively limit access, even when there is a general agreement that those who want to can gain access. On the other hand, hurdles exist both in relation to the computational feasibility of such research and to the technical skills required to make use of APIs.

APIs in the Future

We have sought to show that APIs are an increasingly relevant form of data access, both in academic and applied research, and for civil society more broadly. In addition to the Web APIs provided by large internet companies such as Facebook, Google and Twitter, APIs also proliferate among governments, scientific organizations and NGOs. They are likely to become a more widely used channel, assuming that more people are able to access them. Competency is the key issue here: Web APIs require basic programming knowledge to enable access. This requirement represents a significant hurdle, and one that cannot be overcome easily. The use of a programming language is what makes data access through an API efficient, and alternative, more intuitive forms of access incur costs to the data providers and are unlikely to scale efficiently. A second hurdle is the ability of data suppliers to control access and the ability to distinguish and, if needed, discriminate between users. As society becomes increasingly 'datafied', the relatively informal relationship between API providers and API users will need to be codified in a way that resembles the relationship between providers and users of other (public) services. Public services, such as libraries, and private utilities such as the telephone network point into the direction that this codified relationship may take. As APIs become more and more mundane outside of software development, and our reliance on them increases, the issue of their reliability too will become ever more important.

Acknowledgements

Both authors gratefully acknowledge the support of Volkswagen Foundation.

References

Aitamurto, Tanja & Seth C. Lewis. 2013. "Open Innovation in Digital Journalism: Examining the Impact of Open APIs at Four News Organizations." *New Media & Society* 15 (2): 314–31.

Ausserhofer, Julian. forthcoming. "Die Datenbank verdient die Hauptrolle: Bausteine einer Methodologie für Open Digital Humanities." In *Aufgehoben? Speicherorte, -diskurse und -medien von Literatur*, ed. Susanne Eichhorn, Bernhard Oberreither, Marina Rauchenbacher, Isabella Schwentner & Katharina Serles. Würzburg: Königshausen & Neumann.

Beal, Vangie. 2016. "API – Application Program Interface." Webopedia. Accessed 30 March 2016. www.webopedia.com/TERM/A/API.html.

Bodle, Robert. 2011. "Regimes of Sharing: Open APIs, Interoperability, and Facebook." *Information, Communication & Society* 14 (3): 320–37.

Brennan, Martin W. 2015. "Most Popular APIs Used at Hackathons." *ProgrammableWeb*. Accessed 10 April 2016. www.programmableweb.com/news/most-popular-apis-used-hackathons/elsewhere-web/2015/10/04.

Bucher, Taina. 2013. "Objects of Intense Feeling: The Case of the Twitter API." *Computational Culture* 3 (November). http://computationalculture.net/article/objects-of-intense-feeling-the-case-of-the-twitter-api.

Gerlitz, Carolin & Bernhard Rieder. 2013. "Mining One Percent of Twitter: Collections, Baselines, Sampling." *M/C Journal* 16 (2). www.journal.media-culture.org.au/index.php/mcjournal/article/viewArticle/620.

González-Bailón, Sandra, Ning Wang, Alejandro Rivero, Javier Borge-Holthoefer & Yamir Moreno. 2014. "Assessing the Bias in Samples of Large Online Networks." *Social Networks* 38 (July): 16–27.

Puschmann, Cornelius & Jean Burgess. 2014. "The Politics of Twitter Data." In *Twitter and Society*, ed. Katrin Weller, Axel Bruns, Jean Burgess, Merja Mahrt & Cornelius Puschmann, 43–54. Digital Formations 89. New York: Peter Lang.

Ruths, Derek & Jürgen Pfeffer. 2014. "Social Media for Large Studies of behaviour." *Science* 346 (6213): 1063–64.

Tufekci, Zeynep. 2014. "Big Questions for Social Media Big Data: Representativeness, Validity and Other Methodological Pitfalls." *Proceedings of the Eighth International AAAI Conference on Weblogs and Social Media*. www.aaai.org/ocs/index.php/ICWSM/ICWSM14/paper/view/8062.

Villum, Christian. 2014. "'Open-Washing' – The Difference between Opening Your Data and Simply Making Them Available." Open Knowledge Blog. October 3. http://blog.okfn.org/2014/03/10/open-washing-the-difference-between-opening-your-data-and-simply-making-them-available/.

Zhuang, Yi. 2014. "Building a Complete Tweet Index." Twitter Blogs. November 18. https://blog.twitter.com/2014/building-a-complete-tweet-index.

11. How to Tell Stories with Networks

Exploring the Narrative Affordances of Graphs with the *Iliad*

Tommaso Venturini, Liliana Bounegru, Mathieu Jacomy &
Jonathan Gray

No doubt, networks have become indispensable mathematical tools in many aspects of life in the twenty-first century. They allow us to calculate all kinds of relational metrics and to quantify the properties of their nodes, clusters and global structures. These modes of calculation are increasingly prevalent in an age of digital data. But networks are more than formal analytical tools. They are also powerful metaphors of our collective life, with all of its complexity and its many dependencies. This is why, among the various strategies of data visualization, networks seem to have assumed a paradigmatic position, spreading to the most different disciplines and colonizing a growing number of digital and non-digital objects, sometimes as mere decoration. Contemplating the visual representation of a network, we don't (always) need to compute its mathematical properties to appreciate its heuristic value – as anyone who has ever used a transit plan knows well. Networks are extraordinary calculating devices, but they are also maps, instruments of navigation and representation. Not only do they guide our steps through the territories that they represent, they invite our imagination to see and explore the world in different ways.

Over the past few decades, this visual representation of networks has seen a 'renaissance' thanks to the development of graphical user interfaces and network spatialisation algorithms. The analytical capabilities of graph mathematics have been written into software programs that multiply the visual representation and exploration of graph properties and extend them outside of expert circles (Pousman, Stasko & Mateas 2007). This proliferation of visual representations of networks through digital media shifts focus from the analytic capabilities of networks and raises questions about how such networks may be read narratively (Bounegru, Venturini, Gray & Jacomy 2016).

Can we think of the visual representations of networks as forms of digital storytelling (Couldry 2008; Seegel & Heer 2010)? Can we think of network analysis and visualization software packages such as Gephi, NodeXL and Pajek, as 'authoring systems' (Ryan 2005: 515), that hold specific affordances for the production of narratives and the construction of narrative meaning? And how might the narrative affordances of networks be relevant for those conducting research in an 'age of big data'? It is this storytelling potential of networks that will be the focus of this chapter, not because this narrative potential is more important than the mathematical affordances of networks, but because the latter have a long tradition while the former have only recently become the subject of academic reflection.

A scan of recent literature reveals – perhaps somewhat surprisingly – that 'networks' and 'narratives' have been brought together in recent research in information and communication technology and organization studies. Concepts such as 'narrative networks' and 'narrative network analysis' have been used to describe organizational forms, processes and routines that emerge around information technologies (Pentland & Feldman, 2007; Weeks 2014). Other recent literature that is closer to our line of enquiry in this chapter uses these concepts to describe the application of network analysis to the study of narrative texts. Such work typically aims to bring quantitative methodological approaches to bear on and contribute to narrative and social theory by applying network models and social network analysis to narrative texts (See e.g. Moretti 2011; Bearman & Stovel 2000; Sudhahar, De Fazio, Franzosi & Cristianini 2013).

However, a closer look at these latter studies shows that even when network analysis is applied to the study of narrative forms such as novels or films, the focus of such studies is on the mathematical properties of networks and how they can contribute to the formal or structural analysis of texts rather than on the narrative affordances of networks.

A good illustration of this point is provided by a series of papers that, in the last few years, have analysed the characters' networks in classic epics and, in particular, the *Iliad* (Rydberg-Cox 2011; Mac Carron & Kenna 2012; Miranda, Baptista & Pinto 2013; Kydros, Notopoulos & Exarchos 2015). While offering interesting insights into the formal characteristics of the epic genre, these papers seem to overlook the fact that, beside the structures of the societies they describe, these networks may also be read narratively. However, this privileging of particular styles of analysis of networks is not without good reason. While the mathematical analysis of networks has strong disciplinary roots (such as in graph theory or sociometry), to date the conceptualization of the network visual properties remains comparatively underdeveloped.

It is for this reason that, in this chapter, we will take a different approach. We will temporarily bracket the mathematical properties of networks and instead illustrate the narrative and storytelling potential of networks. We will do so through an examination of the *Iliad*'s network of characters. Much like the way in which a film or game adaptation of the *Iliad* would reconfigure or reassemble the story in accordance with the affordances and constraints specific to the medium, we are interested in exploring how network analysis as an authoring device organizes stories; how it reconfigures and reassembles basic elements of a narrative such as characters, plot, events, setting, temporality and causality; and by doing so how it mediates and structures the phenomena it represents. By this we do not claim network graphs to be narratives per se, but to have the potential of 'possessing narrativity'. The distinction between being a narrative and possessing narrativity is aptly described as follows: 'The property of "being" a narrative can be predicated on any semiotic object produced with the intent of evoking a narrative script in the mind of the audience. "Having narrativity," on the other hand, means being able to evoke such a script. In addition to life itself, pictures, music, or dance can have narrativity without being narratives in a literal sense' (Ryan 2004: 9).

Even though we illustrate our analysis on a literary text, our objective is not to use networks as analytical devices for the study of structural or formal properties of narrative texts. Rather, by taking inspiration from studies of the storytelling potential of data visualizations more generally (as for example in Segel & Heer 2010), we aim to explore the narrative affordances of visual representations of networks. Elsewhere we develop the link between the mathematical properties of networks and the stories they evoke through an analysis of the use of network graphs in a series of journalism projects (Bounegru, Venturini, Gray & Jacomy 2016).

We chose to illustrate the narrative affordances of networks through the *Iliad* because it is a well-known text, allowing the reader to intuitively grasp the stories told by the network, albeit different types of stories – which is partly the point of this chapter. The typology of 'network stories' that we illustrate, however, can be applied to the reading of (almost) any network. As we will try to show, these stories are rooted in the same local and global properties revealed by graph mathematics, only instead of calculating them with numbers, we will visualize them and tell them with words.

Three Perspectives on Networks and Six 'Network Stories'

In this section, we will examine three different ways to narrate a network, corresponding to three different perspectives that can be taken on them. Consider the case of a railway map, a kind of network that we are familiar with using, reading and dealing with. When looking at it, one can observe:

– The overall shape of the network – exploring, for example, which zones are denser in connections (indicating regional agglomerations) and which are sparser (indicating rural regions with few urban centres) and whether the transportation system is more developed in the north or the south, the east or the west.
– The specific situation of a given station – examining, for example, how some cities (the capitals maybe?) are better connected both in terms of the clusters of neighbourhoods around them and routes to further regions of the map.
– The connections between two stations or areas – trying, for example, to find the quickest route from the city where you are to the city that you would like to visit or, conversely, contemplating the possibility of going on a grand tour of the country.

In the next pages, we will exemplify these three perspectives – each translating into two different types of 'network stories' – in the case of the *Iliad*'s network of characters. Before we introduce our six types of 'network stories', however, we need to provide some information about the way in which our example network has been built. The protocol we used for the definition of the nodes and edges of the *Iliad* character graph is not particularly strict. This is because the focus of this chapter is not to contribute to the study of Homer epics, but to illustrate a series of techniques that can be used to narrate a network. Therefore, we contented ourselves with creating a node for all the entities performing one or more actions that influence the development of the story. We have been deliberately liberal in our definition of actors, in accordance with insights from Actor-Network Theory (see e.g. Latour 2005). Thus we have allowed the nodes of our network to represent not only mortals (e.g. Achilles) and divinities (e.g. Zeus), but also groups (e.g. the Myrmidons) and objects (e.g. the Golden Apple). Our definition of edges was equally supple: we connected two entities when the action of one influenced the action of another (e.g. Odysseus is connected to Achilles because if he had not unmasked him from his feminine disguise, the latter would have not joined the war).

Fig. 11.1:   Graph depicting the network of characters in the Iliad.

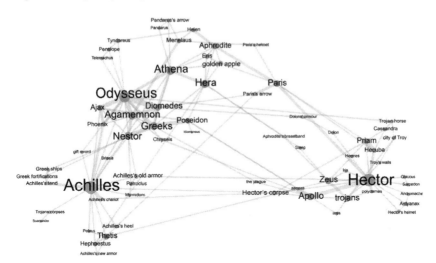

To visualize the network data thus obtained, we performed a number of operations that we will detail below using the network visualization software Gephi[1] (for more details, cf. Venturini, Jacomy and Carvalho Pereira 2015). The most important is the *force-vector spatialisation*. To place our nodes in the space, we used an algorithm that simulates a system of physical forces: nodes repulse each other, while edges act as springs attracting the nodes that they connect (on the specific algorithm we used, cf. Jacomy et al. 2014). Once the algorithm is launched it changes the distribution of nodes until reaching a balance of forces. Force-vector spatialisation minimises edge crossing and, most importantly, confers a meaning to the distribution of nodes in the space of the graph. At equilibrium, the geometrical distance between nodes becomes a proxy for their structural similarity: two nodes being closer the more directly or indirectly they are connected. Once the network was spatialised we gave nodes a size proportional to their degree, i.e. the number of edges adjacent to each node, and a colour corresponding to their nature (pink for humans, blue for gods and green for inanimate entities).

Knowing *Iliad*'s storyline, you can look at this network and recognize familiar elements in the graph (Figure 11.1). You may even discover things you ignored about the relations between characters. However, unless you are a network expert, you may not know the conditions under which your

1   Available at https://gephi.org.

observations are valid. This is not a problem in our case since our goal is to explore new narrative scenarios which may be used in the service of new modes of interpretation and inquiry. We would use different methods – such as statistical methods – to test and validate our hypotheses (cf. Tukey 1977). In this case our challenge is less to consolidate evidence, and more to organize disparate insights into a relevant whole. The six narrative views or reading paths we propose are strategies to achieve this coherence.

The Panorama > The Camps

The first family of narrative readings is called 'panorama' as it is meant to capture the global distribution of connectivity in the graph. In the two 'network stories' associated with it, 'the camps' and 'the (im-)balance of forces', we will not look at any individual nodes, but rather at the varying density of connections in the network. The first reading path, in particular, is intended to narrate the clusters of the network as camps of nodes that gather together in (relatively) tight communities. This view captures two opposing camps of characters, represented through two sets of node clusters separated by a structural hole (Burt 1995). Taking a bird's eye view, one notes the existence of two main regions in the *Iliad* graph, which unsurprisingly correspond to the two main armies deployed in the field (Figure 11.2). Network and cluster properties such as density, position and sub-clustering

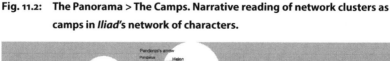

Fig. 11.2: The Panorama > The Camps. Narrative reading of network clusters as camps in *Iliad*'s network of characters.

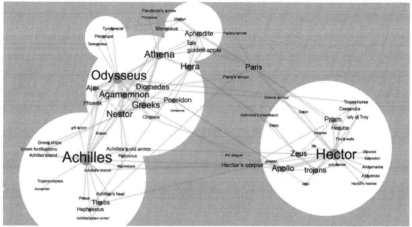

also evoke some of the qualities of these two groups of characters and their protagonists. The right side of the map is occupied by the Trojans mobilized around Prince Hector, King Priam and the city of Troy itself. It is a densely connected cluster showing no interior separations. On the other side of the graph, the Achaeans are, on the contrary, divided in two main sub-clusters: one gathering the main Greek warriors (Odysseus, Agamemnon, Diomedes, Nestor and Ajax) and the other occupied by Achilles and his cohort. As everyone knows, the *Iliad* narration begins by describing the rise of just such a division over a fight between Agamemnon and Achilles for the beautiful slave Briseis (notably positioned between the two factions) and its sore consequences for the Achaeans.

Two other smaller clusters are visible. They both correspond to characters that are relatively marginal in the narration of the *Iliad* itself, but that play a crucial role either before or after it. The first is located above the Greek heroes cluster and notably contains Aphrodite, Helen and the Golden Apple. This cluster is the principal cause of the war of Troy. Eris, goddess of Discord, offended for not having being invited to the wedding of Thetis and Peleus, throws a golden apple inscribed 'to the fairest' between Aphrodite, Athena and Hera. The three goddesses immediately start to quarrel over the apple and soon involve Paris (Prince of Troy and most handsome of the mortals) to judge their beauty. Paris gives the Apple to Aphrodite in exchange for the love of the prettiest woman in the world, the Spartan queen Helen. The Trojan War breaks out over the kidnapping of Helen and the will of Menelaus (Helen's husband) to defend his marriage. The other small cluster (on the top left) contains Odysseus' wife Penelope and son Telemachus who will play a crucial role in the narration of the Odyssey.

The Panorama > The Balance of Forces

The second type of 'panoramic' narrative reading addresses the balance (or imbalance) of the forces expressed in the network (Figure 11.3). To the description of the distribution of nodes and edges in clusters, it adds the discussion of the consequences that such distribution has on the phenomenon described by the graph, reading the nodes as weights and the edges as lines of force. The focus is less on how the network *is* and more on how it may *evolve*.

In our example, despite its duration and its convolution, the outcome of the war is never doubted in Homer's narration. Several prophecies have predicted the destruction of the city of Troy, as characters of both camps

Fig. 11.3: **The Panorama > The Balance of Forces. Narrative reading of cluster size and volume of nodes as imbalance of forces in *Iliad*'s network of characters.**

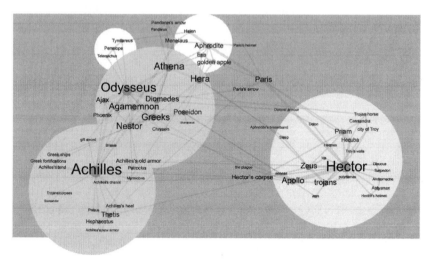

are often reminded. In Book 8, Zeus weighs the fate of the Trojans and the Achaeans on a divine scale and is forced to recognize that (despite his best wishes) Troy is bound to fall.

A similar imbalance of forces is clearly visible in the graph, as the size of the clusters corresponding to the two camps and their volume of nodes shows the Acheans are stronger and more numerous and it is only their division that prevents them from winning the struggle. The bigger size of the nodes of both the mortals and the gods playing in the Greek camp (confronted only by the greatness of Hector) indicates their higher degree of mobilization, suggesting that by uniting forces the Achaeans will have all the means to prevail.

The Vantage > The Crossroads

The second set of narrative views reads the location and size of nodes in order to highlight actors that occupy a vantage position in the network. The first such position is that of central nodes that, being highly connected, find themselves at the 'crossroads' of one or several regions of the graph (Figure 11.4).

In the Greek camp, the most central position is occupied by Odysseus, king of Ithaca. The importance of this character in the *Iliad* is well-known.

Fig. 11.4: **The Vantage > The Crossroads. Narrative reading of the location and size of nodes to identify characters at the crossroads of multiple regions of the *Iliad*'s network of characters.**

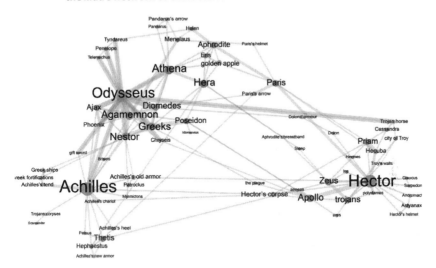

Though ruling over a small and not particularly rich island, Odysseus is by far the most ingenious of the Achaeans. His presence is felt in almost all books of the *Iliad*, not only fighting at the side of most other Greek heroes, but also through his constant work to keep the Greek army united. He repeatedly sermonizes the Greeks to renew their courage; he is the one who enrols Achilles in the war (with the ruse of the gift sword), the one who brings back Chryseis to her father and appeases the anger of Apollo, the preferred referent for Athena interventions; and, of course, the inventor of the stratagem of the wooden Horse which eventually wins Troy.

A similar role is played by Nestor, king of Pylos. Nestor is too old to fight directly, but, being the wisest of the Greeks, he counsels the other heroes. In particular, he is the one who persuades Patroclus to wear Achilles' armour to frighten the Trojans and push them back from the Achaeans' ships.

The Vantage > The Bridge

The second type of vantage position is subtler and characterizes nodes that, although located in a (relatively) marginal position, find themselves between two important and separated regions of the graph. Often located in one of the structural holes of the network, such nodes work as bridges connecting two or more clusters (and sometime serve as the point of passage between them).

In our example, this position is notably occupied by Paris (Figure 11.5). Paris is not nearly as central to the Trojan camp as Odysseus is to the Greeks. In fact, he is located outside that cluster, somewhere in between the cluster of the Trojans and the cluster of Aphrodite and Helen. This position corresponds perfectly to the role of the young prince who fails repeatedly to support the cause of his city – most notoriously in Book 3 when he loses the duel with Menelaus and is saved only by the intervention of Aphrodite who teleports him into Helen's bed. This does not mean, however, that Paris does not have a crucial role in the *Iliad*. On the contrary: by separating Helen from Sparta and associating her with Troy he sets the story into motion by connecting the otherwise separated peoples of the Achaeans and the Trojans.

It is interesting to notice that this capacity to connect different regions of the narration is represented by Paris' ability in archery. The only real feat accomplished by the Trojan prince is to put an arrow (which is the closest node to him) through Achilles's vulnerable heel, thereby depriving the Greeks of their champion.

Fig. 11.5:   The Vantage > The Bridge. Narrative reading of the location and size of nodes to identify characters that occupy 'bridge' positions in the *Iliad*'s network of characters.

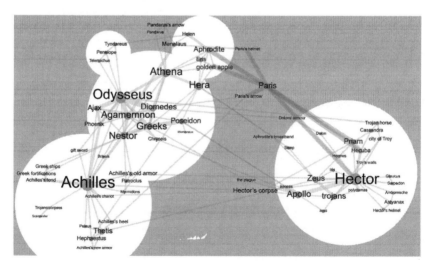

The Journey > The Shortcut

The third and final set of network views pertains to the paths between nodes. Conceptualized as journeys through the graph, these narrative reading paths do not describe the structure of the network but the movements that can be made through it. The first story of this kind is directly related to the peculiar topology of graphs. Although networks can be read to a certain extent as geographic charts, their topology is utterly different. Because of force-vector spatialisation, the spatial distance separating two nodes is not correlated to the length of the travel from one to the other but rather to the number of neighbours that they have in common. This means that distant regions of the network may sometime be connected by unexpected shortcuts. This phenomenon is the source of many surprising findings in graph topologies. The best example of such 'short paths' is provided by one of the most famous paintings by network artist Mark Lombardi, 'George W. Bush, Harken Energy, Jackson Stephens. c. 1979-1990', where the painter shows how unexpectedly connected the Bush and Bin Laden families are due to the entanglement of their respective economic interests.

In our example, we can observe that while occupying two of the furthest and most distanced positions in the graph, Achilles and Hector are more directly connected than one would expect (Figure 11.6). Although

Fig. 11.6:   **The Journey > The Shortcut. Narrative reading of paths that cut across the network as relationships between otherwise distant characters in *Iliad*'s network of characters.**

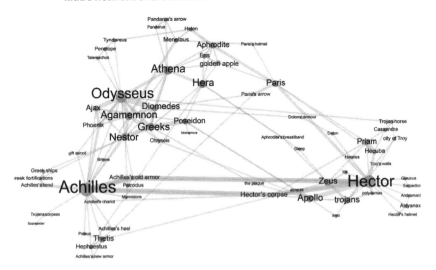

the opposition between them configures the *Iliad* graph digging a large structural hole between them, the two protagonists of the story are also connected by two two-step paths passing through Achilles' armour and Hector's corpse. Both these nodes have an important role in the ecology of the story: it is because Hector wears the spoils of Achilles that the Greek knows through which weak point to stab the Trojan and the *Iliad*'s last two books revolve around the difficulty of persuading Achilles to release Hector's body for proper burial. The symbolic symmetry of these two paths is also remarkable as both the armour and the corpse represent the separation between the heroes' spirit and their mortal remains.

The Journey > The Grand Tour

A second type of graph journey can be construed by following the sequence of creation of the edges between nodes and thereby reconstructing the chronological plot of the network. In this case, the focus is not on the edges that can cut across the network and shorten its diameter, but on patiently following the largest tour of its perimeter.

Reading our example graph (Figure 11.7) from top to bottom (and colouring the nodes with an increasingly saturated shade of red), we set off from Eris' Golden Apple arousing Aphrodite's yearning. Aphrodite persuades

Fig. 11.7:   The Journey > The Grand Tour. Narrative reading of the story timeline by 'taking a tour' of the perimeter of *Iliad*'s network of characters.

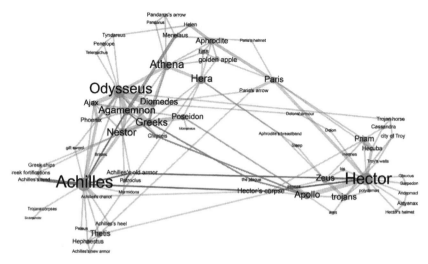

Paris to call her 'the fairest of goddesses' (over Athena and Hera) and in exchange helps the young prince to abduct the queen of Sparta and bring her to Troy.

The kidnapping of Helen pushes her husband Menelaus to ask his brother Agamemnon, king of Argos, for help. Agamemnon calls upon the other kings of Greece and convinces them to bring war upon Troy. Nine years after the beginning of the siege, the Greeks ransack Chryse (a town allied with Troy) and enslave its residents who implore Apollo to send a plague on the Achaeans. To appease Apollo, Agamemnon agrees to return Chryses but in exchange takes Briseis, one of Achilles' slaves. Insulted by this action, Achilles withdraws from the fight and retires to his tent.

After several reversals, the war seems to turn in the Trojans' favour and Achilles is implored by his friend Patroclus to lend him his armour. Disguised as Achilles, Patroclus enters the fight and succeeds in pushing the Achaeans back. He is, however, killed by Hector, prince and champion of the Trojans, who then takes Achilles' armour. Mad with grief for the loss of his friends, Achilles re-enters the fight and ends up killing Hector, thereby definitively tipping the scale against the Trojans.

Conclusion

This chapter has illustrated how narrative meaning can be construed from visual properties of network graphs such as topology, density of connections, absence of connections, size, position and colour of nodes. While the narration of networks is as old as social network analysis (cf. Moreno 1934 for some beautiful examples), such techniques have so far been taken for granted. By exploring six narrative readings evoked by the visual properties of the *Iliad*'s network of characters, we hope to have made a modest contribution towards explicating and formalizing them. The six network narrative views we introduced ('The Camps', 'The Balance of Forces', 'The Crossroads', 'The Bridge', 'The Shortcut', and 'The Grand Tour') should not be considered exclusive or exhaustive. They can be mixed and matched at one's pleasure, and can be complemented by other narrative strategies that we have not yet acknowledged.

Why should the narrative affordances of networks be of interest to media scholars? As powerful and indispensable as they are, we do not believe that the mathematical uses of networks exemplified by graph theory are in themselves sufficient for describing relational phenomena, nor do they fully account for the ways in which networks can be used to organize human attention by bringing certain elements into the foreground and allowing others to recede into the background. No matter how many metrics they compute, network analysts will always have to provide some description of their objects. And this is all the more true for the humanities and social sciences, for which textual narration remains the main argumentative tool.

For this reason, the approaches that we outline above do not attempt to produce new knowledge about the literary text and advance the understanding of Homer's epic, nor to innovate the methods of graph analysis. In reading the graph of the *Iliad*'s characters, we restricted ourselves to using our lay knowledge of the *Iliad*'s plot, deliberately restraining from original interpretations or innovative findings. We leave the task of using networks to investigate narration to another equally interesting but somewhat symmetric area of research (cf. Franzosi 2004; Moretti 2015).

Our interest in this chapter was in how narration can help to convey findings about networks. In doing so we have, more modestly, tried to fill a gap in the toolkit for scholars working with networks, a gap that does not concern the analytical capacities of networks, but rather the construction of meaning from the results of such analyses. Common metaphors that compare network visualizations to 'hairballs' or 'bowls of spaghetti' may be considered to point to this gap. Over the many years in which statistics has been employed in journalism, sociology, policy and advocacy, we have developed a literacy around its visual representations (such as charts and tables) and an ability to read them narratively. Similarly, in order for networks to become powerful knowledge instruments, we now need to advance not just their formal analytical and computational affordances but also their narrative ones. It is the latter that this paper has tried to contribute to through the development of six narrative views or readings of networks.

References

Bearman, Peter S. & Katherine Stovel. 2000. "Becoming a Nazi: A model for narrative networks." *Poetics* 27, no. 2: 69-90.

Bounegru, Liliana, Tommaso Venturini, Jonathan Gray & Mathieu Jacomy. 2016. "Narrating Networks: Exploring the Affordances of Networks as Storytelling Devices in Journalism." *Digital Journalism.* pp. 1-32.

Brandes, Ulrik, Stephen P. Borgatti & Linton C. Freeman. 2016. "Maintaining the duality of closeness and betweenness centrality." *Social Networks* 44: 153-159.

Burt, Ronald S. 1995. *Structural Holes: The Social Structure of Competition.* Cambridge, MA: Harvard University Press.

Couldry, Nick. 2008. "Mediatization or mediation? Alternative understandings of the emergent space of digital storytelling." *New Media & Society* 10 (3): 373-391.

Franzosi, Roberto. 2004. *From Words to Numbers: Narrative, Data, and Social Science (Structural Analysis in the Social Sciences)*. Cambridge: Cambridge University Press.

Jacomy, Mathieu, Tommaso Venturini, Sebastien Heymann & Mathieu Bastian. 2014. "ForceAtlas2, a continuous graph layout algorithm for handy network visualization designed for the Gephi software." *PLoS one* 9, no. 6: e98679.

Kydros, Dimitrios, Panagiotis Notopoulos & Georgios Exarchos. 2015. "Homer's Iliad – A Social Network Analytic Approach." *International Journal of Humanities and Arts Computing* 9 (1): 115-132.

Latour, Bruno. 2005. *Reassembling the Social*. Oxford: Oxford University Press.

Mac Carron, Pádraig & Ralph Kenna. 2012. "Universal properties of mythological networks." *EPL (Europhysics Letters)* 99 (2): 28002.

Miranda, Pedro J., Murilo S. Baptista & Sandro E. de S. Pinto. 2013. "Analysis of communities in a mythological social network." *arXiv preprint arXiv:1306.2537*.

Moreno, Jacob Levy. 1934. "Who shall survive? A new approach to the problem of human interrelations."

Moretti, Franco. 2005. *Graphs, Maps, Trees: Abstract Models for a Literary History*. London: Verso.

—. 2011. "Network Theory, Plot Analysis." Pamphlet 2. Stanford Literary Lab.

Newman, Mark. 2010. *Networks: An Introduction*. Oxford: Oxford University Press.

Pentland, Brian T. & Martha S. Feldman. 2007. "Narrative networks: Patterns of technology and organization." *Organization Science* 18 (5): 781-795.

Pousman, Zachary, John Stasko & Michael Mateas. 2007. "Casual information visualization: Depictions of data in everyday life." *IEEE transactions on visualization and computer graphics* 13 (6): 1145-1152.

Rieder, Bernhard. 2012. "What is in PageRank? A Historical and Conceptual Investigation of a Recursive Status Index. Computational Culture." http://computationalculture.net/article/what_is_in_pagerank.

Ryan, Marie-Laure. 2004. "Introduction." In *Narrative Across Media: The Languages of Storytelling*, ed. Marie-Laure Ryan. Lincoln and London: University of Nebraska Press.

—. 2005. "Narrative and Digitality: Learning to Think with the Medium." In *A Companion to Narrative Theory*, ed. James Phelan and Peter J. Rabinowitz, 515-528. Oxford: Blackwell.

Rydberg-Cox, Jeff. 2011. "Social networks and the language of Greek tragedy." *Journal of the Chicago Colloquium on Digital Humanities and Computer Science* 1 (3).

Segel, Edward & Jeffrey Heer. 2010. "Narrative visualization: Telling stories with data." *IEEE transactions on visualization and computer graphics* 16 (6): 1139-1148.

Sudhahar, Saatviga, Gianluca De Fazio, Roberto Franzosi & Nello Cristianini. 2015. "Network analysis of narrative content in large corpora." *Natural Language Engineering* 21 (01): 81-112.

Tukey, John. 1977. *Exploratory data analysis*. Reading, MA: Addison-Wesley Pub.

Venturini, Tommaso, Mathieu Jacomy & D. Carvalho Pereira. 2015. "Visual Network Analysis." Sciences Po médialab working papers (www.medialab.sciences-po.fr/publications/visual-network-analysis). Paris.

Weeks, Michael R. 2014. "Toward an Understanding of Online Community Participation through Narrative Network Analysis." In *Cyber Behaviour: Concepts, Methodologies, Tools, and Applications*. Hershey: Information Science Reference.

12. Towards a Reflexive Digital Data Analysis

Karin van Es, Nicolás López Coombs & Thomas Boeschoten

Introduction

As mentioned in the introduction to this book, in April 2010 flights across Europe were grounded due to the prospect of an enormous spreading ash cloud caused by the eruption of the Icelandic volcano Eyjafjallajökull. Computer simulations depicted how the volcanic ash would likely disperse. The mathematical models used in these simulations, however, were not supplemented with actual samples of the ash concentrations in the region. The EU administration received widespread criticism for their blind trust in the images produced by the simulations, which not only lacked empirical validation but were based on controversial mathematical models (Gelernter 2010; Schäfer & Kessler 2013).

Although data analysis is hardly a novel practice, the amount of data available to us has drastically increased in recent years. This explosion of data has provided researchers with exciting resources to explore social practices and relationships and has made new approaches to cultural analysis possible (Berry 2011: 1). The current wealth of data can tempt the humanities researcher to adopt new forms of empiricism. However, data are not natural phenomena, but always exist within a particular social context. It is all too easy to lose sight of the fact that 'all data provide oligoptic views of the world: views from certain vantage points, using particular tools, rather than an all-seeing, infallible God's eye view' (Kitchin 2014b: 4). When it comes to sifting and analysing this data, a critical attitude is therefore necessary. Scholars, indeed required by our datafied society to develop new literacies and competencies (see Uricchio in this volume; Rieder & Röhle in this volume and Montfort 2016), can also rely on the skills they already possess. Trained in critical inquiry, they are particularly well equipped, we would suggest, to consider the ways that data are 'cooked' (Bowker 2013). By raising questions at the various stages of digital data research, this chapter brings into focus how researchers and their tools shape data. In so doing it advocates for a reflexive form of data analysis and data visualization that can serve as a critical intervention to dispel the blind optimism and faith in the objective quantification of human behaviour and sociality through

Big Data (Van Dijck 2014). We seek to expose the limitations and biases of contemporary data analysis, which can result in rash, consequential and regrettable decision-making, as was the case with the Eyjafjallajökull ash cloud.

We begin with a brief review of two misconceptions concerning Big Data research that need to be addressed, since they conceal implicit choices made prior to starting research. We then consider questions that correspond to each phase of data analysis. These by no means exhaustive explorations represent an initial attempt to outline a reflexive, transparent procedure to guide digital data research. We recognize that the publication space for documenting methodologies is limited (Bruns 2013) and that choices need to be made in what to communicate to others. This does not, however, alleviate scholars from the obligation to consider and document their decision-making process. Although we draw primarily from our own experience of working with social media data, the reflections provoked by these questions are fruitful for data analysis more generally.

Two main misconceptions

Among the many misconceptions about Big Data (see, for example, boyd & Crawford 2013), there are two widespread assumptions that are arguably the most crucial to correct before embarking on data-driven research, as their implicit choices have serious consequences for the subsequent research process.

First, Big Data is presumed to have the inherent 'authority' to speak for itself – as when Chris Anderson (2008) notoriously declared that the current deluge of data has rendered the scientific method obsolete. Scholars such as Rob Kitchin (2014b) and Nick Couldry (2016) have criticized the idea that knowledge production is free from theory or human bias and interpretation. Kate Crawford concurs: 'Data and data sets are not objective; they are creations of human design. We give numbers their voice, draw inferences from them, and define their meaning through our interpretations. Hidden biases in both the collection and analysis stages present considerable risks' (2013: para. 2). We can add that algorithmic tools are, by nature, opaque to most researchers (see Paßmann & Boersma in this volume).

Because data are not natural resources existing *a priori* to be extracted, but rather cultural entities that are co-produced (Vis 2013), both Johanna

Drucker (2011) and Kitchin (2014a) make the distinction between *data* ('given' in Latin) and *capta* ('taken'), each preferring the latter term. Whichever term is used, data/capta are selected and shaped by humans and their technologies. We intend to reflect on this process through the questions we raise in this chapter.

Second, there is the common misconception that digital data analysis involves amassing large amounts of data and using calculations to detect underlying patterns. This view ties in with, or derives from, two other mistaken assumptions: that all data analysis is quantitative, and that any analysis involving calculations seeks solely to establish patterns. As in other academic fields, scholars within media studies use different methods to answer different types of research questions. Such an approach also applies (or should apply) when data are involved. Some researchers aim simply to ascertain how often something has happened (e.g. how often certain words are used); others, however, seek to discover *how* or *why* it has happened – requiring, in the latter case, a qualitative approach (Crawford 2013: para. 7). This observation is particularly relevant for the humanities. As Kitchin argues, quantitative approaches, while useful 'in regards to explaining and modelling instrumental systems', are limited when it comes to trying to understand human life (2014a: 145).

In the humanities, data analysis often combines quantitative and qualitative approaches. For example, Lev Manovich (2012), referring to Franco Moretti's notion of 'distant reading',[1] sees more benefit in an oscillation between the two than in simply sticking to one of these orientations. Likewise, Burdick et al. (2012) propose a digital humanities practice in which 'toggling' between both perspectives (and their attendant methods) would become the norm (30). However, we should not forget that even research that relies heavily on computational tools for the calculation of large amounts of data and the visualization of patterns still requires the researcher to interpret these patterns. As Manovich observes, '[w]hile computer-assisted examination of massive cultural data sets typically reveals new patterns in this data [...] a human is still needed to make sense of these patterns' (2012: 468–69). Making sense of such patterns, Kitchin stresses, 'requires social [or, we might add, cultural] theory and deep contextual knowledge' (2014: 144).

---

[1] The identification of large-scale trends, patterns and relationships in large numbers of literary texts, as opposed to the 'close reading' of individual texts, a common endeavour in literary studies.

Doing Digital Data Analysis

Because digital data analysis involves many possible methods, each of which functions best in conjunction with a theoretical framework that invests the collected data with meaning, one must carefully reflect on the procedures for working with data. The following section discusses how to work with data in a reflexive fashion – that is, in which researchers consider their own role in the construction of the data. Moreover, this approach entails that researchers take responsibility to discern how the given tools work with and shape the data. To fully adopt such a reflexive approach, researchers must consider important questions that relate to each of the three stages of digital data analysis: acquiring, cleaning and analysing. These phases, inspired by the seven stages of visualization (acquiring, parsing, filtering, mining, representing, refining and interacting) that Ben Fry (2007) explores in *Visualizing Data*, are meant to elicit a critical review of the data-making process. The researcher should be able to answer each of the questions and consider which ones to highlight in the analysis; communicating these questions to others helps keep the research process transparent. The answers need not necessarily be addressed at length in the final research product; they can often be referenced as footnotes, summarized in an attachment or, in the case of visualizations, supplied via explanatory captions.

1.   Acquiring: Selecting Sources and Obtaining Data

No matter what the goal of the analysis, the researcher must identify and gather the relevant data at an early stage in the process in order to answer the research question. In digital data analysis there are four principal ways to acquire such data sets. First, researchers can create their own data – through surveys and interviews, the counting of phenomena, or the tracking of uses and practices (for example, by using A/B testing or analytics software). Second, they can download (open) data made available by governments or institutions such as WikiLeaks or the Pew Research Center. Third, they can extract data from the application programming interfaces (APIs) of popular platforms such as Google Maps, Twitter and Flickr through the writing of code or the use of readymade data extraction applications that enable researchers to retrieve data from the company's database in standard file formats. Finally, they can purchase access to data through social media API aggregation companies such as Gnip, Topsy and

DataSift. However, researchers should be aware that the existence of such commercial resellers limits free access to social media data (Manovich 2012). Indeed, each form of data gathering carries its own limitations and biases. APIs, for instance, not only provide data but are themselves 'data makers' as well: they construct and provide access to certain (meta)data (Vis 2013). This raises further questions about the reliability and validity of the data, as well as how representative it is (see Cornelius Puschmann and Julian Ausserhofer in this volume). Moreover, biases already exist in data sets in that data collection privileges certain social groups (see Leurs and Shepherd in this volume).

Although online data are readily available, such accessibility does not necessarily mean that it is ethical for researchers to use them (boyd & Crawford 2013; Zimmer 2010). Despite such data being 'public', people have expectations as to how this information will be presented and employed (see Markham & Buchanan 2012). Undertaking large-scale online research thus prompts a series of ethical questions. As a result of the significant changes in the scale and scope of data, traditional ethical guidelines relating to 'informed consent' and privacy, as well as the definition of 'human subjects' and the concept of 'harm' in relation to participants, need to be revisited (see Van Schie, Westra & Schäfer in this volume). Prior to embarking on any research project, one must consider research ethics (Markham & Buchanan discuss guidelines in their contribution to this volume) and assess *who* is doing the asking – and how that shapes research outcomes.

The researcher's first challenge is to define the research data. This process should be guided by theory, a research question or preliminary explorations. Note here that not all research requires 'big' data, and in some cases 'small data' (e.g. a focus on a single individual) can be more productive (boyd & Crawford 2013: 670). Small data afford different kinds of questions and methods than Big Data, and therefore yield different kinds of knowledge. The type of data collected depends on the research question (although the first analysis of a data set can also lead to the formulation of a research question). When acquiring data for research, whether big or small, the following questions should be considered:

– What ethical considerations have been taken into account when collecting the research data?
– What kind of data is being used?
– How was the data collected? Which tools or software were used, or who supplied the data?

–   Which criteria were used to select the data set? Who is included or excluded from the data set?
–   What are the limitations of these data-gathering methods? How reliable is the method of data collection?
–   What metadata does the data set contain (for example, location, time, date of a tweet)?
–   When combining data sets, what biases might result from the different contexts in which the data originated?

2.   Cleaning: Parsing and Filtering Data

After reflecting on how the data was retrieved, the researcher needs to explain the decisions made to prepare for subsequent analysis, which also involves removing certain data from the data set. This part of the process concerns how the data has been organized into categories and which data has been retained. Researchers may find that a single data set is not sufficient to realize their objectives. This problem can often be addressed by combining data sets or enriching the data. One may include answers to the following questions in the analysis:

–   What categories are used to organize the data?
–   What do the categories assume about the meaning of the data to be measured and/or calculated?
–   How has irrelevant data (that is, spam or 'noise') been dealt with?
–   What is the 'quality' of the data (for example, were some data wrongly formatted and did they have to be restored)?
–   How has the data(set) been enriched? For what purposes?

Here, it is important to recognize that when we organize data into categories (according to population, gender, nation, etc.), these categories tend to be treated as if they were discrete and fixed, when in fact they are interpretive expressions (Drucker 2011).

3.   Analysing: Mining, Representing and Refining Data

To understand the data and discern underlying patterns, researchers will often use statistical and data-mining methods (Fry 2007: 5). Digital data analysis requires a basic knowledge of math and statistics (that is, sampling and calculating mode/mean/median), so that researchers can assess whether patterns in the data are the result of chance and determine what biases are at play. Moreover, when studying social networks, one should also be aware that 'the degree distribution typically follows a power law distribution, i.e. most people have a few friends, while few people have [a great] many friends' (Tang et al. 2012: 5). In such instances it is futile to discuss averages.

Prior to finding correlations and making statistical claims, researchers should provide for the reader an assessment of the value and meaning of the metrics they are using. For example, in working with information gleaned from social media, it is generally taken for granted that 'shares', 'likes', 'follows' and 'retweets' are salient research material, although the *meaning* of each online gesture is not self-evident. Although it is easy to figure out which users have been retweeted most often, it is not clear what this means (why people have retweeted others' tweets); to discover the answer requires different, qualitative methods. The prestructured actions one finds on social media are not always similar and comparable (see the interview with Carolin Gerlitz in this volume). To put it simply, not all 'likes' are created equal.

Although large data sets are useful for detecting patterns and connections, Big Data research risks having its practitioners see correlations everywhere (Marcus & Davis 2014). The opposite of abductive reasoning, this tendency is called 'apophenia', defined by Dan Dixon as 'pattern recognition gone wrong, seeing only the pattern expected, no matter what data leads to it' (2012: 202). It is a particular pitfall in Big Data research since not all patterns and relationships found in the data are meaningful or truthful (Kitchin 2014: 13). We should recall here the commonplace of statistics that 'correlation does not imply causation' and the fallacy that data is self-evident.

In addition to statistical methods, there are numerous ways to visualize data and many tools for doing so. Visualizations 'may be used as analytical and interpretive tools – to reveal patterns or anomalies or concurrences – or they may be produced to illustrate findings or serve as the distillation of an argument' (Burdick et al. 2012: 43). They can also be used to tell stories in new ways, emphasizing different relations (see Venturini et al. in this volume). Instruments of visualization range from easy-to-use tools that provide WYSIWYG (what you see is what you get) interfaces for data taken directly from cloud services, databases, APIs (social-media-metrics providers such as Buzzcapture, Salesforce, OBI4wan, etc.) or imported spreadsheets such as Tableau and Gephi, to more sophisticated means that require programming (for example, R and D3) or designing in programs such as Illustrator.

Although each tool raises its own specific questions, the following will apply in most instances:
– How was the data prepared and combined for visualization (by filtering, transforming, calculating and enriching)?
– What purpose does the visualization serve?
– Why has this type of visualization been selected?
– How have the colours, sizes and shapes in the visualization been determined?
– What software has been used and why? What computational methods does the research employ?
– Which settings and algorithms were applied?
– How have the decisions related to the above-mentioned questions highlighted or downplayed aspects of the underlying data set?

Each graph and illustration should be provided with a number and a description, and in the analysis itself, it is important to differentiate between description (for example, an explanation of the content, type of graph, sample size, etc.) and the interpretation of what is shown.

Conclusions

The Icelandic ash cloud debacle caused cancellations of some 100,000 flights, stranded 10 million people and collectively cost airlines and airports over 2 billion dollars (*The Telegraph* 2011). For many EU citizens, it was also their most memorable exposure to data research, understandably triggering academic criticism over the objective appearance of the visuals (Schäfer & Kessler 2013). To overcome this significant blot on the field of digital data analysis, we need to engage critically and transparently with data. It is crucial for researchers to reveal how they and the tools they use have shaped their research, and how the data they employ has been influenced by the platforms they originated on. When undertaking data analysis, therefore, the researcher must reflect on the following considerations:
– where the data came from;
– who produced the data and for what purposes;
– what data are selected and how they relate to the larger data set;
– which tools were used for collection and analysis;
– why certain data and metrics were used for the research.

These considerations are mirrored in the more detailed questions relating to the phases of the research process; they can help create awareness of the choices made by researchers during their research and debunk the common misconception that data and data visualizations are neutral and objective. They represent a first attempt to cast light on the inner workings of Big Data research and join the plea that we as researchers have to be more transparent in our procedures in working with data. For consumers of data, these efforts will hopefully contribute to an increased awareness of the stages involved in the production of data and the adoption of a critical stance towards the data they interpret and make sense of. As we come to live in an increasingly datafied society, these aims seem more relevant than ever.

Acknowledgments

The authors would like to thank Eef Masson, Fernando van der Vlist and Mirko Tobias Schäfer for their critical remarks and suggestions to earlier drafts of this article.

References

Anderson, Chris. 2008. "The End of Theory: The Data Deluge Makes the Scientific Method Obsolete." www.wired.com/2008/06/pb-theory/.

Berry, David M. 2011. "The Computational Turn: Thinking About the Digital Humanities." *Culture Machine* 12: 1–22. www.culturemachine.net/index.php/cm/article/viewArticle/440.

Bowker, Geoffrey C. 2013. "Data Flakes: An Afterword to *'Raw Data' Is an Oxymoron*." In Lisa Gitelman, ed., *"Raw Data" Is an Oxymoron*. Cambridge, MA: The MIT Press, 167–72.

boyd, danah, & Crawford, Kate. 2012. "Critical Questions for Big Data: Provocations for a Cultural, Technological, And Scholarly Phenomenon." *Information, Communication & Society* 15 (5): 662-679.

Bruns, Axel. 2013. "Faster Than The Speed of Print: Reconciling 'Big Data' Social Media Analysis and Academic Scholarship." *First Monday* 18 (10). http://firstmonday.org/ojs/index.php/fm/article/view/4879/3756.

Burdick, Anne, Johanna Drucker, Peter Lunenfeld, Todd Presner & Jeffrey Schnapp. 2012. *Digital_Humanities*. Cambridge, MA: The MIT Press.

Couldry, Nick. 2014. "Inaugural: A Necessary Disenchantment: Myth, Agency and Injustice in a Digital World." *Sociological Review* 62 (4): 880–97.

Crawford, Kate. 2013. "The Hidden Biases in Big Data." *HBR Blog Network*, 1. https://hbr.org/2013/04/the-hidden-biases-in-big-data/.

Dijck, José van. 2014. "Datafication, Dataism and Dataveillance: Big Data Between Scientific Paradigm and Ideology." *Surveillance & Society* 12 (2): 197–208.

Dixon, Dan. 2012. "Analysis Tool or Research Methodology: Is There an Epistemology for Patterns?" In *Understanding Digital Humanities*, ed. David M. Berry. New York: Palgrave Macmillan, 191–209.

Drucker, Johanna. 2011. "Humanities Approaches to Graphical Display." *Digital Humanities Quarterly* 5 (1): 1–21. www.digitalhumanities.org/dhq/vol/5/1/000091/000091.html.

Fry, Ben. 2007. "The Seven Stages of Visualizing Data." In *Visualizing Data*. Sebastapol, CA: O'Reilly Media, 1–18.

Gelernter, David. 2010. "Gefahren der Softwaregläubigkeit: Die Aschewolke aus Antiwissen." *Frankfurter Allgemeine Zeitung*, April 26. www.faz.net/aktuell/feuilleton/debatten/digitales-denken/gefahren-der-softwareglaeubigkeit-die-aschewolke-aus-antiwissen-1606375.html.

Kitchin, Rob. 2014a. *The Data Revolution: Big Data, Open Data, Data Infrastructures and Their Consequences*. London: Sage.

—. 2014b. "Big Data, New Epistemologies and Paradigm Shifts." *Big Data & Society* 1 (1): n.p.

Manovich, Lev. 2012. "Trending: The Promises and the Challenges of Big Social Data." In M.K. Gold, ed., *Debates in the Digital Humanities*. Minneapolis: University of Minnesota Press, 460–75.

Marcus, Gary & Ernest Davis. 2014. "Eight (No, Nine!) Problems with Big Data." *New York Times*, April 6, Op-Ed pages. www.nytimes.com/2014/04/07/opinion/eight-no-nine-problems-with-big-data.html?_r=1.

Markham, Annette & Elizabeth Buchanan. 2012. "Ethical Decision-making and Internet Research 2.0: Recommendations from the Association of Internet Researchers Ethics working committee." (Downloaded from http://aoir.org/reports/ethics2.pdf).

Schäfer, Mirko Tobias & Frank Kessler. 2013. "Trust in Technical Images." *Mtschaefer.net*. http://mtschaefer.net/entry/trust-technical-images/.

Tang, Jiliang, Xufei Wang & Huan Liu. 2012. "Integrating Social Media Data for Community Detection." In Martin Atzmueller, Alvin Chin, Denis Helic & Andreas Hotho (eds.), *Modelling and Mining Ubiquitous Social Media*. Berlin: Springer, 1–20.

The Telegraph. 2011. "How the 2010 Ash Cloud Caused Chaos: Facts and Figures," 24 May, sec. Finance. www.telegraph.co.uk/finance/newsbysector/transport/8531152/How-the-2010-ash-cloud-caused-chaos-facts-and-figures.html.

Vis, Farida. 2013. "A Critical Reflection on Big Data: Considering APIs, Researchers and Tools as Data Makers." *First Monday* 18 (10). http://firstmonday.org/ojs/index.php/fm/article/view/4878/3755.

Zimmer, Michael. 2010. "'But the Data Is Already Public': On the Ethics of Research in Facebook." *Ethics and Information Technology* 12 (4): 312–25.

Section 3
Research Ethics

13. Get Your Hands Dirty

Emerging Data Practices as Challenge for Research Integrity

Gerwin van Schie, Irene Westra & Mirko Tobias Schäfer

Introduction

In November 2014 two interns (the first two authors of this chapter listed above) at the Utrecht Data School started investigating an online discussion forum for patients under the supervision of Mirko Tobias Schäfer (this essay's third author). Without his knowledge and without any prior knowledge of scraping websites, the two students downloaded 150,000 patient profiles (which included, amongst other information, age, location, diagnoses and treatments related to these patients), using a (90-euro) off-the-shelf scraper tool[1], without informing these patients or requesting consent from them or the platform providers. The plan to first explore the data (taking the necessary precautions to keep the data confidential) and later, after formulating a research question and hypothesis, to ask permission to conduct in-depth analysis of data relevant for our research, was never realized. After a few days of acting like 'information flâneurs' (Dörk et al. 2011), browsing through the data without specific questions or goals in mind, we were notified that our department's supervisors had terminated the project due to concerns about research ethics.[2] Their decision prompted us to rethink our actions and to question our research practices as well as existing research standards. Assuming that the rather novel data sources and practices of analysis were disrupting the traditional research process and contradicting established guidelines in research ethics, we found that these events provided the inspiration to revisit research ethics concerning big data research.

---

1   Outwit Hub, www.outwit.com/products/hub/.

2   After learning about the data scraping, the project supervisor (Mirko Tobias Schäfer) immediately reported the project to the director of the research school who informed the vice dean of research and the ethics committee. While the decision was pending all data were stored in a secured environment and access was limited to the investigators and documented accordingly. After the board's decision to terminate the project the data were securely deleted. It must be emphasized that the students' activities – despite being disputable – were considered legal as the information was openly available.

Although the forum we investigated was not technically a social network site (SNS), we think that the issues we will discuss in this chapter are very similar to the ethical issues relevant to the investigation of SNSs. The characteristics of available (big) data sets and emerging data practices do not always afford a practice that complies with traditional standards of research integrity. Such standards were very much informed by events marked by severe human rights violations and scholarly misconduct. They responded to incidents in which the lives of 'human subjects' were harmed. Although current research practices do not necessarily cause physical pain, they may violate personal integrity and fail to meet privacy standards by accidentally revealing someone's personal identity or sensitive information about individuals who are part of the sample. When investigating a Web forum for patients afflicted with a specific disease, the authors of this chapter experienced the various promises and pitfalls of digital methods. Drawing from this experience, we reviewed existing standards of scholarly research practice, focusing particularly on media studies. This chapter revisits the formative guidelines that provided the historical basis for current ethical research guidelines, including the Nuremberg Code (1947), the Declaration of Helsinki (World Medical Association 2013) and the Universal Declaration on Bioethics and Human Rights (UNESCO 2006). We will argue that the existing ethical guidelines are relics of discourses and eras that have very little to do with Big data research as it is now conducted. In addition, referring to a case study that describes our own experiences, we will explain how big data research on social networking sites makes the concept of informed consent, a basic principle of all current guidelines, practically infeasible. Building on the guidelines that have been written for internet researchers (Markham & Buchanan 2012), we will conclude with a proposal for a research structure consisting of three stages, each with its own ethical considerations: design, safe data exploration and data analysis.

Big Data and the Humanities

Under the label 'digital humanities', several novel research practices have been developed within social research and media and cultural studies (e.g. Berry 2012; Burdick et al. 2012). For a long time these domains have been strongholds of qualitative research, participatory observation and hermeneutic approaches to textual analysis. Now, new data-driven and computer-aided methods have stirred up dust within departments that had seldom been compelled to question their professional standards of conduct. The rapidly changing situation is now marked by unprecedented access to vast data resources and innovative tools to collect and connect large numbers of data points. As a result, some of these digital humanities projects require skilful interdisciplinary cooperation. Researchers even seek out collaborations with programmers, entrepreneurs, corporations and organizations who contribute technology support, data collection, data hosting or other services. On the other hand, as in our case study, there are now tools that allow researchers with relatively limited technical skills to adopt some of the new practices. Additionally, researchers and their academic institutions have become concerned with the data samples and the practices of investigating the data (Rieder & Röhle 2012). The so-called T3 study (Lewis et al. 2008) and the more recent Facebook study (Bond et al. 2012) have come to the attention of institutional review boards and scholars alike, who point to the need to consider privacy concerns and informed consent when using (big) data from social media platforms (Zimmer 2010).

However, scholars cannot neglect the unprecedented access to new data resources. Historians, literature scholars and information and library scientists quickly recognized that digitized texts provide rich data with which to address novel research questions. Within media studies, the added value of 'natively digital' elements was quickly recognized and used for research (Rogers 2009). Pioneered by media scholar Richard Rogers, it led to the emergence of a set of practices and tools to systematically collect and analyse these data from Web platforms (Rogers 2013). Using digitized cultural artefacts from films to graphic novels to the metadata of Instagram photos, Lev Manovich (2012) applied his approach of 'Cultural Analytics' to use analysis software to detect patterns of cultural production and media use. These new practices are rapidly changing the field of media studies in general and new media studies in particular, as knowledge of these tools and practices is increasingly a requirement in academic hiring. In the field of sociology, the emergence of newly accessible data sources and novel analysis tools has led to a debate that revisits the notion of the 'empirical'. It became clear that the sheer size and variety of the data problematize 'stock-in-trade analytic methods' (Abbott 2000: 298) and that the existing methods of explanation were not suited to the 'increasing availability of a wide range of data that previously was not easily accessible, but is now routinely collected as part of information and communication techniques' (Adkins & Lury 2009: 15).

In this article, we consider how these recent changes in tools and practices affect research methods and ethics. Informed consent – the principle value of research ethics in the social sciences – is under pressure due to two technological advances: the rise of the internet and big data technologies. In the following paragraphs we will explain the origins of informed consent and the way it should be dealt with in the field of big data research on SNSs.

Finding Suitable Guidelines

As early as 2002, Michelle White discussed the limitations of the use of one single guideline to govern the spectrum of possible ways of conducting research on the internet:

> It seems unlikely that any single guideline for Internet research ethics can resolve conflicts between the disciplines. For instance, the 'Protection of Human Subjects' document requires that 'risks to subjects are reasonable in relation to anticipated benefits, if any, to subjects, and the importance of the knowledge that may reasonably be expected to result' and MLA mandates that 'whether a line of inquiry is ultimately useful to society, colleagues, or students should not be used to limit the freedom of the scholar pursuing it' (Code of Federal Regulations. 2001, Title 45, Part 46). Obviously, a more careful articulation of both 'subject' and 'representation' would aid in these considerations. At the moment, guidelines for Internet research have not addressed such disciplinary conflicts and have instead almost completely ignored the conventions in a number of Humanities disciplines. (White 2002: 255-256)

As an emerging digital humanities discipline, big data research has exactly these problems. First, because it takes a hypothesis-generating approach to data, often the usefulness of a line of inquiry is not known beforehand. On an institutional level this is problematic, since requesting funds or grants for research often requires that research objectives be described in advance. In other instances, ethical guidelines can complicate the application, as many issues are ambiguous and unclear, such as the extent to which public profiles and publicly posted information are subject to privacy regulations. Other cases have sparked criticism after publication for the supposed disregard of ethical guidelines. Frequently mentioned in this regard is the so-called Facebook study, which received wide media coverage (Bond et al. 2012). A massive outcry about the researchers' supposedly reckless behaviour arose when it was revealed that user timelines were being manipulated to investigate the emotional impact of Facebook's news feed on users (Puschmann & Bozdag 2014; Schroeder 2014). Informed consent was construed as being given through the user's acceptance of Facebook's terms of use at sign-up. This act was conveniently interpreted to signify the user's agreement to their data being used for research. The data for the study was generated by manipulating the timelines of a large group of Facebook users, in total 60,055,176 profiles. Facebook employees anonymized the data before handing it over to the researchers. Because the researchers were not dealing with data that could be connected to identifiable individuals, they did not classify the research as human subject research and assumed they did not have to comply with regulations regarding such practices (Carberry 2014, in a press release by Cornell University Media Relations). In countries not making use of IRBs, the solution to the problem of possible ethical breaches has to be sought in more general guidelines governing the conduct of individual researchers. Michelle White makes a good start by proposing the use of ethical principles stemming from other disciplines. Regarding informed consent in internet research, she offers an argument based on the relation and difference between human subjects and their online representations in the form of profiles and accounts (2002: 249).

Informed Consent

Informed consent has been an integral part of all guidelines concerning human subject research in the medical, sociological and psychological fields. How this principle should be used in the field of internet research on SNSs is still heavily debated. Psychologist Ilka Gleibs (2014) has discussed ethics in large-scale online studies on social network sites. She argues that informed consent of participants is needed when one wants to use data from these sites:

> The use of informed consent is important because it allows participants to make a choice and signals their willing participation. As researchers we show respect for the individuals' autonomy, which is a fundamental ethical principle. (Gleibs 2014: 5)

Referring to the controversial T3 study (Lewis et al. 2008), Michael Zimmer (2010) emphasizes the need to hold on to existing research standards, arguing that one cannot be ethically lax simply because these data are freely available via Facebook. The recent controversy about the Facebook study (Bond et al. 2012) mentioned above, which manipulated Facebook timelines without users' consent, indicates that certain research practices conflict with the traditional understanding of research integrity. Indeed, for many SNS research projects, informed consent represents the underlying pact between researcher and the subjects in the 'field':

> [I]n order to represent and analyse pertinent social phenomena, some researchers collect data from social media without considering that the lack of informed consent would in any other form of research (think of psychological or medical research) constitute a major breach of research ethics. (Zwitter 2014: 5)

To understand the conflicting visions of how to investigate social phenomena on Web platforms, we recall how ethical standards for research including human subjects came into being. The Nuremberg Code, the Declaration of Helsinki and the Universal Declaration on Bioethics and Human Rights are three regulatory guidelines that are often cited in academic discourse on human subject research (White 2002; Buchanan & Ess 2008; Markham & Buchanan 2012; Gleibs 2014; Dumas et al. 2014: 375). The Nuremberg Code[3] is one of the first documents on human rights that characterizes voluntary informed consent as a fundamental ethical principle (Grodin 1994). But one of its problems, according to physician researchers, is that it did not take clinical research on children, patients or mentally impaired persons into account (Annas 1992: 122) The Declaration of Helsinki can be seen as a more elaborate and more easily applicable document than the Nuremberg Code (*ibid.*). One big difference concerns the expertise of the writers who wrote the documents: the Nuremberg Code was issued by judges (who adopted and expanded ethical principles initially provided by psychiatrist and neurologist Leo Alexander), whereas the Declaration of Helsinki was written by physicians. Another difference is that the latter has been revised regularly: six revisions have been made since the first version appeared in 1964. After all these years, the Declaration is even referred to as 'the most widely accepted guidance worldwide on medical research involving human subjects' (Christie 2000: 913). Ethical guidelines should not be static, and the Declaration of Helsinki proves to be a good model of a set of protocols that has been adapted to meet evolving needs and situations.[4] The Universal

3   'Trials of War Criminals before the Nuremberg Military Tribunals Under Control Council Law 10' (Washington, D.C.: Superintendent of Documents, United States Government Print Office, 1950). Military Tribunal 1, Case 1, United States v. Karl Brandt et al., October 1946 – April 1949, Vol. I, pp. 1-1004; Vol. II, pp. 1-352 (1949).
4   For more substantive information, the article 'The Revision of the Declaration: the past, present and the future' by Robert V. Carlson, Kenneth M. Boyd and David J. Webb (2004), is recommended.

Declaration on Bioethics and Human Rights is the first document that binds UNESCO member states – 195 countries – to one declaration (Berlinguer & De Castro 2003). As its title indicates, its purpose is to provide guidelines for ethical issues 'related to medicine, life sciences and associated technologies as applied to human beings, taking into account their social, legal and environmental dimensions' (UNESCO 2006).

Ethical Decision-making in Internet Research

The Nuremberg Code, the Declaration of Helsinki and the Universal Declaration on Bioethics and Human Rights were all binding (to varying degrees), but each was written under different circumstances, employed different discourses, and was conceived with different kinds of research in mind. According to Dumas et al. (2014: 375) there are, in general, two features evident in most research regulations around the world: first, regulations are often written in reaction to unacceptable research practices (as with, for example, the origins of the Nuremberg Code, which was formulated in the wake of Nazi atrocities); second, these regulations often do not take into account evolving forms of technology (such as possibilities for data gathering). Writers who have accounted for the current state of technology, such as Zwitter (2014: 375) and boyd & Crawford (2012), have been vague. The closest attempt to a set of guidelines for internet research has been written by the Association of Internet Researchers (AoIR), an academic association focused on the cross-disciplinary field of internet studies. This association promotes critical and scholarly internet research. It drafted a first version of the AoIR Ethical Decision Making document in 2002. A second version appeared in 2012, as the association had decided that a revision was in order because the scope and context of internet research had changed rapidly. The AoIR encourages internet research independent of traditional academic borders (AoIR 2015); its basic ethical principles rely on, amongst others, the Nuremberg Code and the Declaration of Helsinki: 'We accept them as basic to any research endeavour' (Markham & Buchanan 2012: 4). The problem of internet research that has to be faced, according to AoIR, is caused by the dynamic evolution of the field of research:

> This dynamism is reflected in the fact that as of the time of this writing, no official guidance or 'answers' regarding internet research ethics have been adopted at any national or international level. (*ibid.*: 2)

The association has no intention of providing 'definitive' regulations that would foreclose further discussion about how to do internet research in an appropriate way: 'We emphasize that no set of guidelines or rules is static; the fields of internet research are dynamic and heterogeneous' (*ibid.*: 2). Thus the Ethical Decision Making document – and this is ultimately a short-coming – proposes an extensive list of 'Internet Specific Ethical Questions' to 'prompt reflection about ethical decision making within the specific confines of one's study' (*ibid.*: 8): it is up to the researcher to determine which questions are relevant for the research being conducted, and which ones are not. The field of big data has not yet been discussed extensively; however, in earlier work, Markham has discussed certain characteristics of qualitative research ethics that have interesting similarities with the way big data research is being done:

> Ethics is considered an a priori stance, often regulated more than felt by the researcher. Research design is often considered a procedural or logistic matter, mostly followed, not questioned, particularly if the researcher is within junior ranks of the profession or working within a discipline that values adherence to particular approaches. The considera-tion of research design as a given is founded in epistemologies that value precision, replicability, validity, and objectivity, all of which require a priori determination of activities. Any interference in the procedures or disruption of pre-determined standards is discouraged because it may invalidate the study. This is antithetical to the idea of context sensitivity and reflexivity. (Markham 2006: 43)

Several problems need to be addressed to ensure that in the future, researchers focusing on big social data can do their research in an ethi-cal way. Markham & Buchanan (2015) notice the different fundamental values expressed in the European and American guidelines. Whereas the UNESCO code takes a de-ontological approach (some boundaries should never be crossed), the American Belmont Report has a utilitarian basis (benefits can outweigh downsides). In the following paragraph we will explain how one need not be forced into a choice between a utilitarian and a de-ontological approach if one adopts a stance of ethical pluralism (Ess 2006; 2007). The underlying question here concerns the possibility of research interest trumping research ethics. This matter can entail harsh consequences when one is dealing with, for example, found (or stolen) data sets. One well-known case is the Ashley Madison data leak, in which user profiles on a popular adulterous dating site were made public. The leak of hacked data revealed not only subscribers' personal information but also the site's heavy use of bots so that it would appear to have far more female users than it actually did and to encourage communication on the site (Newitz 2015). Also well known is the so-called Cablegate case. At the end of 2010, WikiLeaks publicized internal communications of the American diplomatic corps (*The Guardian* 2010). As these cables have still not been declassified by the American government, several US-based journals of political science have been declining papers that use the cables as sources of information, effectively preventing scholars from using crucial information for research (Michael 2015).

Another important issue is the possibility of using new tools for data gathering or scraping. With these tools, websites and online communities can be studied even if they would not like to participate in research. Software like Import.io and Outwit Hub make it incredibly easy to scrape databases from public websites and make them searchable and usable for research. Additional tools can be used to anonymize individuals in the data sets. Platform providers prevent automatic scraping through the blocking of suspicious IP addresses, but such measures can be circumscribed through the use of VPNs or proxies. Marketeers, spammers and researchers routinely employ such tools to gather information. Often neither the tools nor the collection of data are illegal, even if the terms of use of a platform state otherwise. Researchers therefore find themselves in a dilemma. Their fair use guidelines and the widely shared imperative of informed consent require them to inform populations on platforms and platform providers about what they are doing. Michael Zimmer emphasizes that the frequent excuse that the data is being made publicly available is unacceptable (2010). However, as we will point out below, it is not always feasible or desirable to comply with the consent requirement.

Case Study: Big Data Research Without Informed Consent

In November 2014, we started to conduct a big data research project on a discussion board of patients afflicted with the same illness. After logging in, the profiles of all members were open for inspection. This included all the information they chose to share with the community. To explore this information we used a scraping tool to scrape all information from all profiles. We found out that about 15 percent of the community had filled in quite detailed information about their specific condition. Similar to what happens quite often in a big data research project, we focused on the

Fig. 13.1:   New members of Forum X over time.

information that seemed most valuable at first, only to find ourselves at a dead end after about a week. The medical information could be of value only if we could connect it to specific behaviour on the forum itself. Since we gathered only profiles, and not the conversations in the fora and topics sections of the discussion board, we considered this direction of study to be a dead end. In the following few days, two dates quickly became important in our research: the date the profiles were created and the date a profile was last active. We could measure the forum's growth over time by adding up all the dates of profile creation (see Figure 13.1).

We thought that to understand the function of this forum in this particular community of patients we had to gather qualitative data, too. Therefore, we tried to find a representative sample of people that looked most promising for providing information about their use and media practices: namely, the long-time forum users who were still active. To do so we created two graphs: one with all the profiles sorted by the date of last activity (see Figure 13.2), and one with all the profiles sorted by length of activity (see Figure 13.3). We measured the length of membership activity by subtracting the date of creation from the 'last seen' date. When the groups that were active for more than two years (8 percent of the profiles) and had visited the site within one month before the research began (4 percent of the profiles) were combined, we were left with a sample of 1.2 percent of the total population for further qualitative research. As a by-product we found out that 59 percent of all members had been active only for one day. These 'one-day flies' had either only made an account and never logged in,

Figs. 13.2 and 13.3:   Length of activity and 'last seen' date

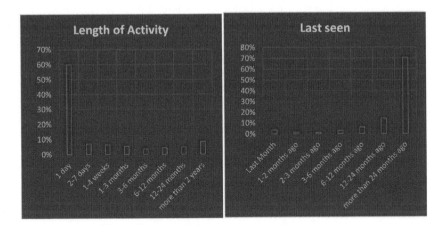

or had logged in the next day and never returned. In addition, we found that about 70 percent of the profiles had not visited in the last two years. As can be expected, there is a big overlap of almost fifty percent between these groups of people.

The inactive group and the 'one-day flies' make visible the problem of informed consent for this forum. The 70 percent of inactive users would probably never reply to a request for consent, simply because these users were no longer active on the forum. We also expected that a big part of the group of one-day flies represented people who would never respond to a request for informed consent – for two reasons. First, amongst the one-day flies there were a certain number of fake profiles (used, for example, for spamming), since there were a lot of homepage URLs that referred to websites concerned with porn, cosmetics, real estate and other subjects not related to the specific disease or the forum's other conversations. Second, we expected that a large part of the one-day flies also represented inactive users, even if their accounts had been made within the previous two years. In reality, the amount of non-responding accounts, accounting for overlap between the two inactive groups, will be close to 80 percent of the total population. Adding to that, we would like to state that, since we were taking a different direction in our research, these accounts were not of any interest to us and would never have been part of the final sample. Still, existing ethical guidelines would have demanded informed consent from all of these users.

The approach of this case-study can be seen as exemplary for big data research with data generated through user activities on an SNS. As we showed, it is highly impractical and maybe even impossible to get informed consent from the entire community or network. A second observation is that the use of the term 'human subjects' is debatable in the context of big social data as not all profiles represent actual users. We strongly believe that big data research can be performed in an ethical fashion without getting informed consent from the whole population of an online service. We therefore propose an alternative way of dealing with these subjects in big data research on SNSs.

Proposal for a Three-step Research Process

Drawing from practical experience, we developed a concept for integrating ethical decision-making into the research design process. With reference to Markham and Buchanan, we also argue for guidelines rather than strict codes. It is necessary to adapt the research design to the need for ethical decision-making. The degree of the potential privacy breach or damage that can result from research will have a significant effect on ethical decision-making: when a scholar investigates an SNS, a user forum or an online community, the vulnerability of the target demographic is relevant to the decision-making.

The research that initiated this paper dealt with an online discussion forum for patients afflicted with a certain illness. The website advertised that it had more than 100,000 members. When two interns with limited technical abilities started to investigate the forum we, naively, thought that the ethical framework could be formed simultaneously with the design of the scraping process. We never expected to be able to acquire the complete database in less than two days. Requesting informed consent would have meant that a vast number of inactive profiles would never have been found. Fake, deceased or inactive members are not able to give consent.

Only after discussion with our supervisors did we understand the magnitude of the actions we had undertaken. It was decided that we should immediately terminate the research and destroy all the data we had acquired. The argument that we had only gathered data that was publicly available could not cancel out the fact that we had not asked for consent. We have the strong conviction that researchers should be able to carry out this type of research in the future. A lack of consent from the users of public fora or platform owners or administrators themselves does not have to be an obstacle to an ethically sound research design. To support this hypothesis, we point to Richards & King (2014), who recognize a difference between privacy and confidentiality: 'With the power of big data to make secondary uses of the private information we share in confidence, restoration of trust in the institutions we share with, rests not only with privacy but in the recognition that shared private information can remain "confidential".' (*ibid.*: 413) To test the boundaries, they advocate experimentation:

> A central part of this experimentation, if we are to have privacy, confidentiality, transparency, and protect identity in a big data economy, must involve informed, principled, and collaborative experimentation with privacy subjects. (*ibid.*: 431)

With this in mind, we propose a research design that starts with exploration, making sure that we provide the necessary precautions regarding the four points Richards and King bring forward: privacy, confidentiality, transparency and identity protection. Ess (2006) advocates a practical view of doing research ethics. Researchers are perfectly capable of making ethical decisions within their own fields, assessing a variety of ethical considerations depending on the context. We therefore choose a perspective of ethical pluralism over dogmatism.

Reviewing the research process, we made an attempt to propose a way of implementing ethical reasoning as well as risk limitation and the safeguarding of personal data confidentiality. It must be emphasized that we want to ensure a maximum degree of academic freedom while identifying possible risks and limiting them.

Stage 1: Design

In this stage an idea will be turned into a research design. This process might start with a 'found data set' or a platform that triggers the researchers' interest and provides a starting point for possible research questions to be developed. The three elements listed in this stage in Figure 13.4 are therefore exchangeable and do not have to follow one upon the other. A topic will be combined with a possible forum or database. An inventory of the stakeholders regarding the information will be made. It lists the amount of personal information, the degree of vulnerability and possible risks such as confidentiality breaches. As a result, a decision will be made about which data will be scraped and how this will be done. This will raise issues concerning the terms of use of the data source, the quality of the gathered information, the legal status and the feasibility of data collection. Researchers must argue why they are collecting data in a specific way. The process of data collection will be developed and data will be scraped accordingly. The risks of the next phase will be defined and limited as much as possible.

Stage 2: Safe Data Exploration

The second stage is an exploratory inquiry into the data set. It leads to the identification of patterns and samples and the formulation of a hypothesis. By exploring the data, researchers find out what the data is about and how it can be used. Several conceptual research questions and possible hypotheses are proposed. To conclude this stage, a definitive hypothesis is chosen with its corresponding sample. In this phase the data will be protected physically by using a stand-alone 'air gapped' computer. Prabhu (2015: 165) emphasizes that data usage needs to be governed tightly. Access to the data will be documented carefully, and only the necessary people will be allowed to work with the data. The data will be explored and filtered. Special attention will be given to patterns that might occur in the data. Research questions will be formed and a sample will be selected. At the end of this stage a decision will be made about whether a part of the data will be carefully anonymized and used in the third stage. Anonymization has to be processed carefully and must take into consideration the possibility of the existence of another data set consisting of partly similar data. The combination of two data sets has proved to be an effective method of de-anonymization (Narayana & Shmatikov 2006; Sweeney 2002). Completely wiping the data is also a possibility.

Stage 3: Research Process

The third stage involves testing the hypotheses which are formulated during the first stage. The use of the data now shifts from an exploratory environment to a research environment. The research should comply with the rules and ethical guidelines that are part of its specific scientific tradition and institution. If informed consent is stipulated by required guidelines, it should be requested. An opt-in or opt-out can be provided to people so they can actively make a choice about their data (Gleibs 2014; Prahbu 2015). Before possible publication, special attention will be given to the anonymization of sensitive data.

Fig. 13.4:   Research process with safe data exploration.

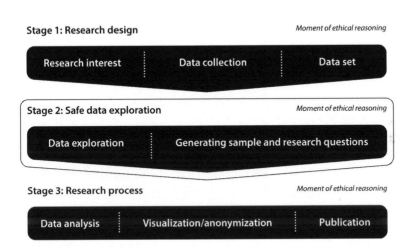

Big Data research process
Moments of ethical reasoning

—

Stage 1: Research design   *Moment of ethical reasoning*

| Research interest | Data collection | Data set |

Stage 2: Safe data exploration   *Moment of ethical reasoning*

| Data exploration | Generating sample and research questions |

Stage 3: Research process   *Moment of ethical reasoning*

| Data analysis | Visualization/anonymization | Publication |

Conclusion

Emerging new branches of humanities research dealing with the use of digital methods are raising questions about methods and ethics. Informed consent as the principle value affiliated with research ethics in the social sciences is under pressure due to two technological advancements: the rise of the internet and big data technologies. Informed consent has been an integral part of all guidelines concerning human subject research in the medical field and the social sciences. First, we demonstrated that the basis of these ethical guidelines in the Nuremberg Code, the Declaration of Helsinki and the Universal Declaration on Bioethics and Human Rights are from eras and discourses that have very little to do with big data research as it is currently being done. Although these guidelines can be very useful or even necessary in the final stage of a big data research project studying an SNS, in the second stage they would only limit the researcher.

Second, we showed that online user accounts and profiles are not equal to human subjects. Online profiles can better be seen as representations of people, not the people themselves, and, depending on the SNS being investigated, many users may provide fake or false information. Receiving informed consent from the whole population of a social network or service is therefore unrealistic. And those who positively respond to a request might constitute a biased and unrepresentative sample. Another practical problem are the numerous inactive profiles online: a request for informed consent will not be answered by those who are no longer members of the community. We showed that in our own research this group would have amounted to close to 80 percent of the profiles. Again, expecting informed consent as a requirement for research to be ethical is unrealistic. This does not mean that researchers must not take all possible precautions to safeguard the confidentiality of the data collected.

To deal with the problems we described above we propose using a system of three stages in big data research on SNSs. Rather than favouring one ethical framework over another, we adopt a view of ethical pluralism, leaving it to the researcher to choose which to use, making appropriate reflections within their context. In the first stage a research design will be made, taking into consideration the stakeholders, type of data and a general direction of inquiry. After the gathering of data, in the second, exploratory stage hypotheses and samples are generated. Informed consent is not necessary in this stage, but since the nature of the data can still be very delicate, protection of the data is of the utmost importance. In the third stage, researchers have to adhere to the rules and guidelines that are mandatory in their specific field of research. In most social sciences informed consent is part of these guidelines and will therefore have to be respected. With this proposal we expect to catalyse both the philosophical and practical discussions about informed consent. To ensure that future research with new tools can be carried out in an ethical way, we need to experiment not only with methods but also with ethical frameworks. In order for us to find practices to protect research integrity we need to get our hands dirty.

References

Adkins, Lisa & Celia Lury. 2009. "Introduction: What is the Empirical?" *European Journal of Social Theory* 12 (1): 5.

Annas, George J. 1992. "The Changing Landscape of Human Experimentation: Nuremberg, Helsinki, and Beyond." *Health Matrix* 2 (2): 119.

Berlinguer, Giovanni & Leonardo De Castro. 2003. *Report of the IBC on the Possibility of Elaborating a Universal Instrument on Bioethics*. Paris: UNESCO.

Berry, David M. (ed.) 2012. *Understanding Digital Humanities*. New York: Palgrave Macmillan.

Bond, Robert M., Christopher J. Fariss, Jason J. Jones, Adam D.I. Kramer, Cameron Marlow, Jaime E. Settle & James H. Fowler. 2012. "A 61-Million-Person Experiment in Social Influence and Political Mobilization." *Nature* 489(7415): 295-298.

boyd, danah & Kate Crawford. 2012. "Critical Questions for Big Data: Provocations for a Cultural, Technological, And Scholarly Phenomenon." *Information, Communication & Society* 15 (5): 662-679.

Buchanan, E.A. & Charles Ess. 2008. "Internet Research Ethics: The Field and Its Critical Issues." In Himma, K.E. & H.T. Tavani (eds.), *The Handbook of Information and Computer Ethics.* John Wiley & Sons, 273.

Burdick, Anne, Johanna Drucker, Peter Lunenfeld, Todd Presner & Jefffrey Schnapp. 2012. *Digital_Humanities.* Cambridge, MA: The MIT Press.

Carberry, John. 2014. "Media Statement on Cornell University's Role in Facebook Emotional Contagion Research." *Cornell University Media Relations.* 30 June 2014. Retrieved from http://mediarelations.cornell.edu/2014/06/30/media-statement-on-cornell-universitys-role-in-facebook-emotional-contagion-research/.

Carlson, Robert V., Kenneth M. Boyd & David J. Webb. 2004. "The Revision of the Declaration of Helsinki: Past, Present and Future." *British Journal of Clinical Pharmacology* 57 (6): 695-713.

Christie, Bryan. 2000. "Doctors Revise Declaration of Helsinki." *BMJ* (321): 931.

Dörk, Marian, Sheelagh. Carpendale & Carey Williamson. 2011. "The Information Flaneur: A Fresh Look at Information Seeking." Proceedings of the SIGCHI Conference on Human Factors. *Computing Systems*: 1215-1224. ACM.

Dumas, Guillaume, David G. Serfass, Nicolas A. Brown, & Ryne A. Sherman. 2014. "The Evolving Nature of Social Network Research: A Commentary to Gleibs." *Analyses of Social Issues and Public Policy* 14.1: 374-378.

Ess, Charles. 2006. "Ethical Pluralism and Global Information Ethics." *Ethics and Information Technology* 8 (4): 215-226.

—. 2007. "Internet Research Ethics." In Joinson, Adam, Katelyn McKenna, Tom Postmes & Ulf-Dietrich Reips (eds.), *Oxford Handbook of Internet Psychology.* Oxford University Press: Oxford.

Gleibs, Ilka H. "Turning Virtual Public Places into Laboratories: Thoughts on Conducting Online Field Studies Using Social Network Sites." *Analyses of Social Issues and Public Policy* 14.1 (2014): 352-370.

Grodin, Michael A. 1994. "Historical Origins of the Nuremberg Code." In *Medicine, Ethics and the Third Reich: Historical and Contemporary Issues*, edited by John J. Michalcyzk, 169-194. Kansas City, MO: Sheed and Ward.

The Guardian. 2010. "WikiLeaks embassy cables: the key points at a glance." Retrieved from www.theguardian.com/world/2010/nov/29/wikileaks-embassy-cables-key-points (accessed 2 January 2016).

Lewis, Kevin, Jason Kaufman, Marco Gonzalez, Andreas Wimmer & Nicholas Christakis. 2008. "Tastes, Ties, and Time: A New Social Network Dataset using Facebook.com." *Social Networks* 30 (4): 330-342.

Manovich, Lev. 2011. "Trending: The Promises and the Challenges of Big Social Data." In *Debates in the Digital Humanities*, edited by Matthew K. Gold, 460-475. Mineapolis, MN: University of Minnesota Press.

Markham, Annette & Elizabeth Buchanan. 2012. "Ethical Decision-making and Internet Research: Recommendations from the AoIR Ethics Working Committee (Version 2.0)". USA: Association of Internet Research. Sciences, 2nd edition, Vol 12. Oxford: Elsevier, 606-613.

Markham, A., & E. Buchanan. "Ethical Considerations in Digital Research Contexts." *Encyclopedia for Social & Behavioral Sciences* (2015): 606-613.

Michael, G.J. 2015. "Who's Afraid of WikiLeaks? Missed Opportunities in Political Science Research." *Review of Policy Research* 32(2): 175-199.

Narayana, Avind & Vitaly Shmatikov. 2006. "Robust De-anonymization of Large Datasets (How to Break Anonymity of the Netflix Prize Dataset)." Retrieved from http://arxiv.org/pdf/cs/0610105.pdf (accessed 24 February 2014).

Newitz, Annalee. 2015. "Is Cheater Site Ashley Madison Actually Growing by over a Million Users Per Month?" *Ars Technica*. Retrieved from http://arstechnica.com/tech-policy/2015/12/is-cheater-site-ashley-madison-actually-growing-by-over-a-million-users-per-month/ (accessed 2 January 2016).

Nuremberg Code. 1996 [1947]. "Permissible Medical Experiments." BMJ 1996 (313): 1448. Prahbu, Robinha. 2015. "Big Data? Big Trouble!" In *Internet Research Ethics*, (ed.) Halvard Fossheim & Helene Ingierd, 157-172. Oslo: Cappelen Damm Akademisk.

Puschmann, Cornelius. & Engin Bozdag. 2014. "Staking Out the Unclear Ethical Terrain of Online Social Experiments." *Internet Policy Review* 3(4).

Richards, Neil M. & Jonathan H. King. 2014. "Big Data Ethics." *Wake Forest Law Review* 49: 393-432.

Rieder, Bernhard & Theo Röhle. 2012. "Digital Methods: Five Challenges." In *Understanding Digital Humanities*, ed. David M. Berry. London: Palgrave Macmillan. 67-84.

Rogers, Richard. 2009. *The End of the Virtual: Digital Methods*. Amsterdam: Amsterdam University Press.

—. 2013. *Digital Methods*. Cambridge, MA: The MIT press.

Schroeder, Ralph. 2014. "Big Data and the Brave New World of Social Media Research." *Big Data & Society* 1 (2).

Sweeney, Latanya. 2002. "k-Anonymity: A Model for Protecting Privacy." *International Journal of Uncertainty, Fuzziness and Knowledge-Based Systems* 10 (05): 557-570.

UNESCO. 2006. "Universal Declaration on Bioethics and Human Rights." Paris.

White, Michele. 2002. "Representations Or People?" *Ethics and Information Technology* 4 (3): 249-266.

World Medical Association. 2013. "Declaration of Helsinki."

Zimmer, Michael. 2010. "But the Data is Already Public': On the Ethics of Research in Facebook." *Ethics and Information Technology* 12 (4): 313-325.

Zwitter, Andrej. 2014. "Big Data Ethics." *Big Data & Society* 1 (2): 2053951714559253.

14. Research Ethics in Context

Decision-Making in Digital Research

Annette Markham & Elizabeth Buchanan

Introduction

In 2012, we published *Ethical Decision-making and Internet Research*, which consolidated the Association of Internet Researchers (AoIR) Ethics Working Committee's recommendations into a comprehensive document. In 2015, we revisited the subject with *Internet Research: Ethical Concerns*, which took a practical approach to internet research ethics by reviewing the work of other researchers in the field. With the article you are reading now, we attempt to reconcile the abstract and the practice-based methods of our previous two articles by unpacking ethical decision-making in view of principles.

Digital media's fast development, expansion and increasing integration into our day-to-day lives does not just mean opportunity but also new ethical challenges for internet researchers. Each new data set entails its own potential quandaries and insights. By placing other researchers' work within AoIR guidelines, we seek to create a more cohesive framework to assist internet researchers, review boards, students and ethicists in ethically navigating the murky waters of internet research.

Recent evolutions in our field, especially surrounding big data, have evolved quickly and still need to be addressed. The task ahead is to expand the more developed concepts and incorporate these new issues into the discussion. We do, however, feel confident that the core issue remains the same: understanding how and to what extent basic principles affect ethical decision-making.

Ethical Fundamentals

A discussion of ethics in any research field must be rooted in the wide array of policy documents, such as the UN Declaration of Human Rights, the Nuremberg Code, the Declaration of Helsinki, and the Belmont Report. Given the extent to which these documents have been discussed elsewhere, we will limit our focus to issues of digital methodology and encourage readers to see the resources mentioned above and in the appendix for more on those fundamental issues.

Flexibility

As seen throughout our publications, our stance supports a flexible set of guidelines over stricter codes of practice. This allows researchers to respond and adapt to the ever-evolving nature of their field. In the end, it is their responsibility to conduct ethical research according to their individual judgements and values, in addition to their disciplinary norms. The core principles of such an ethical approach are dialogic, inductive, case-based and process-focused.

Privacy Concepts

The manner with which humans engage in public spaces continues to evolve as the spectrum of public-private spaces becomes less discernible. Researchers may find themselves vexed by the practical and methodological difficulties of tackling such a nebulous issue, one with little historical precedent to offer guidance. Expectations of privacy increasingly hinge on specific contextual factors as to how information is presented and used, as opposed to the antiquated binary conception of public/private.

Rather than attempting to place information in one box or the other, researchers such as Sveningsson (2003) offer new ways of perceiving this idea. Her grid expands the binary public/private spectrum to include an additional axis of informational sensitivity, so that researchers might better predict users' expectations for how their data may be used.

This diagram is still built around a conception of public and private as two opposite spaces. Attempting to identify within this binary is the wrong

Fig. 14.1:   Sveningsson's (2003) model of internet privacy.

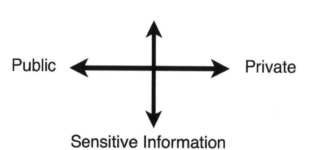

tack, since digital research means dealing with constant and open data flows between always connected parties in an environment where editing, sharing and other mashup practices are carried out within complex global networks.

McKee and Porter's (2009) diagram focuses on the necessity of consent by attempting to balance competing factors. It, too, presents public/private as a binary, but it is a useful tool for approaching ethical dilemmas in research.

Users are often unaware of the extent to which their data may be picked up and used by data aggregators. Nissenbaum's insight remains significant, pointing out that in media contexts 'what people care most about is not simply restricting the flow of information but ensuring that it flows appropriately' (2010: 2). Many internet users do not want their information to be private so much as they want it to only be used publicly in ways they find acceptable. Given the complications of such a stance, we encourage researchers to focus on a person's relationship to their information in a given context when making ethical considerations.

Fig. 14.2:   McKee and Porter's (2009) dimensions for informed consent.

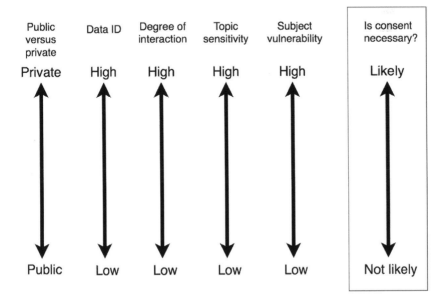

Identifiability

The ubiquity of freely available information on individuals has shifted the internet research ethics discussion from the Sisyphean task of preserving the privacy and anonymity of online parties to a discussion around the sheer quantity of data we both generate and access. The flood of personal data being created by individuals' devices (e.g. geolocation, physical data, online trackers) combined with big data collection tools creates increasingly complicated criteria for ethically conducting internet research. As of yet, there is no consensus on the best way to interact with personally identifiable information. For an in-depth exploration of the topic, see the chapter by Schäfer, Van Schie and Westra.

Informed Consent

The long-standing principle of informed consent becomes problematic when applied to internet or digital research. The ethical, as opposed to regulatory, question, 'when is consent needed?', becomes tricky to answer when applied to anonymous chatrooms and online forums. Moreover, consent may be difficult or impossible to obtain, since one's data may include outdated profiles or contact information. Ikonomidis Svedmark and Nyberg (2009) make a strong argument for making informed consent optional and leaving it to the researcher's discretion. Svedmark (2012) suggests that informed consent be a secondary priority to avoiding harm.

The AoIR ethics document advocates a case-based approach that acknowledges and considers ethical tensions, such as conflicts with legal, disciplinary, institutional and cultural considerations, even when a resolution is not easily found. By consistently posing ethical questions and reflecting on the research process, researchers will better balance their different obligations. In terms of consent, this means deciding whether and how to go about obtaining consent on a case-by-case basis.

Diagram on Internet Specific Ethical Questions

This diagram should function as a guide to forming ethical questions for internet research. It outlines considerations researchers should have in mind when forming these questions. We encourage students to form example questions following this form.

Table 14.1.   Internet Specific Ethical Questions

Defining and conceptualizing context	– Definitions from owners, users, members, etc. – Contextual norms, regulatory frameworks – Ethical expectations of user individuals and community
Accessing context	– Contextual situation of participants and researcher – How researcher approaches participants – Participants' perception of privacy – Accommodating participants' feelings on appropriate flow of information
Involved parties	– Ethical expectations of community, participants, authors and commercial or corporate parties – Future implications of stored data for individuals and communities
Primary object of study	– Ethical expectations associated with particular types of data – Range of persons and texts affected (in)directly by study – Treatment of potentially identifying information – Public availability of data acquired for research
Management, storage and representation of data	– Methods for securing and managing potentially sensitive data – Risks of storing research data for future use – Unanticipated breaches in stored data – Ensuring adequate anonymity of data – Ethical consequences of anonymizing data – Potential distortions of data from removal of selected information – Possible future risks to anonymity from technological advances
Potential harms and risks associated with study	– For individuals, online communities, researchers, research, etc. – Risk assessment in advance and throughout study – Definitions and operationalization of 'vulnerability' and 'harm' – Determination of vulnerability in ambiguous contexts – Potential privacy-related harms – Harms to participants from parties besides researcher – Unknown identity, age or ability of participants
Verifiability	– Relation between profiles and individuals – Representativeness of data sets – Potential for verification of results by later researchers – Influence of data providers/platform – Influence of data analysis and collection tools
Publication	– Ways data visualization shapes/supports argument – Context of research audience

Human Subjects and Personhood

A lively debate continues over how to treat data created by humans and collected through digital means. While the concept of 'human subjects' has historically been very important for preventing harmful treatment, traditional ideas of what that entails become harder to apply when dealing with online profiles and large, semi-anonymous data sets. For a deeper exploration of this topic, see the chapter by Van Schie, Westra and Schäfer.

Deeper, more constant crossover between our internet lives and our physical lives problematize definitions of personhood. This includes avatars and online profiles. Inconsistencies abound, as researchers' perception of their research subjects as persons is often based on the directness of contact, which we described through 'the distance principle' in 2015. This principle states that an increase in experiential or conceptual proximity between researchers and participants prompts the former to identify more closely with the latter. They are then more prone to perceive the latter as 'humans' and to better consider the ethical implications and liability which that implies.

Seeing a photo on a profile may humanize the subject in a way that reading their metadata may not. Yet the consideration of a research object as a human subject should not be reduced to whether information is apparently linkable to an individual. There is a body of evidence suggesting that data sets that have been 'anonymized' often leave individuals identifiable. The question becomes: 'Does the connection between one's online data and one's physical person enable psychological, economic or physical, harm?' By recalling the distance principle, researchers might be more able to keep in mind the hidden ethical issues at play that may become visible later on.

Harm and Vulnerability

Despite understanding and conducting ethical research, researchers must be prepared to respond to harms. The recontextualization of information can produce unplanned outcomes, as innocent beginnings may lead to true harm down the road. The same information found within various contexts may require different privacy judgements. A user may feel comfortable broadcasting tweets to a public audience, following the norms of the Twitter community. Yet knowing that these 'public' tweets had been collected within a data set and combed over by a researcher could quite possibly feel like an encroachment on their privacy. In spite of what a simplified concept of public/private might offer, there is no categorical way to discern all eventual harm. The notion of 'downstream' harms must be considered.

Harm is a flexible and subjective concept. A researcher could feasibly take the 'public' nature of tweets or Facebook posts to indicate that a user has given tacit consent. However, without considering the conceivable harm to a subject, that researcher has not taken proper precautions. In such a context, guidelines for decision-making can be applied using our diagram on forming Internet Specific Ethical Questions.

Conclusions

To contextualize, we urge researchers to begin thinking about the ethical issues we have outlined herein before starting research, during research and after it has concluded. In our 2012 *Ethical Decision-making and Internet Research*, we developed key guiding principles we believe remain crucial in relation to the ethical considerations of digital research:

The greater the vulnerability of the community/author/participant, the greater the obligation of the researcher to protect the community/author/participant.

Because 'harm' is defined contextually, ethical principles are more likely to be understood inductively rather than applied universally. That is, rather than one-size-fits-all pronouncements, ethical decision-making is best approached through the application of practical judgement attentive to the specific context.

Because all digital information at some point involves individual persons, consideration of principles related to research on human subjects may be necessary even if it is not immediately apparent how and where persons are involved in the research data.

When making ethical decisions, researchers must balance the rights of subjects (as authors, as research participants, as people) with the social benefits of research and researchers' rights to conduct research. In different contexts the rights of subjects may outweigh the benefits of research.

Ethical issues may arise and need to be addressed during all steps of the research process, from planning, research conduct, publication, and dissemination.

Ethical decision-making is a deliberative process, and researchers should consult as many people and resources as possible in this process, including fellow researchers, people participating in or familiar with contexts/sites being studied, research review boards, ethics guidelines, published scholarship (within one's discipline but also in other disciplines), and, where applicable, legal precedent.

These basic guidelines help to address the challenges a digital researcher might face, though the conversation does and must continue. Research practices are diverse; while the United States and the United Kingdom have institutional review boards to monitor researchers' ethical decisions, many countries do not. Research ethics conferences are increasingly common as researchers grapple with challenges presented by the emergence of big data and found data; discussions, too, are ongoing around the differences between performing research for professional or commercial parties. We need academic associations to continually expand the ways in which we address these areas.

For the moment, consider that no single ethical or methodological approach can fit every situation. Yet we hope that by considering ethical issues throughout the research process, researchers will be able to confidently and conscientiously develop ethical practices that are appropriate for their individual situations.

References

Ikonomidis Svedmark, Eva & Annakarin Nyberg. 2009. "Om det privata i publika och digitala rum." *Se mig: Unga om sex och internet.*

McKee, Heidi A. & James E. Porter. 2009. *The Ethics of Internet Research: A Rhetorical, Case-Based Process.* Peter Lang Publishing, New York.

Markham, Annette & Elizabeth Buchanan. 2012. "Ethical Decision-making and Internet Research 2.0: Recommendations from the Association of Internet Researchers Ethics working committee." (Downloaded from http://aoir.org/reports/ethics2.pdf).

—. 2015. "Internet Research: Ethical Concerns." In *International Encyclopedia of the Social & Behavioural Sciences*, 2nd edition, Vol 12, ed James D. Wright, 606-613. Oxford: Elsevier.

Nissenbaum, Helen. 2010. *Privacy in Context: Technology, Policy, and the Integrity of Social Life.* Stanford: Stanford University Press.

Svedmark, Eva. 2012. Att skydda individen från skada. En forkninsetusj balansakt. In *Etiska dilemman. Forskningsdeltagande samtycke och utsatthet*, ed. H. Kalman & V. Lövgren, 106-107. Malmö, Sweden: Gleerups.

Sveningsson, Malin. 2003. "Ethics in internet ethnography." In *Readings in Virtual Research Ethics: Issues and Controversies*, ed. E. Buchanan, 45-61. Hershey: Idea Group.

15. Datafication & Discrimination

Koen Leurs & Tamara Shepherd

Introduction: Why Datafication and Discrimination?

Popular accounts of datafied ways of knowing implied in the ascendance of big data posit that the increasingly massive volume of information collected immanently to digital technologies affords new means of understanding complex social processes. The development of novel insights is attributed precisely to big data's unprecedented scale, a scale that enables what Viktor Mayer-Schönberger and Kenneth Cukier note is a shift away from causal inferences to modes of analysis based rather on 'the benefits of correlation' (2013: 18). Indicating the vast implications of this shift, Mayer-Schönberger and Cukier's influential framing of big data describes a revolutionary change in the ways 'we live, work and think', as phrased by the book's subtitle. But the 'we' in this proclamation tends to go unspecified. Who exactly benefits from a shift toward correlative data analysis techniques in an age of big data? And by corollary, who suffers?

Our claim is that big data, given its origins in a Western military-industrial context for the development of technology and concomitant mobilization within asymmetrical power structures, inherently discriminates against already marginalized subjects. This point has been raised in a number of critiques of the big data moment, for example in danah boyd and Kate Crawford's (2012) cautionary account of the mythologies of big data that obscure the ways it engenders new divides in data access, interpretation, representation and ethics. Frank Pasquale (2015) has further illustrated the perils of 'runaway data' that asymmetrically order our social and financial institutions through hidden algorithmic practices that tend to further entrench inequality by seeking to predict risk. An overview of the social inequalities perpetuated across various applications of big data can be found in the Open Technology Institute's series of primers on data and discrimination (Gangadharan 2014). And yet, as the present collection attests, there may be ways of approaching big data with a critical lens in order for researchers to also benefit from new methods (see also Elmer et al. 2015). In the present collection, many authors make efforts to trouble the politics of big data by admonishing researchers to take alternative perspectives on data-based methods for social research: Nick Couldry, in line with his previous work on media's ontological implications (e.g.

2012), asserts that researchers should strive to demistify big data (p. 238); Carolin Gerlitz describes measurement as valuation that needs to be de-naturalized (p. 243); and Lev Manovich develops Cultural Analytics to get past demographic generalizations through a process of 'estrangement' that prompts researchers to question their cultural assumptions (p. 67). Such actions – demystifying, denaturalizing, estranging – seem to offer important directives for highlighting the often invisible discriminatory functions of big data, but how exactly do they work? Who and where are the actual people implicated in big data discrimination?

These kinds of questions seek to elaborate on Evgeny Morozov's conten-tion, also in the present collection, that 'social biases exist regardless of whether algorithms or computers are doing the job', and thus, 'plenty of discrimination happens with regard to race, class, gender and so forth' (p. 247). One concrete example of this sort of discrimination is offered by Richard Rogers's explanation of query design, which describes how keyword searches illuminate the discursive operations of language within power dynamics (p. 81). His chief examples of keywords being used in this way, as part of 'efforts at neutrality' between politically charged actors, include the BBC's use of the term 'barrier' rather than 'security fence' or 'apartheid wall' to describe the Israeli-Palestinian border structure, and the preference for using the term 'conflict' diamonds or minerals above 'blood' diamonds or minerals on the part of industries attempting to inhabit a corporate social responsibility. These examples usefully point toward modes of political obfuscation that lie at the heart of data sets, as they are constituted from what are seen as legitimate sources of information to query. Even in these cases, however, what is getting queried are certain privileged accounts of political struggle, such as BBC coverage or industry discourse. Clearly, determining what counts in the first place as a legitimate object for big data analysis is a process that implicates deep-seated social biases at a number of levels, not only on the part of programmers and researchers but more fundamentally at the level of the organization of knowledge.

As a rejoinder to existing modes of talking about big data and what it means for social research, this chapter suggests an epistemological intervention from a critical, anti-oppressive stance that seeks to reinstate people within datafied social life. Rather than taking as its premise that big data can offer insights into social processes, this approach starts from the perspective of the people caught up in programmes of social sorting, carried out by computational algorithms, particularly as they occupy marginalized positions within regimes of power-knowledge (to use Foucault's term). As a specifically situated case study, we examine the ways data are mobilized in

European border control and how this phenomenon can be studied, framed through the Eurocentric legacies of population measurement in colonial disciplinary surveillance. The connection between power and knowledge here is meant to implore researchers to consider how their deployments of big data, even from critical perspectives, may serve to replicate structures of discrimination by denying less 'data-ready' ways of knowing. To that end, the conclusion of the chapter suggests some alternative methodological avenues for reinstating people – specifying who the 'we' permits – in light of big data supremacy.

Datafied Migration Management and Border Control

Consider the following anecdote, placed here to illustrate a contemporary case example of the discriminatory workings of algorithmic sorting that separates the privileged from the unprivileged. Flashback to spring 2001. The first author, Koen, found himself sitting in an office cubicle on the 7th floor of a leading mobile phone provider in the Netherlands. Working as an activation and security & compliance officer in a life before academia, every once in a while he would get requests from local mobile phone shop managers to look into activation requests which were 'rejected': 'Why can't you activate this mobile phone contract?' Upon receiving a fax with signed contracts, passport copies and bank statements, Koen and his fellow team of about fifteen would assess applications in two ways. First, they would manually check for the applicant's financial history in the national credit registry. Second, the application would undergo an automated algorithmic risk assessment. The second process was opaque because the employees did not know exactly which variables were evaluated. Frequently, applicants who had a clean credit report were denied a contract after the algorithmic risk assessment. Over time, Koen discerned a pattern: those denied a contract were usually young men of non-Dutch descent who held temporary resident permits rather than Dutch passports and who were living in certain low-income areas. After asking his floor manager about this process, he received confirmation that the mal-payment prediction system targeted specific subgroups: 'especially those Somalis, they never pay'.

Many years later, algorithmic security assessments have become even more commonplace in the corporate world and have also gained prominence in various forms of state governance and surveillance. These systems are typically put in place to ensure greater predictive accuracy, according to a widespread faith in the insights generated through large data sets and statistical calculations since the development of statistical methods in the 1880s, when 'the unflappable stance of quantitative method acquired a prestige that is still in force and whose power derives from the long valorization of impersonality' (Peters 2001: 442). But what the anecdote illustrates is that, far from the imagined objectivity of social sorting through computation, people are still making the decisions at every step of the process (Gillespie 2016).

Moreover, on a wider scale, the story of young male Somalis whose digital data traces algorithmically rendered them as undesired consumers finds parallels in the current moment of 'refugee crisis' in Europe. Automated social sorting at state borders has become commonplace practice as part of governments' efforts to control flows of undesired migrants. For those privileged subjects carrying desirable passports, e-borders and iris scans sustain liquid flow across borders and planetary nomadic mobility as an effortless normality. By contrast, undesired subjects have to provide fingerprints – a genre of biometric data with a long history of criminal connotations – to be cross-referenced among a host of other identifiers in data-based risk calculations. Border control across the Global North and South is increasingly augmented by data collection and processing techniques developed by industry and ported to government applications. This digital policing of unwanted movement has been explored in previous studies on the Australian (Ajana 2013) and Indian (Arora 2016) contexts. In Europe, the division between desired and undesired migration plays out with its own specific contours, where although the internal Schengen Area is borderless, it controls against undesired external populations in the capacity of Fortress Europe.

Fortress Europe presents a particularly relevant context to study datafied discrimination because its contemporary practices of social sorting at the border show lingering traces of colonial-era human classification, measurement and ordering, which were pioneered and mastered on 'subject populations' in its peripheral territories throughout the last centuries. In recent years, continental Europe has prided itself on the premise of 'unity in diversity' but as a 'postcolonial location', it operates at its centre according to a mostly hidden logic of 'European apartheid' (Balibar 2004: 121; Ponzanesi 2016). Also spurred by the IS attacks in Paris in November 2015 and Brussels in March 2016, once again it mobilizes the colonial 'idea of European identity as a superior one in comparison with all the non-European peoples and cultures' (Said 2014: 7). Through various discursive, symbolic, material and datafied processes, it decides who rightfully belongs to Europe by distinguishing between the West and the rest, or 'the Orient' and the 'Occident' (*ibid.*). Through this process the EU justifies who it retains, detains or relocates, thereby distinguishing between lives worth living and 'bare life': those non-citizens stripped of status who become unprotected by the law (Agamben 2005).

Residual colonialism can be located in contemporary border policing. EU member states together manage nearly 2,000 official entry ports and 60,000 kilometres of land and sea borders (Broeders & Dijstelbloem 2016: 247). In 2015, Europe welcomed a record of 611 million international tourist arrivals across these borders (UNWTO 2016), while it sought to control over one million refugees who reached Europe across the Mediterranean sea, half of whom were fleeing war in Syria (UNHCR 2016). This human sorting process of differentiating desired from undesired migrants is increasingly datafied through proliferating, non-linear and non-geographically-bound electronic border governance processes, as a result of economic incentives, opportunistic political motives and the expansion of the security industry. Alongside the other centralized databases of the Schengen Information System and the Visa Information System, the European Dactyloscopy (EURODAC) biometric database, which holds fingerprints of asylum seekers and so-called 'third-country nationals', is the most prominent datafied border control mechanism against unwanted others. EU counterterrorism measures have developed toward increased securitization and an outspoken desire to connect 'data fragments' on non-Europeans through achieving higher 'interoperability' between these and other architectures and databases (European Commission 2016:3).

According to EURODAC regulations, 'individuals from 14 years on should be fingerprinted, whether they are asylum seekers, aliens apprehended in relation with the irregular crossing of an external border or aliens found illegally present in a Member State' (EDPS 2009: 15). 28 EU countries and four associated states have access to the fingerprint data in EURODAC. EURODAC is managed by the European Agency for the operational management of large-scale IT systems in the area of freedom, security and justice. Its data are stored at the headquarters in Tallinn (Estonia), its operational management is housed in Strasbourg (France), and backup systems are in place in Sankt Johann im Pongau (Austria). In EURODAC jargon, 'asylum applicants' and 'aliens' become 'data subjects' as their fingerprints are processed through three categorizations: 1) data of asylum applications; 2) data of 'aliens' apprehended in connection with irregular border crossings; and 3) data related to 'aliens' 'illegally present' in member states (euLISA 2015: 13-14). Through algorithmic social sorting, the 'Automated Fingerprint Identification System' classifies some data subjects as undesired, resulting in 'digital deportability' (Tsianos & Kuster 2013). Digitally sanctioned deportation may happen when a 'hit' occurs: when a searched individual appears in the database, cross-referenced between the categories listed above.

The Central Database held over two million entries as of 2012 (Jones 2014: 3), but evidencing the growing stream of Syrian refugees, it processed a total of 750,000 transaction requests in 2014, an 84% increase compared to 2012. Observing migration management in practice in Germany, researchers witnessed how the EURODAC system automatically played a James Bond melody whenever it 'produced a hit' (Tsianos & Kuster 2013: 10). This example of smart border gamification blurs the boundaries between fact and fiction and exemplifies risks of dehumanization and depersonalization inherent to datafied social sorting. Individual people, faces, stories and motives are not of interest to 'smart' border processes. Furthermore, this echo of the popular culture version of espionage contrasts the automated, computational process of categorizing data subjects as undesirable, where the political struggle inherent in classification becomes naturalized through its bureaucratic manifestation (Bowker & Star 1999: 196). Seemingly without human intervention, EURODAC operates as a disciplinary truth machine, making data-driven decisions. In 2014, 24% of EURODAC entries produced a hit proving a 'data subject applied for asylum on two or more occasions', which means 121,358 people could be internally deported to a European member state where their fingerprints were previously taken. For 72,120 hits, data confirmed a data subject's 'illegal' presence in Europe (euLISA 2015: 4, 15), which rationalizes and normalizes deportation to countries of origin, where individual deportees may experience persecution, torture or worse (Bloch & Schuster 2005: 496-497).

The United Nations High Commissioner for Refugees (UNHCR) has rightly criticized EURODAC for breaching the human right to privacy and family life – placing data subjects at significant risk, as data may be shared with countries of origin – and for stigmatizing groups, as fingerprints are associated with criminal activity and can result in latent fingerprint errors that cannot be eliminated (UNHCR 2012). Although commonly presented as the perfect migrant management solution, such errors abound. In 2014, for example, from one million data entries, over one hundred thousand were rejected, largely due to data validation issues, fingerprint errors or insufficient data quality (euLISA 2015: 18). These errors are typically attributed to tactics used to contest machine readability, including migrants' attempts to purposefully damage their fingertips with glue for this purpose (European Commission 2015: 5). However, aging and heavy manual labour such as farming and construction work can also wear out fingerprints, causing insufficient image quality (Storisteanu et al. 2015: 137; see also Tsianos & Kuster 2013: 33-35). Despite these problems, the EU has since made fingerprinting mandatory in response to the trend in 2014-15 for Syrians and Eritreans refusing to be fingerprinted: 'In cases where a EURODAC data-subject does not initially cooperate in the process of being fingerprinted [...] it is suggested that all reasonable and proportionate steps should be taken to compel such cooperation,' including steps like detention and coercion by force (European Commission 2015: 4-5). And fingerprints are only one subset of potential biometric data collection. If EURODAC officials encounter difficulties establishing the age of data subjects as over 14, they corroborate fingerprints with medical examinations that can include visual, dental, bone X-rays, blood tests and sexual development tests, cross-referenced with connected data sets including census records.

The actions of EURODAC show how data subjects come to be constituted through a mixture of invasive and institutional strategies. The agency's own use of the term 'data subjects' implies that people have a say over how their data is compiled across diverse sources. And in fact, according to article 18(2) of the EURODAC regulation, migrants as data subjects have the right to access their data. But there is a huge gap between theory and practice. In 2014, data subjects lodged only 26 such requests, a number that has decreased from 49 in 2013 and 111 in 2012 (euLISA 2015: 18). These findings show that concerns previously voiced by the European Data Protection Supervisor (EDPS) over the lack of information available about consequences of being fingerprinted, the transmission of data, and rights of access, rectification and deletion have not been addressed and so 'the information provided to data subjects should be highly improved' (EDPS 2009: 14). But rather than data offering such subjectivity, datafied migration management evidences how migrants are subjected by data, with digital immobility and deportability – a dehumanized form of 'exclusion through registration' (Broeders 2011: 59) – as plausible social sorting outcomes.

Alongside database-led migrant management, the EU's 'smart' border control processes demand scrutiny. Europe's securitization of its external land, sea and aerial borders has resulted in the establishment of Frontex, the pan-European border agency, in 2004. In addition, in 2013, the European Border Surveillance System (Eurosur) was established to support the exchange of information between agencies 'for the purpose of detecting, preventing and combating illegal immigration and cross-border crime' at the 'external borders' (Frontex 2016a). The agency lists 'intelligence', 'risk analysis' and 'situational awareness' among its key missions, alongside its claim to operate in line with the EU fundamental rights charter. Providing lucrative business opportunities for a conglomerate of technology and arms manufacturers, this datafied surveillance arsenal combines radars, offshore sensors, on-shore olfactory sensors such as 'sniffer' and 'snoopy' satellite tracking systems, border patrol robots such as 'Talos' on land and 'Uncoss' at sea. Dronification is the latest step in this process, and a 'common pre-frontier intelligence picture' is established through unmanned aerial vehicles, Remote Piloted Aircraft Systems and Optionally Piloted Aircraft (*ibid.*).

In addition to internal migration management which operates mainly out of the public eye, Frontex also maintains detailed statistics on various border movements such as interceptions, and routinely uses infographics to make such data available to the public. These data visualizations further reify distinctions between insiders and outsiders, the Occident and Orient. Figure 15.1 is an exemplary Frontex data visualization depicting continental Europe and representations of various flows of incoming migrants. The orange arrow on the far right visualizes that between January and March 2016, over 150,000 people, mostly Syrian, Afghani and Iraqi nationals, attempted to illegally cross the border, taking the Eastern Mediterranean route (Frontex 2016b).

Fig. 15.1: Migratory Routes Map (Frontex 2016b)

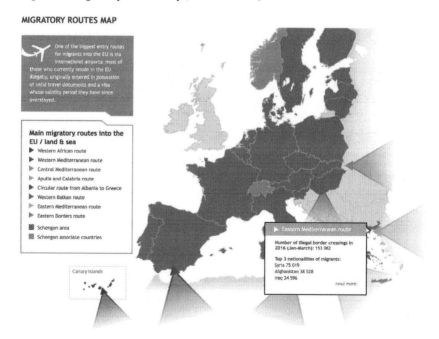

These kinds of data visualizations should be questioned, given emerging representational conventions such as mapping that serve to imbue data with 'objectivity' based on ideological notions of 'transparency, scientific-ness and facticity' (Kennedy et al. 2016: 716). Accordingly, the numerical and symbolic politics of this visualization can be unpacked: the choice to represent people with arrowheads taps into the symbolisms of weaponry, threat and massive contagion, while the proportional size of the arrows does not consistently reflect actual figures of interceptions (blue arrow equals yellow in size, but only visualizes 675 crossings). Frontex's provision of data visualizations is thus illustrative for its appeals to transparency and accountability but also for its ideological thrust. EU bordering is characterized by a paradoxical situation of painful 'exclusion from registration' (Broeders 2011: 59): a significant gap remains between what is recorded and what remains untracked. It is striking, for example, that the agency does not systematically gather data on deaths at the borders (Migrants' Files 2015). Prioritizing one 'smart' border statistic over another reflects a poignant decision, given that Europe has become the 'deadliest migration destiny of the world', with 3771 deaths in 2015 and 3521 deaths in 2016 in the first three quarters of the year alone the Mediterranean is becoming an 'open air cemetery' (Wolff 2015; UNHCR 2016). These crucial representational decisions lie at the heart of discriminatory data practices, which seem to maintain a longstanding appeal to quantitative objectivity despite the historical precedent for 'people in the algorithm' (Gillespie 2016).

From Statistical Subjects to Datafied Society

Contemporary cases around migration and border security offer a salient entry point into the discriminatory implications of a datafied society. But the current faith in big data as a font for accurate representations of and predictions about social groups has a much longer history. In terms of predicting risk, for example, the insurance industry was the site of key innovations that exemplify discriminatory practices at all levels of statistical calculation. Precedents for the cases of predictive discrimination in insurance redlining examined by Pasquale might be found in Dan Bouk's (2015) history of the American insurance industry's expansion in the late nineteenth century. By this time, insurance companies sought to expand beyond their traditional clientele of middle-class white men in the Northeastern states. Bouk charts the development of data-based metrics that asymmetrically created (not simply calculated) the higher risk factor of groups such as women, children, Southerners and African-Americans, which served not only to inform differential insurance policies but also to simultaneously construct vast swathes of the US population as differentially valued 'statistical subjects', the precursors to contemporary 'data subjects'.

One key story in this process was how Prudential's insurance policies were developed in the 1890s based on statistician Frederick Hoffman's measurements and calculations, including data gleaned from the tombstones of pre-Civil War segregated cemeteries and contemporaneous eugenic science (Bouk 2015: 113-120). Hoffman 'created the largest compilation of data about the American Negro then available in print', in support of Prudential's categorization of Southern African-American clients as higher risk (Wolff 2006: 85). While African-American activists mobilizing against this framing successfully pressured lawmakers to introduce anti-discrimination legislation, race-based discrimination in the insurance industry persists to this day:

> Race-based pricing classifications and coverage restrictions proved difficult to dislodge not only because of the structure and legal regulation of private commercial insurance markets, but also because of the strength of the underlying ideologies of racial difference, race separation, and the rhetorical power of actuarial language. Legislation and litigation, despite some progress, proved ineffective in changing industry practice. (Heen 2009: 362)

The historical precedent set by discriminatory insurance practices offers an origin narrative that captures a number of crucial dimensions to the modes of discrimination underlying the faith in big data today. Despite the seeming robustness of large data sets, as the European migration case illustrates, structural biases at every moment of 'calculation' – data gathering, organization, aggregation, algorithmic design, interpretation, prediction and visualization – serve to construct legitimized difference by reproducing existing inequalities across individuals as data subjects.

Despite their conceit to objectivity, data-based calculations reinforce inequalities specific to historical conjuncture. In the story of insurance redlining, it was post-Civil War race relations and the eugenics movement that informed data gathering and organization. In the story of today's 'refugee crisis', datafication is shaped by EU economic policy along with racial and ethnic stereotypes dating back to the colonial era. Whatever the historical moment, social context is key for understanding the specific modes of inequality embedded in quantitative operations. In turn, the application of data-driven insights to perceived social problems – typically framed around mitigating risk – performs a doubling of discriminatory frameworks through the asymmetrical representation of particular social problems that constructs them precisely as 'problems'. Representations of contemporary European migration, as discussed above, draw on disproportionately datafied renderings of certain groups of refugees, replicating fears of the other that stem from the colonial era. These representations show how the social thus becomes an effect of data as a resource to be appropriated (Couldry & Van Dijck 2015). The cycle of discriminatory measurement being used to inform discriminatory representations is one important point of continuity between the early uses of statistics and the current fashion for big data.

Another salient point of historical comparison concerns the role of the military-industrial complex in leading the way with the development and implementation of data-based 'solutions' to what are construed as social problems. Indeed, data-based discrimination as a military-industrial process seems not to be effectively contained by public governance or law; this goes for insurance as well as other sectors working to construct the statistical or data subject. The datafication of credit, medicine, marketing, human resources, policing, urban planning, transportation and security industries over the course of the twentieth century laid the groundwork for the ascendance of big data according to developments in information processing (Danna & Gandy 2002). The exponentially increasing capacity for collecting and tabulating social dynamics as information has been framed in James Beniger's (1989) classic text as a 'control revolution' coalescing around Big Science in the 1950s and 60s. At this time in the US, funding for the development of tools designed to gather, process and store increasingly large data sets was allocated according to a Cold War rationale intended to strengthen national security and military intelligence operations. The internet itself – the meta-network that supports proliferating data – of course emerges from within this context, as is evident in vestiges as such data 'caches' organized according to 'C3I' protocols (command, control, communication and intelligence) which operate behind the screen (Ricker Schulte 2015: 40; see also Gitelman 2006: 114; Norberg & O'Neill 1996). It is this Eurocentric and masculinist ideological nexus that informs the discriminatory considerations designed into data science technologies and techniques that, when combined with the commercialization imperatives of industry, form the basis for the networking of statistical subjects together within a datafied society.

What changes in the move from a statistical society to a datafied society is framed by proponents of big data as economies of scale. Innovative insights emerge from networking between unprecedented large data sets, which creates value far beyond any one set alone (Mayer-Schönberger & Cukier 2013: 135). Yet despite these economies of scale, similar operations that have historically encoded discrimination into statistical calculations remain. The implication of networking large data sets is that at every level, from individual data subjects – and even more finely, 'dividuals' or sub-individual units (Terranova 2004: 34) – up to entrenched industries and institutions, epistemological and ideological contours around what counts and how it is measured still serve to produce and reinforce structural inequality. Unlike traditional statistical analysis, however, big data methods perform these operations in ways that are often automated and invisible. Quintessential examples of contemporary social life being reorganized according to discriminatory datafication include Facebook's profiling of users' 'ethnic affinities' based on their online activities, Amazon's redlined same-day delivery zones, or Google's culturally and linguistically biased search results (Knobel & Bowker 2011; Noble 2016). The invisibility of the algorithmic biases underlying such social platforms enable the 'laundering of past practices of discrimination' so that they become black-boxed, 'immune from scrutiny' (Pasquale 2015: 41).

Further, the development of social sorting algorithms in commercial contexts informs contemporary modes of governance, as seen in the case of migration – enabled by a permanent state of exception preserved through the 'war on terrorism' (Guzik 2009) – where police surreptitiously collect data and run predictive calculations that violate the privacy of people living in racialized communities (Crawford & Schultz 2014), and the State distinguishes citizenship from 'foreignness' according to the hidden logic of the National Security Agency's surveillance assemblage (Cheney-Lippold 2016). The public implication of this shift toward opaque and automated datafied discrimination renders justice through transparency and accountability ever more elusive for data subjects (Barocas & Selbst 2016).

The fact that datafication supports the increasing automation and opacity of discriminatory practices not only accords with what Beniger foresaw as the centrality of information processing for social control, but also points toward immanent surveillance as the crux of domination. The military-industrial invention of the datafied individual can be seen as more deeply embedded within a colonial legacy of surveillance as the means of achieving the dual purpose of value extraction and social control (Mbembe 1992). While in a datafied society one might think instead of 'dataveillance', the continuous monitoring that pervades the social fabric through immanent collection of both data and metadata 'for unstated present purposes' (Van Dijck 2014: 205; see also Zimmer 2008), the ways in which algorithms exert discriminatory 'soft bio-power' find precursors in surveillance as a disciplinary gaze (Cheney-Lippold 2011).

In order to collect people's information, they must be observed, their pertinent information discerned, translated into a notation system and organized. Each of these steps involves a surveillant gaze whose roots can be traced to military-industrial colonial expansion that relied on making use of indigenous populations through techniques based on visible measurement (Glissant 1997). This profit-oriented domination was further justified through European imperial knowledge systems such as medically proven 'inferiority' which rationalized the existence of 'subject races' (e.g. non-whites) that needed to be ruled by white superiors as part of their civilizing mission (Said 2014; Wekker 2015). Disproportionate applications of surveillance to othered bodies characterized the slave trade as a network of power exercised through a monopoly of knowledge comprised of overseers, paper technologies, shipping routes, biometrics, plantations, identification cards and the census (Browne 2015; Siegert 2006). Parallel to contemporary data visualization and the social graph, these various practices of surveillance generated data that could be processed, organized and, most importantly, mapped onto the expanding territories of empire (Shepherd 2015). Moreover, the ways in which diverse data sources could be networked through mapping highlights the Eurocentric conceit of datafication; as José Rabasa (1993: 180) contends, traces of European expansionism continue to imbue measurements and representations of the social world with an underlying Eurocentric universality – this is the basis for the 'we' who benefit from big data in Mayer-Schönberger & Cukier's account.

An epistemological critique thus subtends a look backward to the historical precedents for applications of data processing to social organization. The ways in which knowledge is produced through measurement invokes a culturally specific set of baggage inherent in the very language used to delimit what counts as 'data', as the first step in a series of human processes that seek to make sense of the social world through measurement and organization. Even within a Eurocentric lineage of structuralist and post-structuralist thought (e.g. Foucault's *Les mots et les choses*, 1966), human sciences are acknowledged to be governed by an unconscious set of formative rules as productive of knowledge as power. In this light, the work of nineteenth-century anthropometrist Adolphe Quetelet, who believed that data sets large enough would produce accurate predictions of criminality

(Beirne 1987), might be seen as a formative epistemological touchstone for the contemporary faith in the 'bigness' of big data. Belief in quantification is a hallmark of this episteme, embedded in the language, tools, methods and data itself used to represent social life. In other words, the software that immanently conducts operations of collection, organization and prediction might be seen as the 'frozen organizational and policy discourse' that circulates as a means of legitimizing inequality (Bowker & Star 1999: 135).

Methodological Interventions and Alternative Cartographies

Therefore, the question arises whether we can repurpose big data approaches for anti-oppressive knowledge production, and, if so, how? We explore this question by offering some methodological considerations developed from the situated case of human mobility. Clearly, the methodological debate on big data is polarized. Utopianists celebrate big data as the next lucrative frontier (colonial metaphor intended). In line with this optimistic rhetoric, quantitative and mathematically oriented scholars have praised big data for natural, unmediated, objective, purer and self-explanatory access to social processes. Exemplary of this discourse is the recognition of the 'data scientist' as the 'sexiest job title of the 21st century' (cited in Gehl 2015). On the other end of the spectrum, a dystopian denouncement of big data as a form of 'methodological genocide' highlights its lack of attention to history, culture, context, specificity, meanings, structure and agency (Uprichard 2015).

Realistically, because datafication is a pressing contemporary empirical geopolitical reality, we cannot simply reject dealing with it, nor should we univocally champion it as a silver bullet. Evelyn Ruppert and her colleagues suggest that data mining can be of value for socio-cultural research through 'specific mobilizations' of certain digital methods 'in particular locations' (2013: 32). Similarly, the chapter on reflexive research by Karin van Es, Nicolás López Coombs and Thomas Boeschoten in the present collection (pp. 171-180) offers a promising starting point for opening up onto more critical methodological approaches to the datafied society. However, to date, little attention has been given to how to make data mining a people-centred process, which accounts for dynamism, complexity, reflexivity, diversity and multiplicity (Leurs forthcoming 2017).

The common paradigm of disembodied, impartial knowledge production is often conducted on the basis of a utilitarian research ethics. In large-scale data-driven research projects, ethical safeguards are commonly geared toward managing risk and reputation on the part of the institution, rather than protecting those people involved in the study. This model draws on a cost-benefit analysis and abides by expectations held by biomedical-ethically oriented university Institutional Review Boards. Consider for example the painful example of the 'massive-scale emotional contagion' experiment, where a team of academic and industry researchers manipulated the News Feeds of nearly seven hundred thousand unwitting Facebook users. They took Facebook's Terms of Service as a proxy for informed consent, and no one could opt out from the study (Kramer, Guillory & Hancock 2014).

By contrast, providing distinctive alternative ethical positions stemming from feminist, critical pedagogical, anti-oppressive, community-based and Indigenous paradigms and methods offers ways to rethink big data as a progressive toolkit. Although they have yet to engage in sustained dialogue with data studies, these approaches share a common interest in dialogically involving informants as knowledge co-producers or co-researchers who share valuable insights. They involve consciously highlighting the human in data-based decision-making, where each step in the process of creating and manipulating large data sets involves ethical reflexivity (O'Neil 2016). With ambitions to decolonize dominant disembodied research methodologies that claim positivist objectivity, scholars in alternative paradigms seek to establish greater reciprocity for underprivileged, queer, Indigenous or otherwise non-mainstream voices (Kovach 2010; Walter & Andersen 2013). Rather than neutrally extracting self-explanatory data from an apolitical data void, scholars may account for power relations, and prioritize listening, relationalities, fluidity, journeying, mutual trust and strategic refusals as a way of helping data subjects regain sovereignty over knowledge production. When transposed to the digital context, these approaches may prompt scholars as activists to take seriously the agency of individuals over their own information; this data can be collaboratively repurposed for community advocacy (Gubrium & Harper 2013).

Alternative cartographies and bottom-up initiatives that reinstate what's missing in big data are exemplary for how data-based initiatives can be appropriated for community advocacy, 'civic action' (Schäfer 2016), 'agency' (Kennedy, Poell & Van Dijck 2015) and 'data activism' (Milan & Gutiérrez 2015). Various digital counters and mapping initiatives maintained by consortia of journalists, researchers and activists that combine big and small data (individual cases) have made a growing impact. For example, the Bureau of Investigative Journalism (BIJ) manages wherethedronesstrike.com, visualizing 10 years of drone strikes in Pakistan. The Missing Migrant Project maintained by the International Organization of Migration tracks 'deaths

Fig. 15.2:   Abdul Satar's story (Bureau of Investigative Journalism 2016)

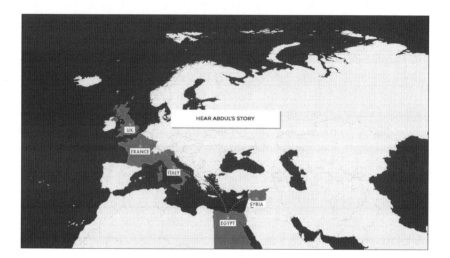

along migratory routes worldwide'. The Migrants' Files similarly maps 'the human and financial cost of 15 years of Fortress Europe', providing 'data-driven insights on migration to Europe'.

The BIJ's recent infographic, 'Which countries treat children like children?' (Figure 15.2), provides access to voices and accounts of 95,000 unaccompanied children seeking asylum in Europe in 2015. Besides numerical overviews, situated individual voices are integrated into the map. For example, we can find out about Abdul Satar's story. We see a young man in a photograph, a 17-year old Syrian currently living in London. He fled from his native country in 2013. In a video, we hear how he narrates his journey in Arabic, with English subtitles. This journey is also visualized, alongside the complete translated transcript of the interview. His claim, 'Someone must talk about us – because no one is listening to us', resonates through the small-data contextual cues juxtaposed against the larger data set.

Such initiatives commonly combine various sources of people-centred information, crowdsourced data gathering and open access databases that accommodate non-specialist public audiences for the information. For further examples of how alternative data corpora can draw attention to marginalized issues, consider the Information Sharing Portal on refugees and migrants emergency responses in the Mediterranean (UNHCR 2016), the Missing Migrant Project listing cross-referenced deaths of migrants at the European borders since 2000 (IOM, 2016), and TMF MoneyTrails an open access spreadsheet listing the costs of EU deportations from 2000 onwards (2016). While combining large and small data sets and toggling between distant and close reading can risk a reification of the methods themselves (Caplan 2016), the point to emphasize in alternative cartographies is the reflexive self-positioning of the observer. In this way, small data might be reconceptualized as 'deep data', information rendered self-aware through cultural continuity that acknowledges data's formative epistemological contexts (Brock 2015). These embodied, situated and re-humanized examples of doing 'deep data' analysis offer incentives to further think about ways in which big data might be strategically mobilized as an anti-oppressive knowledge-power system.

Conclusion: Who Are 'We' in the Datafied Society?

Returning to the proclamation that big data affords a revolutionary change in the ways 'we live, work and think', as phrased by Mayer-Schönberger and Cukier's subtitle, the 'we' might be most fruitfully interrogated from the perspective of power and privilege. Their popular account of big data may indeed be seen as a continuation of longstanding power structures within the mythologies of information processing. Echoing Cisco CEO John Chambers's claim in the 1990s that the internet would 'change the way we work, live, play and learn' (Fryer & Stewart 2008), the rise of big data extends Beniger's control revolution, which opens with the conceit that 'understanding ourselves in our own particular moment in history will enable us to shape and guide that history' (1986: 6). If the goal of data-based inquiry is to shape and guide history, and if 'methods are social practices, means of forming good communities, not just tools for poking at reality' (Peters 2011: 444), then specifying the 'we' who are invested with agency and 'they' who become the excluded others in a datafied society is critical. Data analytics dashboards seductively promise a complete rendering of reality, but any approach to data-based social research must contend with the thorny question: who are 'we'? And how can 'we' be critiqued, opened up, accessed and delineated? As shown in the contemporary case of migration, situated within a colonial history of the statistical measurement of populations, data's inherent discriminatory operations need to be uncovered in order to get at the 'we'. This involves recognizing the politics embedded within technological artefacts (e.g. Winner 1980), and particularly recognizing the asymmetrical power embedded in a doctrine of objectivity 'honed to perfection in the history of science tied to militarism, capitalism, colonialism, and male supremacy' (Haraway 1991: 187). Taking this specific assemblage of privilege into account, researchers working with data can counter the investments in its 'bigness' with anti-oppressive tactics drawn from small and deep data co-construction in order to lay bare the ethical implications of a datafied society.

Acknowledgements

This research was supported by the Netherlands Organisation for Scientific Research (NWO) Veni-grant 'Young Connected Migrants', project reference 275-45-007. We benefited from inspiring discussions with the members of the Canadian Social Sciences and Humanities Research Council funded network 'The Fourchettes: Critical methods in technoculture', and Sandra Ponzanesi, Domitilla Olivieri, Laura Candidatu, Claudia Minchili, Melis Mevsimler, Donya Alinejad. Thanks Karin van Es and Mirko Schäfer for your critical questions and feedback.

References

Agamben, Giorgio. 2005. *State of exception*. Chicago: University of Chicago Press.

Ajana, Btihaj. 2013. *Governing through biometrics: The biopolitics of identity*. Basingstoke: Palgrave Macmillan.

Arora, Payal. 2016. "The bottom of the data pyramid: Big data and the global South." *International Journal of Communication* 10: 1681-1699.

Balibar, Etienne. 2004. *We, the people of Europe?* Princeton: Princeton University Press.

Barocas, Solon & Andrew D. Selbst. 2016. "Big Data's Disparate Impact." *California Law Review* 104. http://papers.ssrn.com/sol3/papers.cfm?abstract_id=2477899.

Beirne, Piers. 1987. "Adolphe Quetelet and the origins of positivist criminology." *American Journal of Sociology* 92(5): 1140-1169.

Beniger, James. 1989. *The control revolution: Technological and economic origins of the information society*. Cambridge, MA: Harvard University Press.

Bloch, Alice & Liza Schuster. 2005. "At the extremes of exclusion: Deportation, detention and dispersa." *Ethnic and Racial Studies* 28(3): 491-512.

Bouk, Dan. 2015. *How our days became numbered: Risk and the rise of the statistical individual*. Chicago: University of Chicago Press.

Bowker, Geoffrey C. & Susan Leigh Star. 1999. *Sorting things out: Classification and its consequences*. Cambridge, MA: The MIT Press.

boyd, danah, & Crawford, Kate. 2012. "Critical Questions for Big Data: Provocations for a Cultural, Technological, And Scholarly Phenomenon." *Information, Communication & Society* 15 (5): 662-679.

Brock, Andre. 2015. "Deeper data: a response to boyd and Crawford." *Media, Culture & Society* 37(7): 1084-1088.

Broeders, Dennis. 2011 "A European 'border' surveillance system under construction', in H. Dijstelbloem & A. Meijer (eds.), *Migration and the new technological borders of Europe*. Basingstoke: Palgrave: 40-67.

Broeders, Dennis., & Huub Dijstelbloem. 2016. "The datafication of mobility and migration management: The mediating state and its consequences." In *Digitizing identities: Doing identity in a networked world*, ed. I. Van der Ploeg and J. Pridmore, 242-260. London: Routledge.

Bureau of Investigative Journalism. "Which countries treat children like children?" www.thebureauinvestigates.com/which_countries_treat_children_like_children/ Accessed 4 October 2016.

Browne, Simone. 2015. *Dark matters: On the surveillance of blackness*. Durham, NC: Duke University Press.

Caplan, Lindsay. 2016. "Method without methodology: Data and the digital humanities." *E-flux* 72(4): www.e-flux.com/journal/method-without-methodology-data-and-the-digital-humanities/.

Cheney-Lippold, John. 2011. "A new algorithmic identity: Soft biopolitics and the modulation of control." *Theory, Culture & Society* 28(6): 164-181.

—. 2016. "Jus Algoritmi: How the national security agency remade citizenship." *International Journal of Communication* 10: 1721-1742.

Couldry, Nick. 2012. *Media, Society, World: Social theory and digital media practice*. London: Polity.

Couldry, Nick & José van Dijck. 2015. "Researching social media as if the social mattered." *Social Media + Society* 1 (2): http://sms.sagepub.com/content/1/2/2056305115604174.full.

Crawford, Kate & Jason Schultz. 2014. "Big data and due process: Toward a framework to redress predictive privacy harms." *Boston College Law Review* 55(1): 93-128.

Danna, Anthony & Oscar H. Gandy Jr. 2002. "All that glitters is not gold: Digging beneath the surface of data mining." *Journal of Business Ethics* 40(4): 373-386.

Dijck, José van. 2014. "Datafication, dataism and dataveillance: Big Data between scientific paradigm and ideology." *Surveillance & Society* 12(2): 197-208.

Elmer, Greg, Ganaele Langlois & Joanna Redden (eds.). 2015. *Compromised Data: From Social Media to Big Data*. New York: Bloomsbury Publishing USA.

EDPS 2009. "Eurodac Supervision Coordination Group Second Inspection Report." https://secure.edps.europa.eu/EDPSWEB/webdav/shared/Documents/Supervision/Eurodac/09-06-24_Eurodac_report2_EN.pdf.

European Commission. 2015. "Commission staff working document on Implementation of the Eurodac Regulation as regards the obligation to take fingerprints." http://ec.europa.eu/dgs/home-affairs/e-library/documents/policies/asylum/general/docs/guidelines_on_the_implementation_of_eu_rules_on_the_obligation_to_take_fingerprints_en.pdf.

—. 2016. "Stronger and smarter information systems for borders and Security. Communication from the commission to the European Parliament and the Council." www.eulisa.europa.eu/Newsroom/News/Documents/SB-EES/communication_on_stronger_and_smart_borders_20160406_en.pdf.

euLISA. 2015. "Annual report on the 2014 activities of the Central System of Eurodac." www.eulisa.europa.eu/Publications/Reports/Eurodac%202014%20Annual%20Report.pdf.

Foucault, Michel. 1966. *Les mots et les choses*. Paris: Gallimard.

Frontex. 2016a. "Legal basis." http://frontex.europa.eu/about-frontex/legal-basis/.

—. 2016b. "Migratory routes map." http://frontex.europa.eu/trends-and-routes/migratory-routes-map/.

Fryer, Bronwyn, Thomas A. Stewart & John Chambers. 2008. "Cisco sees the future: The HBR interview with John Chambers." *Harvard Business Review* 86(11): 72-79.

Gangadharan, Seeta Peña (Ed.). 2014. *Data and Discrimination: Selected Essays*. Washington, DC: Open Technology Institute, New America Foundation. www.newamerica.org/oti/ data-and-discrimination/.

Gehl, Robert W. 2015. "Sharing, knowledge management and big data: A partial genealogy of the data scientist." *European Journal of Cultural Studies* 18(4-5): 413-428.

Glissant, Edouard. 1997. *Poetics of Relation*. B. Wing (transl.). Ann Arbor: University of Michigan Press.

Gillespie, Tarleton. 2016. "Facebook Trending: It's made of people!!" *Culture Digitally*, 9 May: http:// culturedigitally.org/2016/05/facebook-trending-its-made-of-people-but-we-should-have-already-known-that/.

Gitelman, Lisa. 2006. *Always already new: Media, history and the data of culture*. Cambridge, MA: The MIT Press.

Gubrium, Aline & Krista Harper. 2013. *Participatory visual and digital methods*. Walnut Creek, CA: Left Coast Press.

Haraway, Donna. 1991. *Simians, cyborgs, and women: The reinvention of nature*. New York: Routledge.

Heen, Mary L. 2009. "Ending Jim Crow life insurance rates." *Northwestern Journal of Law & Social Policy* 4: 360-399.

IOM. 2016. "Missing migrants project." http://missingmigrants.iom.int.

Kennedy, Helen, Rosemary Lucy Hill, Giorgia Aiello & William Allen. 2016. "The work that visualization conventions do." *Information, Communication & Society* 19 (6): 715-735.

Kennedy, Helen, Thomas Poell & José van Dijck. 2015. "Introduction: Special issue on Data and agency." *Data & Society*. December,

Kovach, Margaret Elizabeth. 2010 *Indigenous methodologies: Characteristics, conversations, and contexts*. Toronto: University of Toronto Press.

Knobel, Cory & Geoffrey C. Bowker. 2011. "Values in design." *Communications of the ACM* 54(7): 26-28.

Kramer, Adam DI, Jamie E. Guillory & Jeffrey T. Hancock. 2014. "Experimental evidence of massive-scale emotional contagion through social networks." *PNAS* 111(29): 8788-8790.

Leurs, Koen. Forthcoming 2017. "Feminist data studies: Using digital methods for ethical, reflexive and situated socio-cultural research. Lessons learned from researching young Londoners' digital identities." *Feminist Review* 115, Feminist Methods themed issue.

Mayer-Schönberger, Viktor & Kenneth Cukier. 2013. *Big data: A revolution that will transform how we live, work, and think*. New York: Houghton Mifflin Harcourt.

Migrants' Files. 2016. "The human and financial cost of 15 years of Fortress Europe." www.themigrantsfiles.com/.

Milan, Stefania & Miren Gutiérrez. "Medios ciudadanos y big data: La emergencia del activismo de datos." *MEDIACIONES* (14): 10-26.

Mbembe, Achille. 1992. "Provisional notes on the postcolony." *Africa: Journal of the International African Institute* 62(1): 3-37.

Noble, Safiya U. 2016. *Algorithms of oppression: Race, gender and power in the digital age*. New York: New York University Press.

Norberg, Arthur L., Judy E. O'Neill & Kerry J. Freedman. 1996. *Transforming computer technology: Information processing for the Pentagon, 1962-1986*. Baltimore: Johns Hopkins University Press.

O'Neil, Cathy. 2016. "How to bring a better ethics to data science." *Slate*, 4 February: www.slate. com/articles/technology/future_tense/2016/02/how_to_bring_better ethics_to_data_science.html.

Pasquale, Frank. 2015. *The Black Box Society: The Secret Algorithms that Control Money and Information.* Cambridge, MA: Harvard University Press.

Peters, John Durham. 2001. "'The only proper scale of representation': The politics of statistics and stories." *Political Communication* 18(4): 433-449.

Ponzanesi, Sandra. 2016. "Connecting Europe: Postcolonial mediations." Inaugural lecture Utrecht University: www.uu.nl/file/43575/download?token=mZlBGt8R.

Rabasa, José. 1993. *Inventing America: Spanish historiography and the formation of Eurocentrism.* Norman, OK: University of Oklahoma Press.

Ricker Schulte, Stephanie. 2015. *Cached: Decoding the Internet in Global Popular Culture.* New York: NYU Press.

Said, Edward. 2014. *Orientalism. 25th anniversary edition.* New York: Vintage Books.

Schäfer, Mirko. 2016. "Introduction to special issue: Challenging citizenship: Social media and big data." *Computer Supported Cooperative Work* 25(2): 111–113.

Shepherd, Tamara. 2015. "Mapped, measured, and mined: The social graph and colonial visuality." *Social Media + Society* 1(1): http://sms.sagepub.com/content/1/1/2056305115578671.full.

Siegert, Bernhard. 2006. *Passagiere und Papiere: Schreibakte auf der Schwelle zwischen Spanien und Amerika.* Munich: Fink.

Storisteanu, Daniel Matthew L., Toby L. Norman, Alexandra Grigore & Tristram L. Norman. 2015. "Biometric fingerprint system to enable rapid and accurate identification of beneficiaries." *Global Health* 3(1): 135-137.

Terranova, Tiziana. 2004. *Network Culture: Politics for the Information Age.* London: Pluto Press.

TMF Money Trails. 2016. "Deportations. https://docs.google.com/spreadsheets/d/1rDThuJ1HV TsWWPEvauOIGuYokd7h8fGkrxebmlMt7h4/.

Tsianos, Vassilis & Brigitta Kuster. 2013. "Thematic report 'Border Crossings.'" *MIG@NET. Transnational digital networks, migration and gender:* www.mignetproject.eu/?p=577.

UNHCR. 2016. "Information Sharing Portal. Refugees/Migrants Emergency Response – Mediterranean". http://data.unhcr.org/mediterranean/regional.php.

UNHCR. 2012. "An efficient and productive EURODAC". http://www.unhcr.org/50adf9749.pdf

Uprichard, Emma. 2015. "Most big data is social data – the analytics need serious interrogation. Philosophy of Data Science." *Impact of Social Science Blog*, London School of Economics and Political Science. Available at: http://blogs.lse.ac.uk/impactofsocialsciences/2015/02/12/philosophy-of-data-science-emma-uprichard/.

Walter, Maggie & Chris Andersen. 2013. *Indigenous Statistics: A Quantitative Research Methodology.* Walnut Creek, CA: Left Coast Press.

Walters, William. 2005. *Rethinking Borders Beyond the State.* Basingstoke: Palgrave.

Wekker, Gloria. 2015. *White Innocence.* Durham, NC: Duke University Press.

Winner, Langdon. 1980. "Do artifacts have politics?" *Daedalus* 109(1): 121-136.

Wolff, Sarah. 2015. "Deaths at the border. Scant hope for the future." *Clingendael:* www.clingendael.nl/publication/deaths-sea-scant-hope-future?lang=nl.

Wolff, Megan J. 2006. "The myth of the actuary: Life insurance and Frederick L. Hoffman's 'Race Traits and Tendencies of the American Negro.'" *Public Health Reports* 121(1): 84-91.

Zimmer, M. 2008. "The gaze of the perfect search engine: Google as an infrastructure of dataveillance." In A. Spink & M. Zimmer (eds.), *Web Search*, 77-99. Berlin: Springer.

Section 4
Key Ideas in Big Data Research

In what follows we have asked four scholars several questions pertaining to ideas they have formulated which we find are key to researchers interested in the datafication of society. In the first two short interviews we tackled fundamental challenges facing online data research. We asked Nick Couldry, Professor of Media, Communications and Social Theory at the London School of Economics, about the myth of big data. He poses concerns about the validity of Web-based data analysis to formulate statements about social interaction and cultural production. Connected hereto is the data point critique formulated by Carolin Gerlitz, Professor of Media Studies at the University of Siegen. She considers the research problem of making data points (e.g. likes and shares) countable and comparable despite emerging from different interpretations, practices and actors. We subsequently zoom out to discuss the role of algorithms in our society and algorithmic exceptionalism with internet critic Evgeny Morozov. He stresses the fact that algorithms provide a continuation rather than a break with previous practices. Lastly we turn to Mercedes Bunz, Senior Lecturer at the University of Westminster, for a discussion on the need for a dialogue with technology. She considers how data and algorithms affect the heart of our society, in that it reshapes our understanding of media industries and public discourses.

16.   The Myth of Big Data

Nick Couldry

Increasingly, institutions in the fields of research and policymaking, as well as the corporate realm, base decision-making and knowledge production on metrics calculated from what is metaphorically called 'big data'. In his 2013 inaugural lecture 'A Necessary Disenchantment: Myth, Agency and Injustice in a Digital World', Nick Couldry discusses the mythical claim that big data is generating a new and better form of social knowledge.

What does/doesn't 'big data' tell us about the social? Or in other words, what type of 'social' is being constructed in social media?

No one disputes that data sets in every domain, including those relating to the social, are very large, or that, because they are so large, there is something to be gained by using automated processing to establish correlations across those data sets; such processing is, of course, beyond the capacity of human interpreters. The issue is how we interpret the value of the outputs of such processing. Already in the latently metaphorical term big data, there is a story being told about human beings' changing relation to the domain we have called social that is highly contestable. Big data, it is implied, is the source of a different order of knowledge, a step change in human self-understanding that precisely bypasses humans' meagre attempts at self-understanding through interpreting the local details of what they think, say and do. This way of putting things obviously prejudges positively the value of the outputs of 'big data' processing. That is the ideological work done by the term 'big', beyond its obvious descriptive force (and, as I said, no one disputes that the data sets involved are very large!). I don't believe we should accept this story, and I will come back later to how we could contest it. But if we simply accept it, it has major consequences for the type of social domain that is accessible to us as researchers and social actors. 'Big data' is only possible on two basic conditions (which actually are composites of many more detailed conditions): first, that data is collected continuously about the states of affairs in various domains (including not just what individuals do and say, but the state of their bodies); second, that data is aggregated and its patterns of correlation computed and 'interpreted'. Because only information of particular sorts conforms to the requirements of data management, and because only processes of particular sorts generates such information, 'big data', however expanded its scope and however fine-tuned its workings, must always be a selection from the actual world of action and interaction. danah boyd and Kate Crawford (in their important 2013 article on the 'myths' of big data) brought out the many specific delusions in relying on 'big data' as a source of knowledge, but in my work I have tried to focus on the overall delusion that, if you like, frames all the specific ones: that is, the overall attempt to reorient us towards big data processes as 'the' new form of social knowledge.

Ideological uses of the term 'big data' however forget that general, yet highly motivated, selectivity, and so inevitably misread the picture of the social obtained through big data processing, but with a constructive force that is difficult to resist, especially when investment in social knowledge (by governments, funders, private corporations) is increasingly focused on 'big data'. Over time, this may obscure our possibilities for imagining, describing and enacting the social otherwise. Meanwhile, the ideological work is going on all around us, whether in Wired magazine editor Chris Anderson's trailblazing article 'The End of Theory' (Anderson 2007) or more critically in a book such as Mayer-Schönberger and Kenneth Cukier's *Big Data: A Revolution that Will Transform How We Live, Work, and Think* (2013) where they predict that, as datafication and big data processing grows, 'we will no longer regard our world as a string of happenings that we explain as a natural or social phenomenon, but as a universe comprised essentially of information' (2013: 96, emphasis added). Note that opposition: not 'natural or social' but 'essentially information'.

Clearly those with skills at interpreting the social 'need not apply' in this new world of 'social' knowledge! The paradox, as with most forms of symbolic violence, lies only just below the surface, but it relies for its effectiveness on us letting it pass without comment – and on us acting out its consequences every day. I will come back to action and resistance in a moment. The long-term consequences of this ideological shift towards 'big data' as the new default source of knowledge about 'the social' takes two contrasting forms.

First, in how the particular details of data collection and data processing recalibrate the possibilities of social existence, the ontology if you like of the social. We feel this at work from hour to hour as we monitor our day to decide whether it is 'worth' a status update on whatever social media platform we use. But the detailed workings are much harder to track, and require exhaustive analysis of the linked data sets on which, for example, automated credit ratings are based. Oscar Gandy was pioneering in seeing the socially discriminatory potential of corporate data collection a quarter of a century ago (Gandy 1993), and my LSE colleague Seeta Gangadharan is doing great work in this area: www.datacivilrights.org/.

And second – and this was more my focus in my inaugural lecture, at LSE (Couldry 2014) – to criticize the overall celebration of social knowledge achieved through automated, processing and, by contrast, the devaluing – even the attempted decommissioning,– of other forms of social knowledge that until fairly recently, were taken seriously. To unpack this, we need 'a hermeneutic of the anti-hermeneutic'; we need to register what Judith Butler calls 'a refusal of discourse' (2004: 36). If we don't, we risk losing touch – in our languages about the social – with a basic truth: that, as philosopher Charles Taylor (1986) put it, the human being is 'a self-interpreting animal' and so the only possible meaning of our lives together stems from its basis in our attempts to interpret what we do to each other. Without a hold on that truth, we accept a risk of inhabiting what the 19th-century Russian novelist Nikolai Gogol called 'dead souls': human entities that have financial value (in his novel, as mortgageable assets; in our new world, as unwitting data producers), but that are not alive, not at least in the sense we have always known human beings to be alive.

But why talk about the claims about big data as mythical? Why should we care so much about the myth of big data?

That goes back to the question of action. In much of my work I have been concerned with how it is that large modern societies have become organized, if you like focused, around the productions of particular institutions with huge symbolic power, whether traditional media institutions or increasingly the organizations that run our digital platforms and also those that generate process and own the data that we, largely unwittingly, generate through our actions online. I have always argued that such a big social 'fix' requires something more than ideology in the traditional sense: it requires us to act in ways that conform to it. Here Žižek's concept of ideology (1990) is more helpful than Marx's, but personally I have preferred to use the term 'myth'. The myth of big data is a fix of that sort: a society-wide rationalization of a certain state of affairs that works not just, or sometimes not even, through what we think, but always through what we do: what we go on doing, whatever we believe ('clicking like' and so on). The myth of big data is particularly broad in how it has emerged and is being played out, but is also particularly important in that it works to challenge the very idea that the social is something we can interpret at all. It works to disable other, older (and no doubt newer) forms of social knowledge. That, I believe, will have huge consequences in the longer term for our understandings of democratic agency and social justice.

So how then do we achieve a more agent-focused account of big data?

This is a long-term collective battle, and there are many levels to it. First, we need to refuse the myth as such: to reject its explicit claims and language. The myth of big data is an attempt to appropriate the possibilities of producing knowledge about the social domain, which needs to be resisted. So specific attempts to claim better understanding of the social based on automated processing of very large data sets need to be closely interrogated as specific claims, stripping away the usual rhetoric about 'how all social knowledge is changing' that often accompanies such specific claims.

Second, and as another LSE colleague, Alison Powell, and I argued in an article called 'Big Data from the Bottom Up', the skills and collaborative practices necessary for those outside the large institutions that benefit from the myth of big data – including civil society organizations – to work with large data sets must be developed and encouraged. It is the case – and this is the good element in some big data rhetoric – that cities might be run better if citizens gathered different types of data about what goes on in cities, and were empowered not only to decide how that data is being analysed to citizens' mutual advantage, but also what sorts of action might flow from the knowledge the analysis of that data generates. Part of that process of opening up civically the black box of 'big data' (but which we would do better to simply call very large data sets) means spreading awareness of how currently vast data sets are collected, sifted, aggregated and then repackaged as sources of truth, but without much, if any, accountability for the rules of operation that drive that process.

This practical civic project holds to a basic principle of social science research, that it should work towards the 'de-reification' of social processes (Sewell 2005). Never have we needed a project of 'de-reification' more than today, I suspect.

References

Anderson, Chris. 2008. "The End of Theory: The Data Deluge Makes the Scientific Method Obsolete." *WIRED*. 23 June. www.wired.com/2008/06/pb-theory/.

boyd, danah, & Crawford, Kate. 2012. "Critical Questions for Big Data: Provocations for a Cultural, Technological, And Scholarly Phenomenon." *Information, Communication & Society* 15 (5): 662-679.

Butler, Judith. 2006. *Precarious Life: The Powers of Mourning and Violence*. Verso.

Gandy Jr., Oscar H. 1993. *The Panoptic Sort: A Political Economy of Personal Information. Critical Studies in Communication and in the Cultural Industries*. ERIC.

Gogol, Nikolay. 2004. *Dead Souls*. New York: Penguin Press.

Mayer-Schönberger, Viktor & Kenneth Cukier. 2013. *Big Data: A Revolution that Will Transform How We Live, Work, and Think*. New York: Houghton Mifflin Harcourt.

Sewell Jr, William H. 2005. *Logics of History: Social Theory and Social Transformation*. Chicago: University of Chicago Press.

Taylor, Charles. 1985. "Self-Interpreting Animals." In Taylor, Charles: *Human Agency and Language*. Cambridge: Cambridge University Press, 45-76.

Žižek, Slavoj. 1989. *The Sublime Object of Ideology*. London: Verso.

17.   Data Point Critique

Carolin Gerlitz

There is a plethora of publications emerging in the humanities, especially media studies, that use data points from social media platforms in order to investigate social interaction and cultural production. Data points taken from social media platforms are used for calculating metrics on the most diverse aspects of users and use. As Carolin Gerlitz has pointed out, research practices tend to treat these data points alike in spite of the fact that they take on different functions (Gerlitz & Rieder 2013) and even though they are used by different social groups (Bruns & Stieglitz 2013). Drawing on Espeland & Stevens (1998), Gerlitz calls this the commensuration of data points and formulates a data point critique.

What does your criticism of making data points countable and comparable for analysis consist of exactly?

Digital media are informed by standardization. What users can do in social media or platforms is usually prestructured into specific forms or – to quote that Agre (1994) – grammars of action. Friending, following, liking, commenting, sharing or favoriting allows users to act in prestructured form in the front end whilst at the same time producing equally prestructured data points in the back end. Action and capture are collapsed and happen simultaneously. A proliferating array of counters, tickers and notifications interfaces between action and capture, presenting users with aggregate counts of grammars performed through like or share counters, numbers of comments and other metrics. Whilst some platforms offer a rather limited set of grammars, like Instagram or Twitter, platforms like Facebook constantly proliferate their grammars. But what is it that we are counting when aggregating tweets, likes or comments? The combination of standardized action and countability is rather suggestive, both to media users and researchers, as it implies that the actions that grammars capture are similar if not comparable. But that is not necessarily the case. First, because users have different reasons to like, share or retweet and deploy the 'interpretative flexibility' (Van Dijck 2012) of platform grammars by assigning different meanings to them. Secondly, these grammars are increasingly being realized outside of the platform through social media clients, cross-platform syndication, automating software, apps and/or custom scripts (Gerlitz & Rieder 2015), which allow the grammars of one platform to be folded into the grammars of other platforms – whilst not necessarily following the same objective or interpretation. Hashtags deployed on Instagram are easily transposed to Twitter through cross-syndication, just as tweets can be automatically created from news articles or RSS-feeds, just to name a few examples. The data points of one platform are thus informed by the interpretations, grammars and politics of a multiplicity of third parties. Espeland and Stevens understand such 'transformation of different qualities into a common metric' (1998: 314) as commensuration. Grammatisation of action and the possibility to build on top of platforms through apps, clients and syndication facilitate the commensuration of heterogeneous actions into a single data point. Rather than treating the data points provided by platforms as unproblematic and straightforwardly countable first order metrics (Callon 2005), I suggest to treat them as already assembled second order metrics, which are composed of heterogeneous interpretations, practices and actors. In order to work with social media data, researchers need to understand what they are counting in the first place, before reassembling data points into new metrics.

How can we avoid the commensuration of data points? And what do you mean by treating data points as 'lively metrics'?

Commensuration cannot be avoided; it is a central element of the politics of platforms which provide infrastructures that cater to a variety of actors and their different objectives. These infrastructures facilitate the relative openness of grammars, as well as the possibility to retrieve and input data from and to the platform through application programming interfaces (APIs) which can be enacted by users and third parties. Commensuration is thus not only enacted by the platform itself, but has to be understood as a distributed accomplishment – or a happening (Lury & Wakeford 2012) – which needs to be realized by multiple actors in local, distributed and specific ways. Thinking of commensuration as happening does not reduce it to a mere effect of the medium or of grammatisation, but takes the various infrastructures, actors, practices and meanings into account that can feed into data points. As the happening of commensuration can play out differently at different times, with different issues, actors and practices involved, I suggest we think of social media metrics as 'lively metrics' which are animated by specific and local dynamics of commensuration. I understand lively in the sense of Marres & Weltevrede (2013) as internally dynamic, animated and variable, pointing to the multiple ways of being on platforms (Gerlitz & Rieder 2015).

Why do you call for a public debate on data points?

There is a delicate relationship between counting and valuation. 'What counts', Alain Badiou argues 'in the sense of what is valued – is that which is counted. Conversely, everything that can be numbered must be valued' (2008: 1). Within social media research, data points are being valuated in regards to the stories they tell, the practices they explicate and the medium-specific dynamics they point to. Before reaggregating platform data into new second order metrics, it is important to understand what is being counted in the first places, as 100k tweets have a different value in research if issued from political protesters, cross-syndicated from Instagram or issued by spam-bot networks. The fact that numbers are easy to be displaced, circulated and reaggregated has led to their constant re-evaluation by a multiplicity of actors, reassembling them for intelligence, indicators for engagement, issue detectors or influence rankings (Gerlitz & Lury 2014), to name only a few. Once reassembled into new second order metrics, the question of what the original data points are composed of descends into the background. However, 'commensuration changes the terms of what can be talked about, how we value, and how we treat what we value. It is symbolic, inherently interpretive, deeply political, and too important to be left implicit' (Espaland & Stevens). As soon as social media data points come to have effects by determining the value or creditworthiness of consumers, or becoming part of governmental intelligence, it is important not to take initial data points as a given, but to understand what they are animated by. Therefore, a critical engagement with social media data needs to unpack and denaturalize especially those data points that appear most naturalized and straightforwardly countable. Their similarity is not a property but an accomplishment and there is a need for public debate on what is rendered equivalent and feeds into public forms of valuation here.

References

Agre, Philip E. 1994. "Surveillance and capture: Two models of privacy." *The Information Society* 10 (2): 101-127.

Badiou, Alain. 2008. *Number and Numbers*. Cambridge: Polity.

Callon, Michel. 2005. "Peripheral Vision: Economic Markets as Calculative Collective Devices." *Organization Studies* 26 (8): 1229–1250.

Dijck, José van. 2012. "Tracing Twitter: The Rise of a Microblogging platform." *International Journal of Media and Cultural Politics* 7: 333–348.

Espeland, Wendy Nelson & Mitchell L. Stevens. 1998. "Commensuration as a Social Process." *Annual Review of Sociology* 24(1): 313–343.

Gerlitz, Carolin & Celia Lury. 2014. "Social media and self-evaluating assemblages: On numbers, orderings and values." *Distinktion: Scandinavian Journal of Social Theory* 15 (2): 174-188.

Gerlitz, Carolin & Bernhard Rieder. 2015. *Tweets are not created equal. The politics of platform metrics.* Manuscript.

Lury, Celia & Nina Wakeford. 2012. *Inventive Methods: The Happening of the Social.* New York: Routledge.

Marres, Noortje & Esther Weltevrede. 2013. "Scraping the Social? Issues in live social research." *Journal of Cultural Economy* 6 (3): 313–335.

18. Opposing the Exceptionalism of the Algorithm

Evgeny Morozov

Evgeny Morozov is one of the most outspoken critics of Silicon Valley and its techno-opportunism. In his publications, he has challenged the claims that social media should be seen as a tool for political emancipation and that technological advancement equates to social progress. He recently addressed the technocratic expectations for big data and algorithms as problem solving machines for public administration and social organization.

It is claimed that algorithms and private companies are better than public institutions at solving societal problems. What is your take on this?

The public institutions that we currently have in place have emerged partly thanks to the emergence of the developers' state and are therefore already predisposed to algorithmic optimization. Welfare for a poor, disadvantaged group presupposes that spending can be optimized by surveillance and in the US, for instance, the system has been expansive in monitoring the recipients of food stamps and other kinds of aid. This was built into the democratic apparatus of the welfare state and public institutions alongside a drive towards effectiveness, efficiency and leanness. The entrance of new players to make things faster, cheaper and more expansive is not unexpected.

I would not necessarily worry about the displacement of public institutions by algorithms because these institutions already have some algorithmic background. For example, institutions that you would associate with the public realm like taxi companies – publicly regulated in a way that Uber is not – have a very rudimentary capacity to match supply and demand. Previously, this was done by phone dispatchers and not a digital algorithm. In a sense, I would argue, even the phone dispatcher can be seen as an algorithm. These dispatchers weren't particularly efficient, but they matched supply to demand nonetheless. The entrance of companies into the market that do this more quickly, cheaply, effectively and efficiently is not necessarily a big departure from that model.

Within the philosophy of law and within the legal tradition, there is a huge debate as to whether judges discover law or whether they apply it.

If you stick to the view that they just apply it, then you argue that judges work in a very mechanistic, algorithmic manner. They take a set of rules and they generate an interpretation of those rules. Where exactly sources of that interpretative power come from is a question you can investigate and debate. But even that process in itself, depending on which philosophy of law you opt for, can be seen from the algorithmic perspective. The process of displacing public institutions with private ones is a different matter. It has to do with the nature of private companies providing services previously provided by the State. In some respects, this displacement is better and in some respects, it's worse. However, I don't think that algorithms are the dividing line between the two. The qualitative difference then would be that the new services or new industries are running on cheaply available data. Before the State was the primary collector of data and now we have those industries collecting data. That enables them to take over certain functions in a different way.

Banks, loan companies and Experion, not to mention all the other data collectors, were in the business way before technology companies. With my work, I consistently try to oppose the exceptionalism of 'the internet'. In this case I don't think that the collection of data by private companies has much to do with the internet. The scale has changed, if you look at the aggregation of banks and how they decide whether to give you a loan or not. The principle that banks use for generating a credit score, which in turn determines whether you are eligible for a loan, is not that different from the kind of reputation economy that Uber and Airbnb want to develop for determining if you are a trustworthy customer. That principle has its origins in banking far more than in the technology industry.

Obviously, there is far more data generated about lifestyle by individuals. This is in part because we have shifted to a society where devices can easily generate data. That data is useful for all sorts of purposes, but I don't think that if an insurance company could have grabbed that data 80 years ago, they wouldn't have grabbed it. Nothing has changed in the epistemic assumptions of how capitalism operates that made companies suddenly realize that data was valuable. It was always valuable but very hard to grab before. I would also challenge the assumption that only governments collected it in the past. If you look at the history of regulation of credit scores in Europe, you can argue that in Germany there were legal barriers as to what kind of data can be legally incorporated and analysed by a bank when they are determining whether to give you a loan, but the data was collected nonetheless.

What impact does delegating public services to algorithms have on society?

You can answer the question in a highly theoretical mode or an empirical mode. I will answer it in the empirical mode, in that I have zero conviction that the decisions that have been taken by humans and institutions have been just or fair in most cases. Plenty of discrimination happens with regard to race, class, gender and so forth. We should not glorify human decision-making just because it is human. Social biases exist regardless of whether algorithms or computers are doing the job. With algorithms you can actually create an audit trail and see the exact reasoning process that led to the decision. The problem is that the corporatization of algorithmic decision-making will also result in more opacity within the algorithms. Because many of them will be proprietary, we won't be able to examine them and look inside them. There will be certain domains where I would like to have human critics, but that has to do with critical thought and the experience of quality rather than decision-making. I would like food critics to go and think about food as opposed to generating an algorithm aggregating Yelp opinions, not because I reject algorithms, but because food is something that requires a very different kind of decision-making.

There is no way I would trust institutions to delegate public services in a fair and responsible manner. But switching back to the theoretical mode, I don't think this should be impossible. Much depends on how much trust and faith you have in the State. In Europe, I see few reasons to trust a State which has been dismantling itself. So why would I trust it to enact a switch to algorithms? But again, here the distrust doesn't have to do with the algorithms, or even with the corporate nature of people doing the shift; it has to do with the nature of the public institutions and the State as it exists in Europe.

What can civil society do to preserve their democratic values?

They should develop long term strategies for rethinking ways of political representation, engagement and process. To some, representative democracy is overrated. In Europe and America, it has lent itself to capture by forces that have more or less deprived it of whatever democratic potential it had. I would be happy to experiment with alternative forms of decision-making and governance beyond representative democracy. Perhaps direct democracy would not be a bad alternative. The specific institutional arrangements can be discussed later, but I think a lot of it would involve not getting confused (which much of Europe is now). People are pursuing fake and false emancipation strategies (e.g. collaborative economy, peer-to-peer, and makerspaces). They find ways to accustom themselves to the rather dire state of affairs and then think that their particular little project, which now involves some kind of technological component, is the way to resolve contradictions. I am not convinced of this.

I am pushing for direct political engagement. I don't mean voting and showing up at elections, but actually analysing questions that we would traditionally qualify as political: Who makes decisions? Who owns what? Who runs what? How much legitimacy do certain institutions have or should they have? These questions are much more relevant for thinking about our future than questions about certain technological aspects. It might not be so useful for your book, but I just can't fake it anymore.

19.   The Need for a Dialogue with Technology

Mercedes Bunz

In her book, *The Silent Revolution*, Mercedes Bunz describes a relentless transformation that unfolds silently. Algorithms and data merge in automatized processes of intellectual labour: algorithms produce journalistic articles, stock reports, and sports news. This slippery slope into an algorithmic society unfolds relatively unnoticed and without the occasional hypes that usually mark milestones of technological progress. However, it has effects on the heart of our society in that it reshapes our understanding of media industries and public discourses. With this, it questions our identity as *zoon politikon*. What once was opinion forming has now been taken over by decision-making machines that have become an inherent part of our social organization. Bunz shows the need to consciously interact and understand technology.

Why do you describe the digital revolution as a silent one?

What we socially want from digital technology is rarely discussed. It is apparent that we understand digital technology and its 'disruption' foremost as an economic sensation. If there is a political promise at all, it is one that can be described with Christopher Kelty (2015) as a 'Fog of Freedom'. Interestingly, this is very different from the role technology played in our past, when the transformative powers that technologies offer our societies were understood as political; here Elizabeth Eisenstein's *The Printing Press as an Agent of Change* but also Donna Haraway's *Cyborg Manifesto* (1987) are prominent examples for research addressing the political side of technology. Following their approaches, my book addresses our approach towards algorithms as a missed chance as much as a problem. I agree with Wendy Chun, who points out in her forthcoming *Habitual New Media* (2016) that media matter most when they seem not to matter at all. Thus, I am interested in the fact that we don't debate what we want from technology. Instead of understanding it as something that *can be shaped* and *turn towards it*, we approach it in a rather stereotypical manner: we are either *for* or *against* technology, as my critical discourse analysis looking into how we talk about technology shows.

What do you mean by 'turning towards technology'? Why is criticality not enough?

Of course, we need to critically analyse technology, but criticizing algorithms must go beyond pointing out its negative aspects. Technology studies (Fuller 2003; Parisi 2012; Brunton 2013) have shown again and again that when it comes to technology, effective critique needs to be followed up with action. The overwhelmingly negative view of Google and its dealing with data we find in Germany is a good example of this: while being highly critical of Google, the market position of its search engine just in that country for 2015 is 94.84%; in the US Google's market share is only 64%. This shows clearly that a negative critique of technology is in danger to fail when it does not actively change anything.

Following the French philosopher of technology Gilbert Simondon (1958), I understand this change as a dialogue with technology. Simondon understood the human as being in an 'ensemble' with the machine, instead of being the master above it. This is where critique that keeps an objective distance to technology goes wrong; apart from the fact that is has not been proven as being very effective. In short, 'turning towards technology' does not mean to become non-critical, but to apply one's critique in a dialogue with technology. Also for political reasons: one cannot leave the detailed knowledge of technology and its technical development in the hands of businesses, simply hoping that hackers like Anonymous or the Chaos Computer Club do their best pointing out the fundamental problems; Gabriella Coleman (2014) has recently shown their important role. As digital technology has become part of our daily environment, as we leave data with every usage, we are all asked to make more of an effort of consciously interacting with technology, and in understanding it; apart from insisting on having a right over our own data, of course.

Your book focuses especially on how the digital revolution is changing skilled work. How are algorithms changing the work of experts?

It is obvious that algorithms and big data change the work culture of skilled work and expertise. Inspired by Erik Brynjolfsson's and Andrew McAfee's research (2012), which gave a general picture of how algorithms transform our economies in the 21st century, my research digs down in some more detail as to what this means for 'skilled work'. My question here was whether the algorithm does to the skilled worker what the machine in the industrial age has done to the manual worker.

That there is change, is clear. Something as simple as the search function performed by various algorithms has fundamentally changed skilled work, which amounts to up to 75% in Western post-industrial societies. So far, expertise was exclusive and as such the decisive factor. Now the knowledge of teachers, doctors, journalists and even plumbers or engineers has become accessible to everyone. Furthermore, skilled work can also partly be automated besides being accessible. In the US, lawyers who were formerly allocated to do a document review are already being replaced by software called 'e-discovery'. It scans 1.5 million documents for less than $100,000. Of course, both developments triggered by algorithms unsettle experts.

Case studies in my book, however, show that algorithms will not replace the expert. Even though information has become accessible and can be automated, the studies show that this information needs contextual knowledge to be judged. This is also the case for the automation of knowledge, which needs to be guarded by experts. In a nutshell, one can say that it is not that the expert is replaced by algorithms. It is more that their areas of work are changing.

What is the role for concerned citizens as knowledge and its distribution are partially shaped by algorithms?

As concerned citizens, we have the duty to be more curious about what an algorithm can do and what it cannot do. Or why a company knows more about me, thanks to analysing data, than I can. I am afraid this concern, however, cannot be outsourced – it is not that Google or Facebook publish their algorithms, and the problem is solved. As our algorithms play a more important part in Western societies, we all need to become more digitally literate. This does not necessarily mean to learn programming, but to understand what programs can do and what they cannot do. As my colleague Luciana Parisi (2013) puts it: when we are interested in what knowledge and thinking is today, we need to study 'algorithmic thought'. For this, we need to turn towards it and not away from it – also for political reasons: technology is way too important for our societies. Following here again Gilbert Simondon, my book tries to understand technological shifts in great detail, and tries to explain how digital technology and its cultural technique of 'search' affects knowledge and with it work as well as the public sphere; besides being a researcher, I have worked for several years as a journalist.

With your experience as a journalist, what would you say is happening to the public sphere in today's media environment?

Regarding the public sphere, we can observe two very different aspects: On the one hand, the internet has a democratizing effect in the sense that it has opened an alternative channel for each single member of the public. Due to this, social media has become one important source for journalism, which my former employer *The Guardian* understood early on. Its digital director, Emily Bell, now director of the Tow Center for Digital Journalism at Columbia University, once said: you have to produce journalism *with* the internet, not *on* the internet. Buzzfeed, profitable since 2013, currently understands this best with their production of sharable entertaining news as well as exciting investigative journalism.

But the digital public is not only a rich source for journalism, it also assists where it is helpless or fails as it allows to voice alternative opinions; we have seen important adjustments to existing reporting for example with the death of teenager Michael Brown in Ferguson, one of far too many incidents that have led to 'Black Lives Matter'. But of course, there is a flipside to this much more populated public sphere. That we can engage there more easily also means that each one of us can be 'reached' more easily – mass surveillance and trolling are the ugly outcomes of this. As it stands, it must be understood that technology is not simply a solution for political problems but also causing some.

Something we also need to be aware of is that the shape of that digital public – the long tail – is one of those problems. From a technical perspective, as long as we have net neutrality, the internet follows an end-to-end-principle in which application-specific functions ought to reside in the *end hosts*. While it is important to fight for this, we also need to be aware of the fact that all ends are not the same. The social functions of those ends are far less democratic than the technical functions. Some ends are far better connected than others and have more reach: the thick 'head' has an advantage over its thin long tail. While the technicality of the internet is democratic, some get all the attention.

What is the role of the university when it comes to digital technology, algorithms and data?

In the future, universities could play an essential role when it comes to exploring technology, which they should not only do in their computer science departments. Today, algorithms are a cultural technique, so from my perspective, it is the humanities that are concerned with human culture. Humanities scholars have been experts of human knowledge storing ever since the invention of, first, writing, and then books. I believe when being open to explore today's knowledge storing more hands-on, they can very productively draw from their past. This is why the humanities scholars should establish their very own dialogue with technology. After all, 'What can we know?' is a classic question posed in the humanities.

How can we make the silent revolution heard?

As things are just about to start babbling with the so-called "Internet of Things" (Bunz 2016), I think it will soon be hard to ignore it. But as a many of my brilliant colleagues have pointed out (Bratton 2016, Chun 2016, Parisi 2015, Pasquinelli 2015, Fuller & Goffey 2012): if we don't want to live with a technology that is a black box, we all need to interact with it more attentively.

References

Bratton, Benjamin H. 2016. *The Stack: On Software and Sovereignty.* Cambridge, MA: The MIT Press. http://mitpress.mit.edu.proxy.library.uu.nl/books/stack.

Brunton, Finn. 2013. *Spam: A Shadow History of the Internet.* Cambridge, MA: The MIT Press.

Brynjolfsson, Erik & Andrew McAfee. 2011. *Race against the Machine: How the Digital Revolution Is Accelerating Innovation, Driving Productivity, and Irreversibly Transforming Employment and the Economy.* Digital Frontier Press. www.change-management.net/Race.docx.

Bunz, Mercedes. 2015. "Things Are Not to Blame: Technical Agency and Thing Theory in the Age of Internet of Things." In *New Media, Old Media: A History and Theory Reader,* ed. Wendy Chun and Anna Watkins Fisher. London: Routledge.

Campbell-Kelly, Martin. 2003. *The History of Mathematical Tables: From Sumer to Spreadsheets.* Oxford: Oxford University Press.

Coleman, Gabriella. 2014. *Hacker, Hoaxer, Whistleblower, Spy: The Story of Anonymous.* London: Verso.

Eisenstein, Elizabeth L. 1980. *The Printing Press as an Agent of Change.* Vol. 1. Cambridge University Press.

Fuller, Matthew. 2003. *Behind the Blip: Essays on the Culture of Software.* New York: Autonomedia.

Fuller, Matthew & Andrew Goffey. 2012. *Evil Media.* Cambridge, MA: The MIT Press.

Haraway, Donna. 1987. "A Manifesto for Cyborgs: Science, Technology, and Socialist Feminism in the 1980s." *Australian Feminist Studies* 2 (4): 1–42.

Kelty, Christopher M. 2014. "The Fog of Freedom." In *Media Technologies: Essays on Communication, Materiality, and Society,* ed. T. Gillepsie, P.J. Boczkowski & K.A. Foot, 195–220. Cambridge, MA: The MIT Press.

Parisi, Luciana. 2013. *Contagious Architecture.* Cambridge, MA: MIT Press.

Pasquinelli, Matteo, ed. 2015. *Alleys of Your Mind: Augmented Intelligence and Its Traumas.* Meson Press by Hybrid.

Simondon, Gilbert. 1980. *On the Mode of Existence of Technical Objects-1958.* Translated by Ninian Mellampy. Ontario: University of Western Ontario.

—. 1989. *Du Mode D'existence Des Objets Techniques.* Paris: Editions.

Tools

We recommend all the programs used in this book and, to help you along, they are listed below alongside the chapters they are featured in. Please see those chapters for more on how those tools have been used by our contributors.

Chapter 2: Cinemetrics, ACTION, Cultural Analytics
Chapter 3: Cultural Analytics
Chapter 4: Cultural Analytics, Gnip
Chapter 5: Google Search, Lippmannian Device (DMI)
Chapter 6: T-CAT tool (DMI)
Chapter 11: Gephi
Chapter 13: Outwit Hub

For a more expansive and updated list, please visit the Utrecht Data School website at dataschool.nl/resources using the password 'udsResources'.

Notes on Contributors

Julian Ausserhofer (@julauss) is a digital communication researcher from Vienna, Austria. He pursues his PhD at the Department of Communication at the University of Vienna, and works for the Alexander von Humboldt Institute for Internet and Society in Berlin. Academically, Julian's areas of interest include computational methods in the social sciences and in journalism, and social media in news and politics. In particular, Julian examines practices in data journalism and interactions in the algorithmic formation of networked publics. Julian has published in *Information, Communication & Society* and recently co-edited an open-access book in German on *digital methods in Communication Science*. He blogs at ausserhofer.net.

Dominikus Baur (@dominikus) is an independent researcher based in Munich, Germany. His research focuses on touch-based visualizations and mobile interaction design. Another of his interests are large-scale data-based installations with projects such as 'Selfiecity' and 'On Broadway'. He has published in *IEEE Transactions on Visualization and Computer Graphics* and *IEEE Computer Graphics and Applications*, among others.

Asher Boersma (@asherboersma) is a PhD researcher in the DFG postgraduate programme 'Locating Media', at Siegen University. His research looks at technologically mediated work (ethnographically) and its representations (media archaeologically). It focuses on the advent of infrastructure control rooms from the 1950s to today and how they have developed from manned stations towards more algorithmic autonomy.

Thomas Boeschoten (@boeschoten) is the founder of and a researcher at the Utrecht Data School (Utrecht University). His current research focuses on (new) media and data. His past publications in outlets such as *M/C Journal* and *First Monday* have explored social TV and Facebook and Twitter as spaces for online deliberation. For more info: thomas@dataschool.nl or www.boeschoten.eu.

Liliana Bounegru (@bb_liliana) is a PhD candidate at the University of Groningen and the University of Ghent and a researcher at the Digital Methods Initiative, University of Amsterdam. Her current research focuses on data journalism, digital methods and new media studies. She is also a visiting researcher at the Sciences Po Paris médialab and research fellow at the Tow Center for Digital Journalism at Columbia University. More about her work and publications can be found at lilianabounegru.org.

Elizabeth Buchanan (buchanane@uwstout.edu) is the Endowed Chair in Ethics and Director of the Center for Applied Ethics at the University of Wisconsin-Stout. Her research focuses on the intersection of research regulations and various forms of internet research. Past publications include articles in the *Journal of Empirical Research and Human Research Ethics*, *Computers and Society*, and in the *Stanford Encyclopedia of Philosophy*. She is currently studying the ethics of university service learning programmes as part of a National Science Foundation grant.

Mercedes Bunz (@mrsbunz) is a senior lecturer of journalism and digital media at the University of Westminster. She writes about digital media and philosophy of technology. She is a co-founder of meson.press, an open-access publishing cooperative; her book, *The Silent Revolution: How Digitalization Transforms Knowledge, Work, Journalism and Politics without Making Too Much Noise*, was published in 2014.

Nick Couldry (@couldrynick) is Professor of Media, Communications and Social Theory in the Department of Media and Communications at the London School of Economics. As a sociologist of media and culture, he approaches media and communications from the perspective of the symbolic power that has been historically concentrated in media institutions. He is interested in how media and communications institutions and infrastructures contribute to various types of order (social, political, cultural, economic, ethical). He is the author of many books, most recently *Ethics of Media* with Madianou and Pinchevski.

Karin van Es (@kfvanes) is Assistant Professor of Television and New Media at Utrecht University and a Senior Researcher at the Utrecht Data School. Her current research focuses on how new forms of knowledge production through data affects Dutch broadcast television. Her past publications in outlets such as *Television & New Media*, *M/C Journal* and *First Monday* have explored social TV and online deliberation. Her recent book *The Future of Live* (Polity Press, 2016) tackles the concept of the 'live' in the social media era.

Daniel Goddemeyer (@dgoddemeyer) is the founder of the New York City-based research and design practice Object Form Field Culture (OFFC), which creates new relationships with technology through research, products, services and experiments. OFFC works with companies such as BBVA Innovation Center, Telefonica Digital and Audi to identify new product applications for emerging technologies. To continuously inspire his work with a unique outlook, he explores – through his own research and the MFA class Urban Fictions at the School of Visual Arts – how the increasing proliferation of technology in our lives will impact and change our future every day. He holds an MFA from the Royal College of Arts. He has received several distinctions and awards from the Art Directors Club, the Red Dot Award, the German Design Prize and the Industrial Designer Society of America. More about his work and publications can be found at danielgoddemeyer.com.

Carolin Gerlitz (@cgrltz) is Professor of Media Studies at the University of Siegen. She conducts research on digital culture and methods. Her research explores the various intersections between new media, methods and economic sociology, with a specific interest in Web economies, platform and software studies, brands, value, topology, measurement, numeracy, social media, digital (social) methods and issue mapping online. Together with Bernhard Rieder, she coordinates the 'Media of Calculation' research group. She has published in *New Media & Society, Theory Culture & Society* and *Sociological Review*, among others.

Jonathan Gray (@jwyg) is Prize Fellow at the Institute for Policy Research, University of Bath. His current research focuses on the politics of open data and public information. He is also Research Associate at the Digital Methods Initiative, University of Amsterdam; Research Associate at the médialab at Sciences Po; and Tow Fellow at the Tow Center for Digital Journalism, Columbia University. He is a regular contributor to *The Guardian* and *Open Democracy*. More about his work can be found at jonathangray.org.

Mathieu Jacomy (@jacomyma) is a research engineer who has been at the Sciences Po Paris médialab since 2010 and leads the Web instrument of Equipex DIME-SHS. His current research focuses on visual network analysis, digital methods applied to social sciences and issue mapping. He created the Gephi network analysis software and is currently developing the Web crawler Hyphe.

Koen Leurs (koenleurs.net) is an Assistant Professor in Gender and Postcolonial studies at Utrecht University. He is a feminist internet researcher who recently completed the EU-funded Marie Curie study on 'Urban Politics of

London Youth analysed Digitally' at the London School of Economics and Political Science (2013-15). Currently, he leads the Netherlands Organization for Scientific Research-funded research project 'Young connected migrants. Comparing digital practices of young asylum seekers and expatriates in the Netherlands' (2016-19). His publications in *Crossings: Journal of Migration & Culture, Feminist Review, Observatorio OBS** and *Social Media + Society* explore gender, race, class, migration, urbanity and youth culture using quantitative and qualitative approaches. He has published *Everyday Feminist Research Praxis* (Cambridge Scholars Press, 2014) and *Digital Passages. Diaspora, Gender and Youth Cultural Intersections* (Amsterdam University Press, 2015).

Nicolás López Coombs is a PhD candidate at the University of Antwerp as part of a research project focusing on the mediated urban experience. He received his MA in New Media and Digital Culture from Utrecht University in 2016, where his thesis took a fan studies approach to citizen journalism related to the podcast Serial. This is his first academic publication.

Lev Manovich (@manovich) is Professor of Computer Science at The Graduate Center, CUNY and a Director of the Software Studies Lab that uses methods from computer science, media design and humanities to analyse big cultural data such as millions of Instagram images. He is the author and editor of eight books including *Data Drift* (RIXC, 2015), *Software Takes Command* (Bloomsbury Academic, 2013), *Soft Cinema: Navigating the Database* (The MIT Press, 2005) and *The Language of New Media* (The MIT Press, 2001) which was described as 'the most suggestive and broad ranging media history since Marshall McLuhan'.

Annette Markham (@annettemarkham) is an itinerant scholar researching and teaching in the broad areas of social media, qualitative methodologies and ethics. She is an associate professor in the Department of Aesthetics & Communication at Aarhus University, Denmark. She has published two books, including *Internet Inquiry: Conversations about method* with Nancy Baym (2009), and has published in *Digital Ethics, Journal of Qualitative Communication Research* and the *Encyclopedia for Social & Behavioural Sciences*, among others.

Eef Masson is an Assistant Professor in the Media Studies department of the University of Amsterdam. Her publications include the book *Watch and Learn: Rhetorical Devices in Classroom Films after 1940* (Amsterdam

University Press, 2012) and articles on historical non-theatrical/utility films and archival issues for various journals (e.g. *Film History, The Moving Image*) and essay collections. Currently, she is shifting her attention to the contemporary uses of screen-based media in museum contexts, and exploring the affordances of data research for film history.

Evgeny Morozov (@evgenymorozov) is a contributing editor at *The New Republic* and the author of *To Save Everything, Click Here: The Folly of Technological Solutionism* (2014) and *The Net Delusion: The Dark Side of Internet Freedom* (2012). He was a visiting scholar at Stanford University and a Schwartz fellow at the New America Foundation from 2010-12. He has written for *The New York Times, The Economist, The Wall Street Journal, Financial Times, London Review of Books, Times Literary Supplement, Slate* and other publications. His research focuses on the social and political implications of technology.

Christian Gosvig Olesen (http://filmhistoryinthemaking.com/) is a PhD candidate at the University of Amsterdam's Centre for Cultural Heritage and Identity. His research project, provisionally titled *Film History in the Making*, investigates the implications that digitization in film archives bears upon film historical research methods in primarily academic settings. He has published articles based on his research in journals such as *NECSUS – European Journal of Media Studies*, Cinema et Cie and The Moving Image.

Johannes Paßmann (@j_passmann) is a media scholar and postdoc at Siegen University. His PhD thesis, finished in March 2016, was a media ethnography researching popular amateurs on German-speaking Twitter both online and offline. This was done over a five-year period and combined ethnography with digital methods. The research focused on Twitter's media practices, i.e. retweeting, faving (or liking), following etc. These practices were differentiated into information organization practices on the one hand and recognition practices on the other hand, drawing on German recognition theory (especially Hegel and Axel Honneth) and French gift theory (especially Marcel Mauss and Marcel Hénaff).

Cornelius Puschmann (@cbpuschmann) is a senior researcher at the Alexander von Humboldt Institute for Internet and Society as part of the research group Networks of Outrage, funded by the VolkswagenStiftung under its data journalism funding scheme. Additionally, he is a project leader and coordinator of the postdoc research group Algorithmed Public Spheres (APS) at the Hans Bredow Institute for Media Research at the University of Hamburg. In addition to coordinating the APS postdoc group, Cornelius is chair of the annual conference of the Association of Internet Researchers. Cornelius's research interests include interpersonal communication in digital platforms (particularly hate speech), the role of algorithms in the selection of media content, as well as methodological, ethical and epistemological aspects of computational social science.

Bernhard Rieder (rieder@uva.nl) is Associate Professor of New Media and Digital Culture at the University of Amsterdam and a collaborator with the Digital Methods Initiative. His research focuses on the history, theory and politics of software and particularly on the role algorithms play in social processes and in the production of knowledge and culture. This includes work on the analysis, development and application of computational research methods as well as investigation into the political and economic challenges posed by large online platforms.

Richard Rogers (@richardrogers) is the Department Chair of Media Studies and Professor of New Media & Digital Culture at the University of Amsterdam. He is director of the Digital Methods Initiative (Amsterdam) and author of *Information Politics on the Web* (MIT Press, 2004), awarded the best book of the year by the Association for Information Science and Technology, and *digital methods* (MIT Press, 2013), awarded the outstanding book of the year by the International Communication Association (ICA).

Theo Röhle (theo.rohle@kau.se) is a Senior Lecturer at the Department of Geography, Media and Communication, Karlstad University. His current research focuses on comparative software history and historical intersections of gaming and control. His past publications in outlets such as *New Media and Society*, *First Monday* and *Computational Culture* have focused on search engines, surveillance and the mass media aspects of the Open Graph protocol.

Mirko Tobias Schäfer (@mirkoschaefer) is Assistant Professor of New Media & Digital Culture at Utrecht University and project leader at the Utrecht Data School. In 2016, Mirko was a Mercator Research Fellow at the NRW School of Governance at University of Duisburg-Essen. His research interest revolves around the socio-political impact of media technology. His publications cover user participation in cultural production, hacking communities, politics of software design and communication in social media. He is co-editor and co-author of *Digital Material. Tracing New Media in Everyday Life and Technology* (Amsterdam University Press, 2009) and author of *Bastard Culture! How User Participation Transforms Cultural Production* (Amsterdam University Press, 2011).

Gerwin van Schie is a Teaching Assistant in New Media and Digital Culture at Utrecht University and a Junior Researcher at the Utrecht Data School. In 2015, he received his MA with honours in New Media and Digital Culture at Utrecht University with a thesis on moral mediation of privacy in the mobile messaging applications Whatsapp and Telegram. His current research focuses on big data ethics for scientific research and policymaking.

Tamara Shepherd (tshepski.com) is an Assistant Professor in the Department of Communication, Media and Film at the University of Calgary. She studies the feminist political economy of digital culture, looking at labour, policy and literacy in social media, mobile technologies and digital games. She is an editorial board member of *Social Media + Society*, and her work has been published in *Convergence, First Monday, Triple C*, and the *Canadian Journal of Communication*.

Moritz Stefaner (http://truth-and-beauty.net) works as a 'truth and beauty operator' at the crossroads of data visualization, information aesthetics and user interface design. With a background in Cognitive Science (BSc, University of Osnabrück) and Interface Design (MA, University of Applied Sciences Potsdam), his award-winning work beautifully balances analytical and aesthetic aspects in mapping abstract and complex phenomena. His work has been exhibited at the Venice Biennale of Architecture, SIGGRAPH, Ars Electronica and the Max Planck Science Gallery. He also publishes the *Data Stories* podcast with Enrico Bertini (http://datastori.es).

Natalia Sánchez-Querubín is a PhD candidate at the Amsterdam School for Cultural Analysis, and Lecturer at the New Media & Digital Culture at the University of Amsterdam. Her graduate research is concerned with how patients use social media platforms for narrating their experiences of illness and with care practices currently being developed online.

William Uricchio is Professor of Comparative Media Studies at MIT, where he's also Principal Investigator of the MIT Open Documentary Lab, and Professor of Comparative Media History at Utrecht University. His research focuses on the early phases of various media forms both as technologies and social practices, tracing the processes by which affordances are embraced, forgotten, or deferred to subsequent media forms. He has written extensively on 19th Century television, early film, and immersive technologies from the panorama to VR to AR and other locative media, and his publications can be found at http://williamuricchio.com

Tommaso Venturini is a lecturer at King's College London (Digital Humanities Dept.). He is also associate researcher at the médialab of Sciences Po Paris, which he founded with Bruno Latour and coordinated for six years. He was the leading scientist of the projects EMAPS (climaps.eu – EU FP7) and MEDEA (projetmedea.hypotheses.org – ANR). His research focuses on Digital Methods, STS and Social Modernization. He teaches Controversy Mapping, Data Journalism and Information Design at graduate and undergraduate level. He was trained in sociology and media studies at the University of Bologna, completed a PhD in Society of Information at the University of Milano Bicocca and a postdoc on social modernization at the Department of Philosophy of the University of Bologna. He was also a visiting student at UCLA and visiting researcher at the CETCOPRA of Paris 1 Pantheon Sorbonne. During his studies, he founded a Web design agency and led several online communication projects.

Irene Westra is a recent graduate of Utrecht University's undergraduate sociology programme where she received an award for best bachelor thesis of the Faculty Behavioural and Social Sciences at UU. Her thesis focused on how institutions influence organizational performance via the network structure. She is currently part of the Utrecht Data School as executive secretary. Irene is interested in how the emergence of 'big data' changes the way (scientific) research can be performed. Her research aims to combine a sociological approach with data science.

Index

ACTION 19, 39-41, 47-51
Actor-Network Theory 158
affordances 157
Agre, Philip 114, 241
Akrich, Madeleine 82, 92, 110
algorithmic 75, 77, 112, 125-137, 211-215, 222, 245-247
  culture 16
  exceptionalism 233, 245, 246
  society 249
  thought 21, 251
algorithms 50, 57, 66, 75, 76, 87, 117-119, 125-137, 222, 233, 245-252
  as black boxes 20, 139-142
Anderson, Chris 14, 172, 236
Anscombe, Francis John 119, 120
Application programming interfaces (APIs) 14, 20, 61, 112, 147-153, 174, 242
Association of Internet Researchers 189, 201

Beer, David 112
Berry, David 13, 20, 26, 27, 109, 111, 114, 122, 171, 184
bias 104, 112, 172, 175-177, 212, 222, 247
  algorithmic 222
  linguistic 222
  social 212, 247
Big data research 19, 21, 172, 177, 179, 183-186, 190-194, 197, 198, 233
Bordwell, David 41-44
Bourdieu, Pierre 62
Bowker, Geoffrey 142, 171, 216, 222, 224
boyd, danah 15, 172, 175, 189, 211, 236
Bucher, Taina 112, 139, 149

calculation 33, 34, 105, 155, 173, 214, 219, 220, 222
Casey, Michael 39, 50, 51
Cinemetrics 39-51
close reading 33, 55, 173n, 227
Communication Studies 57, 58
computational methods 15, 17, 30, 33, 35, 52, 58, 110-113, 115, 122, 178
computational turn 13-16, 19, 91, 109
computer science 56-58, 121, 252
computer simulation 63, 65, 171
constructivist 30
Couldry, Nick 15, 155, 172, 211, 221, 235-238
Crawford, Kate 15, 139, 172-175, 189, 222, 236
crawling 76
Cultural Analytics 29, 39-41, 47-51, 55, 56, 60-62, 67, 69, 93, 109, 119, 185, 212
cultural production 126, 128, 131, 185, 233, 241, 263

Daston, Lorraine 18
data 11-21, 31, 172, 175-177, 183-190, 193-198, 201-208, 211-214, 219-227, 236
  bias and discrimination 21, 172, 175-177, 211-214, 219-222, 227, 236
  ethics 17, 21, 175, 183-190, 193-198, 201-208, 224, 225
  point 21, 61, 66, 72, 130, 185, 233, 241-243
  practice 12-21, 31, 183-185, 219
data point critique 233, 241-243
data visualization 30, 39-41, 44, 46, 48-51, 155, 157, 171, 179, 218, 219, 223
datafication 11-16, 220-224
dataveillance 222
De Certeau, Michel 40, 52
Declaration of Helsinki 184, 188, 189, 197, 201
deep data 227, 228
democracy 14, 95, 99, 247
digital Bildung 20, 111, 114, 115, 117, 122
digital data analysis 20, 173-178
digital humanities 15, 16, 19, 26-29, 31-34, 55-60, 109, 111-114, 121, 122, 173, 18-186
digital methods 20, 27, 30, 75-79, 91-93, 97, 99, 101, 103, 109-114, 123, 139, 184, 197, 201, 224
digital rhetoric 238
discourse analysis 83, 249
distant reading 93, 173
Drucker, Johanna 16, 25, 29-32, 34, 45, 51, 112, 173, 176

empiricism/empiricist 15, 32, 39, 171
  fallacies of empiricism 15
epistemic/epistemology 15, 18-20, 25-31, 39, 40, 76-79, 87, 92, 109, 111-113, 116-119, 122, 125-127, 190, 212, 222-224, 246
ethical 21, 175, 184, 186-190, 193-198, 201-208, 225, 228
  decision-making 189, 194, 201, 207, 208
  guidelines 21, 175, 184, 186, 188, 193, 196, 197

Facebook 14, 63, 128, 147, 149-153, 185-187, 207, 222, 225, 241, 251
  data 147, 150-152, 187, 222
  pages 187, 207
  statistics 63, 187
  study 185-187, 225
  terms of use 187, 225
filter bubble 77
Foucault, Michel 212, 223
Fry, Ben 174, 176

Galison, Peter 18
gatekeepers 131-133
Gelernter, David 19, 171

Gephi 117, 118, 145, 155, 159, 177
Gerlitz, Carolin 21, 100, 102, 151, 177, 212, 233, 241-243
Gillespie, Tarleton 127, 128, 131, 214, 219
Google 14, 20, 58, 64, 72, 75-77, 79-81, 83, 87-93, 127, 128, 139, 149, 174, 222, 250, 251
  algorithms 75, 77, 87, 127, 139, 251
  flu 64, 75, 81
  terms of service 90n
Google Pagerank 76, 87
Greenpeace 78, 79

hashtag 20, 95-105, 242
  ethnography 105n
  politics 96, 99, 102
  publics 99-102
  stream 20, 95-99
Heidegger, Martin 133-136
hermeneutic(s) 19, 28, 41, 48, 50, 93, 125, 184, 237
humanists 19, 26-31, 33, 34, 48, 56, 58, 60, 112, 114, 115, 121
  digital 27, 29, 33, 56, 60, 112, 114, 121
Humanities 11-17, 19-21, 25-35, 47, 55-58, 60-63, 65, 109, 111-114, 122, 136-139, 149, 168, 171, 173, 184-186, 197, 241, 253
digital 15, 16, 19, 26-29, 34, 55-58, 60, 109, 111, 114, 173, 184-186

Iliad 21, 155-168
ImagePlot 29, 48-51
Informed consent 21, 175, 184-188, 191-198, 203, 204, 225
Instagram 14, 20, 48, 55, 58-61, 63-66, 69, 71, 72, 149, 150, 185, 241-243
  photos 20, 58-61, 72, 185
issue crawler 98
issue networks 20, 95-100, 103, 104

Kitchin, Rob 11, 15, 17, 29, 32, 34n, 171-173, 177
Knorr Cetina, Karin 25n, 46, 140, 141
Kuhn, Thomas 41n, 109

literacy 118, 135, 139, 168
long data 66

machine learning 33, 50, 64, 65n, 113, 127, 133
manga 61, 119, 120
Manovich, Lev 19, 29, 33, 39, 48-51, 59, 61, 69, 93, 119, 120, 128, 173, 175, 185, 212
Markham, Annette 21, 175, 184, 188-190, 194
Marx, Karl 62, 63, 66, 142, 237
Merleau-Ponty's, Maurice 143, 144
metadata 49, 76, 99, 100, 151, 176, 185, 206, 223
Methodenstreit 110
methodology 19, 27, 39-41, 47-51, 95, 110-118, 121, 156, 172, 201, 202, 208, 224, 225
metrics 100, 118, 121, 152, 155, 168, 177, 178, 214-217, 219, 223, 235, 241-243
  bio 214-217, 223

socio 118, 121
Moretti, Franco 50, 156, 168, 173
Morozov, Evgeny 21, 212, 233, 245

narrative affordances 157
Negroponte, Nicholas 77
Netflix 130
network analysis 20, 95, 117, 118, 155-157, 167, 168, 259
network visualization 21, 98, 112, 117, 118, 145, 155, 159, 168
N-Gram viewer 58

objectivity 13, 18, 25, 30, 63, 112, 127, 131, 172, 178, 190, 214, 219, 220, 227
On Broadway 20, 61, 66, 69-73
ontology 11, 132, 190, 211
open data 15, 69, 148, 149, 203

Pariser, Eli 77
Pasquale, Frank 15, 211, 219, 222
personalization 77, 80, 127, 132-135
Petric, Vlada 41, 43
Photosynth 134-136
politics of association 95-99, 104
politics of circulation 112
positivism/positivist 19, 25, 30-33, 39, 51, 63, 66, 122
Positivismusstreit 110
power-knowledge 212
predictive analytics 127
privacy 149, 150, 175, 184-186, 194, 195, 202-207, 216, 222
programming 16, 48, 111, 114-118, 121, 122, 131, 148, 149, 153, 177, 212, 251
  language 149, 153
  skills 115, 121, 122

qualitative 27, 55, 98, 110, 111, 125, 173, 177, 184, 190, 192, 246
quantitative 16, 25, 27, 30, 39-43, 47, 55, 62, 92, 109-111, 125, 156, 173, 214, 219, 221, 224
queries 77, 80-83, 87-89, 92, 93, 98
  ambiguous 87-89
  search 81, 93, 98
  unambiguous 87-89, 93
query design 20, 80-82, 87-89, 92-94, 212

Redfern, Nick 44n, 45
regression 116, 120
repository 11, 118
research design 151, 190, 194, 195, 198
Rieder, Bernhard 20, 29, 109-112, 115, 139, 140, 145, 151, 171, 185, 241, 242
Rogers, Richard 20, 85, 95-98, 185, 212
Röhle, Theo 20, 29, 109-111, 139, 140, 145, 171, 185

Salt, Barry 41-47, 50
sampling 93, 150, 151, 177

scientific 16, 18, 30, 39-43, 46-52, 56, 63, 65, 97, 109, 140, 141, 149, 150, 228
  accuracy 18
  image 18, 46, 47
  realism 41, 52
  self 18
scientism 18, 26, 39, 46, 48, 50, 141
scraping 21, 29, 76, 183, 191, 194
search engine 14, 75, 77, 80, 81, 87, 250
Shannon, Claude 119
Simondon, Gilbert 122, 123, 250, 251
social computing 19, 55-62, 65
social graph 223
social media 14, 57, 60, 64, 66, 71, 96, 99, 104, 105, 112, 131n, 147-152, 172-175, 177, 185, 188, 235, 236, 241-243, 245, 252
  content 57, 96, 104, 152
  data 64, 150, 172-175, 241-243
  metrics 152, 177, 242
social networks 55-61, 65, 149, 156, 167, 177, 184, 187, 198
social science 11, 60, 63, 66, 109-116, 148-151, 168, 185, 197, 198, 238
social sorting 77, 80, 89, 212-217, 222
sociology 14, 60, 62, 110, 140, 185
software studies initiative 29, 48, 55, 59, 71
SPSS 116
statistical subjects 219-221
statistics 29, 45, 62, 64, 110, 116-122, 168, 176, 177, 218, 221

style analysis 39-44, 47, 48, 52
Sustein, Cass 77

techno-images 18
the Nuremberg Code 184, 188, 189, 197, 201
Thompson, Kristin 42-44
Time magazine 61
trained judgement 18
transparency 20, 29, 30, 139-145, 178, 195, 219, 222
  practical 140-145
Tukey, John 50, 111, 160
Turow, Joseph 77
Twitter 14, 20, 55-58, 66, 69-72, 100-103, 105, 145, 147-153, 174, 206, 241, 242

unambiguous queries 87-89, 93
Underwood, Ted 59
user-generated content 56, 58, 61, 65
Utrecht Data School 9, 17, 183

Van Dijck, José 13, 172, 221, 223, 225, 241
Vis, Farida 172, 175
Weltbild 133, 135, 136
wide data 66, 67, 69
Wikipedia 75, 76, 80, 89, 92, 134
Williams, Raymond 82, 83, 92

YouTube 14, 55, 57, 59, 80
  video 57, 80